*The Wealthy Boomer*

# The Wealthy Boomer

## Life After Mutual Funds

Jonathan Chevreau
with Michael Ellis, CIM, FCSI, and S. Kelly Rodgers, CFA

*Foreword by Malcolm Hamilton*

KEY PORTER BOOKS

**Canadian Cataloguing in Publication Data**

Chevreau, Jonathan, 1953-
    The wealthy boomer : life after mutual funds

Includes index.
ISBN 1-55263-006-4

1. Investments. 2. Securities. I. Ellis, Michael, 1966-   . II. Rodgers, S. Kelly, 1956-   .
III. Title.

HG4521.C43  1998        332.6        C98-931397-2

The Canada Council | Le Conseil des Arts
FOR THE ARTS | DU CANADA
SINCE 1957 | DEPUIS 1957

The publisher gratefully acknowledges the support of the Canada Council for the Arts and the Ontario Arts Council for its publishing program.

Key Porter Books Limited
70 The Esplanade
Toronto, Ontario
Canada  M5E 1R2

www.keyporter.com

Design: Peter Maher

Electronic formatting: Heidi Palfrey

Printed and bound in Canada

98 99 00 01  6 5 4 3 2 1

Page 16: cartoon reprinted courtesy of Andy Donato; page 35: cartoon reprinted courtesy of Jamie Wayne and Graham Chevreau; pages 40 and 73: cartoons reprinted courtesy of Ed Franklin; pages 95 and 169: DILBERT reprinted by permission of United Feature Syndicate, Inc.

# Contents

# Foreword

Fees are important.

Most investors are familiar with the "rule of 72." Take 72. Divide by the rate of return you expect to earn on your investment. And presto, you've got the number of years it takes to double your money. Earn 12% per annum and you double your money in six years. Earn 6% and it takes 12.

For mutual fund investors there's an equally important rule—the "rule of 40." Take 40. Divide by your mutual fund's management expense ratio (MER). And presto, you've got the number of years it takes management expenses to consume one-third of your investment. Choose a mutual fund with a 2.1% MER, the Canadian average, and in 20 years one-third of your investment has been lost to fees. Pick a more glamorous fund, one with a 3% MER, and in 13 years one-third of your investment is gone.

Many investors think "no-load" mutual funds are "no fee" mutual funds. They aren't. Each month, whether you know it or not, you're paying the people who manage the money. You're paying for the systems that track your account. You're paying for the statements that tell you how you're doing. You're paying for brokers who execute the trades. You're paying for the prospectus and the regulatory filings. In many instances, you're paying the high cost of promoting and selling the fund: advertising, marketing departments, trailer fees—it all adds up. Paying a 2% MER for 20 years is like paying a 33% front-end load. That's a lot to give up!

None of this would matter if investment managers could beat the markets by 2% or 3% per annum. Then, even after paying a hefty fee, mutual fund investors would do as well as the markets.

But most won't. It isn't that investment managers lack skill. They are conscientious, knowledgeable, experienced professionals with sound judgement. They can't beat the market because they *are* the market. They are competing against equally conscientious, knowledgeable, experienced professionals. In the long run, only a few managers will beat the markets by enough to cover the cost of running their funds, and the average investor won't be astute enough, or lucky enough, to find these managers.

Low fees are particularly important to those saving for retirement, because retirement savings are invested for 20 to 25 years. Compare a member of the Ontario Teachers' Pension Plan to someone saving for retirement in a mutual fund. The Ontario Teachers' Pension Plan can manage a teacher's retirement savings for 0.15% per annum. The mutual fund investor pays over 2% per annum. Compounded over 25 years, the teacher will get 60% more for each dollar invested.

There may be a hundred good reasons why Canadian mutual funds have high MERs, but from the investor's perspective, it doesn't make any difference what those reasons are. High fees have a materially adverse impact on your retirement savings. If you can find a way to lessen this impact without sacrificing performance, you should do so.

There are circumstances where mutual funds make sense. If you're just starting out and you don't have much money to invest, mutual funds are a convenient way to capture the benefits of diversification and professional money management. The MERs are high, but a high percentage of a small account balance is still a small amount. Using mutual funds to fill gaps in your portfolio—small cap stocks, foreign equities, or emerging markets—can be a good idea. If you are financially inept, plagued by poor judgement and indecisive, paying others to manage your money is a good idea regardless of the cost. You won't do well, but you wouldn't have done well anyway.

American investors can find no-load mutual funds with MERs under 0.25%. Canadian investors can't. For this, Canadians have only themselves to blame. We aren't price sensitive. We either don't know what we're paying, or we don't care. If the customer doesn't care what the product costs, the producer has no reason to economize. High MERs mean better incomes for investment managers. They mean bigger profits for fund companies. They mean larger trailer fees for brokers. They mean fat advertising budgets. In the long run, everyone is happy—except the customer. Until investors demand a better product by rewarding those who provide it and punishing those who don't, Canadian mutual funds will have high MERs. And as long as MERs stay high, using mutual funds intelligently means using them less.

Fortunately, there are ways for investors to earn decent returns with or without mutual funds, but you need to work at it. You need to know what to do and how to do it. This book points you in the right direction, but good advice helps only those who act on it. If you want others to do the work for you, they will; but in the long run you'll pay—probably more than you know.

*Malcolm Hamilton, MSc, FSA, FCIA is a prominent actuary and pension consultant.*

# Acknowledgments

Many people were involved with this book, particularly the many sources who give so generously of their time and expertise when talking to *The National Post*.

The authors would like to give particular thanks to Malcolm Hamilton, who penned the foreword; and to the GOOD financial planners who vetted all or parts of the manuscript: Warren Baldwin of T.E. Financial Consultants Ltd., and Jim Rogers of The Rogers Group Financial Advisors Ltd. The Ontario Securities Commission's Glorianne Stromberg was, as always, an enormous help.

Numerous individuals within the brokerage and mutual fund industry made contributions but did not want to be identified.

*The National Post*'s director of strategic development, John Rowsome, and Key Porter publisher and CEO Anna Porter, took care of the business end of the project, with a view to contributing a measure of wealth to their firms and the boomer authors.

# Preface

Is there life after mutual funds?

Yes, if you're a young investor just starting out on the road to building a retirement nest egg. If you're a near-retiree or senior intending to cash out into a RRIF, there may also be life after mutual funds in another sense.

But that's not the primary focus of this book. The authors believe that the "next big thing" for baby-boom investing—and for anyone on the cusp of real wealth—is Managed Money. For many, mutual funds will serve as their first introduction to Managed Money. But there are many more efficient and inexpensive alternatives at the retail level other than open-end mutual funds carrying high annual management expense ratios (MERs).

This book is primarily addressed to baby-boom investors— defined as people born between 1946 and 1964—but will also benefit people of any age who have started to accumulate real wealth. While the phrase "high net worth" usually describes those with $250,000 to $500,000 or more, some of the concepts in this book apply to individuals with assets of as little as $10,000 or $50,000. We assume you already know what mutual funds are and that you are probably invested, either partly or wholly, in mutual funds.

The book is organized into three main parts: Problems with Mutual Funds; Alternatives to Mutual Funds; and Eat Well and Sleep Well with Managed Money.

Part 1 addresses the strengths and weaknesses of open-end mutual funds. Gradually, it may have occurred to you that mutual funds may not be the one-size-fits-all infallible panacea for investing ills that the mass media and its advertising support team make them out to be. You have noticed that equity mutual funds can be costly, can't be customized to your particular needs, and are forced to be fully committed to the stock markets, no matter where in the economic cycle we may be. You may have encountered some annoying taxation implications of mutual funds or some of the inherent inefficiencies of funds. You may even have a fund portfolio skewed by the tainted advice of a financial adviser who put his or her commissions and self-interest ahead of yours.

In short, mutual funds may be the best way to get you from zero to $50,000 or $150,000 in assets. But at some point your net worth—especially if combined with your spouse's—will reach the point that you need to consider the many alternatives that do exist, and always have existed, above and beyond mutual funds. These alternatives are the subject of Parts 2 and 3.

We recognize that some investors may prefer mutual funds, or don't yet have enough money to move to the next level. We therefore look at how to "minimize the damage" from the tainted advice you may have received along the way. Some of the strategies are "hybrid" ones that may use mutual funds as a part of the overall approach. Some involve complete or gradual cashing out of certain types of mutual funds over a number of years.

Part 2 is Alternatives to Mutual Funds. We look at the investment fund cousins to mutual funds that may have certain advantages: closed-end funds, offshore funds, real estate investment trusts, life insurance segregated funds, and so on. Then we consider passive investing, in which one abandons actively high-cost managed approaches and invests in low-cost index solutions; a guaranteed variant of this from the banks called index-linked GICs (Guaranteed Investment Certificates); and finally the pros and cons of building what is in effect your own mutual fund by using a traditional stock broker to buy stocks and bonds directly.

Part 3, Eat Well and Sleep Well with Managed Money, looks at the products and services available for the wealthy—and we argue that if you're a baby boomer or married to one with a good job, have a paid-for home or your own business, or are likely to inherit, you may already be wealthier than you think. Eating well refers to the need for growth investments that outstrip taxes and inflation. That's the "stocks for the long run" formula baby boomers have absorbed perhaps too well. Sleeping well is the other half of the equation, balancing an all-equity portfolio with fixed income, cash, and other asset classes diversified away from pure growth stock investments.

Historically, Managed-Money products were aimed at the most affluent segments of society—people with more than $250,000 in investable assets. Such individuals have tended to be older: over age 50. Much of the closing part of this book focuses on this market, which until recently comprised the generation ahead of the boomers: i.e., the parents of the boomers. It looks at some "Cadillac" products available at a lower-per-unit cost than mass-market mutual funds, options such as "pooled funds," "Wrap accounts," and "segregated management," the last being the most elite of the products in the Managed-Money hierarchy. Ironically, mutual funds are an entry-level Managed-Money product. If you'd already rejected the alternatives in Part 2 and shied away from picking your own stocks in favor of mutual funds, you may already have been on the right track!

Why haven't you heard about these alternatives? First, they're not usually advertised. The wealthy heard about them "by invitation only" and were referred to them through their exclusive network of accountants, lawyers, and tax professionals. Second, your current financial planner or broker may not be highly motivated to tell you about these alternatives. Third, since these products or services are less extensively advertised than mutual funds, or not advertised at all, the mass media tend to give them short shrift.

Mutual funds have been a mass-market phenomenon. But the move by baby boomers to equity mutual funds has caused the high-net-worth market to gradually reach "down market" with increasingly attractive alternatives to mutual funds. Many of the entrepreneurs at the center of the fast-growing "high-net-worth" market have themselves started out in the mutual fund industry.

There's a sea change coming and it's merely coincidental that it is starting to happen as the new century, and new millennium, is dawning. Many boomers have already passed age 50. They're closer to retirement now than to Woodstock. For most of them, Freedom 55 will be nothing more than a life insurance industry marketing slogan. The boomers may be on the way to building wealth, and some may inherit significant amounts from their parents, but they have a long way to go before gaining true financial independence. Today's young people may be highly conscious that when it comes to their retirement, they're on their own. But when it comes to personal finance and saving money, most boomers are late bloomers. Now they're saving in earnest but it's only when the RRSPs of dual-career couples are combined that you can start to describe the average boomer as wealthy. Mutual funds have allowed them to share in the greatest stock-market boom of the century. Keeping that wealth, and making it work harder by shaving the associated costs to the bone, is the subject of this book.

What if you're not officially a member of the baby boom? Near-retirees and retirees can certainly benefit from the concepts outlined here. While it is not our original intent, one interpretation of our title can be that mutual fund RRSP portfolios eventually grow up into Registered Retirement Income Funds (RRIFs). In the past, RRIFs may have consisted primarily of fixed-income products. But with the advances in health care and longevity, managed portfolios exposed to the bond and stock markets are just as relevant to retirees in their 70s and 80s as to boomers who wish they'd arrived at that point in their financial lives.

As for Generation X and those born after the baby boom, it could be that mutual funds are still the perfect product for you. If you have less than $50,000, it's hard to get the kind of diversification and convenience that mutual funds provide. If so, we refer you to the companion book to this volume, *The National Post's Smart Funds 1999*. But even if mutual funds are still the appropriate product for you at this stage in your financial life, you may wish to refer to *The Wealthy Boomer* to prepare a strategy for the day you're ready to "graduate" from mutual funds. If you learn nothing else but that you should avoid high-MER and rear-load mutual funds, the flexibility you'll gain of being ready to switch to the kind of products or services outlined here will make it well worth the modest investment of the price of this book.

There are three co-authors, each bringing a different perspective to the theme.

**Jonathan Chevreau** is also the co-author of the five *Smart Funds* volumes published to date and is *The National Post*'s Personal Finance columnist. He also writes the *Post*'s biweekly "Serious Money" column, which is aimed at high-net-worth investors and focuses on the products in Part 3.

The main source on the "Serious Money" column is the second co-author, **S. Kelly Rodgers**, CFA, who is an independent investment consultant. Her firm, Toronto-based Rodgers Investment Consulting, matches investors with investment counselors. She has self-published *The Insider's Guide to Selecting the Best Money Manager*. She has also created several regional directories of investment counselors, which are free upon request directly from Rodgers.

The third co-author is **Michael Ellis**, CIM, FCSI, an investment adviser at a leading bank-owned investment dealer. He is a Certified Investment Manager, a Fellow of the Canadian Securities Institute, and a nine-year veteran of the financial industry.

# Introduction

## Chapter One

# The Next Big Thing in Boomer Investing

As books such as David Foot's *Boom, Bust & Echo* have clearly demonstrated, demographic trends are so powerful that they can be used to explain "two-thirds of everything."

When it comes to a sea change in modes of investing, one need look no further than the baby-boom generation to divine the near future.

If you're a boomer, you probably don't think of yourself as being on the cusp of possessing real wealth. But if you think that the "high-net-worth" tag doesn't apply to you, think again. If you're reading *The National Post* or its competitors, odds are you may have control over more financial assets than you think, or you soon may have to start worrying about these things.

Ask yourself these questions:

- Do relatives ask you for investment advice? Perhaps your parents are selling their main house and moving to a retirement apartment. Suddenly, they're looking to you for advice on where to put the proceeds.
- Are you part of a dual-income family with $200,000 or $300,000 stashed into RRSPs between both husband and wife?
- Is your home mortgage almost paid off (even if it took two incomes to do it)? Once it is, are you starting to think about putting aside some money outside your RRSP?
- Do you expect to receive an inheritance in the next 10 or 20 years?
- Do you donate time and energy to charities or foundations? Are you on the board of local hospital foundations or service organizations? Do you own your own business, or do you plan to sell soon?

If you answered yes to any of these questions, then either today or in the near future you may have to deal with the issue of how to manage relatively large amounts of money.

Indeed, one of the fastest growing sectors of the Canadian financial services industry is the "high-net-worth" market, defined as individuals with more than $1 million in investable financial assets.

A 1997 study by Ernst & Young shows that this segment of the Canadian market will almost triple from 225,000 in 1996 to 365,000 in 2000 to 630,000 in 2005. There may be as many as 300,000 Canadians with $1 million when dual-income households are included.

Furthermore, the fastest growing segment will be baby boomers aged 40 to 59. Ernst & Young's numbers are conservative, since they do not include real estate, pension plan assets, CPP entitlements, annuities, and non-liquid assets such as private company shares and limited partnerships. Even defining wealth so narrowly, the pool of investable financial assets held by individual Canadians will rise from $1.2 trillion in 1996 to $2.6 trillion in the year 2005, according to E&Y. One-quarter of people make between $100,000 and $500,000 a year and just 3%—or 6,000 individuals—make more than $500,000 a year.

There are two main routes to achieving high-net-worth status. A lifetime of saving, even from modest incomes, has created many in the $1-million to $2-million camp. This can be achieved by saving 15% of a $75,000 annual salary over 30 years, according to Ernst & Young principal Colin Deane. Dual-income RRSPs can be expected to reach millionaire status well before that. The pot can also be sweetened by inheritances, pension conversions, and severance payments.

If you think such levels of wealth are attained only by older people, think again. Just over a third, or 36.3%, are more than 70. One in ten is under 40. The 40–49 age group comprises 13.5% of this market, 50–59 makes up 16.4%, and 60–69 24.4%.

It's interesting that the term high net worth is not necessarily synonymous with high income. Almost three quarters (72%) of the 225,000 high-net-worth Canadians identified by E&Y have annual incomes below $100,000.

## Profiles of High-Net-Worth Canadians

High net worth is defined as those with over $1 million of investable financial assets.

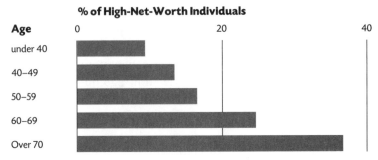

More than one-third of high-net-worth people are over 70.

## High Net Worth Doesn't Necessarily Mean High Income

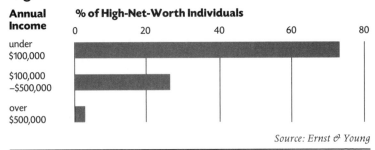

Source: Ernst & Young

Those who get to the elite $2-million camp tend to get there through entrepreneurship. Ninety percent of this group are owners of their own businesses or founding members of public companies who struck gold with stock options.

How to go about investing this capital once it's created is the subject of this book. After building such nest eggs, these individuals are understandably as concerned about keeping it as growing it further. That's why our later chapters talk about the need both to "sleep well" as well as "eat well."

As anyone who hasn't been on sabbatical in another galaxy

during the past decade is no doubt aware, the current "big thing" in investing is mutual funds. While not limited to any one generation, it's clear that the baby-boom generation's enthusiastic embrace of equity mutual funds—funds that invest in the stock market—has fuelled much of the boom in mutual fund investing. Boomers have embraced the notion of "stocks for the long run," "buy the dips," and similar passions, as well as two other forces driving the ongoing bull market: globalization and technology.

Part of this emphasis on growth (owning companies)—as opposed to fixed income (lending money for interest)—comes because the boomers came relatively late to the notion of planning for their retirement. Let's face it, back in the tie-died psychedelic 1960s and early 1970s, it would have been very "uncool" to have dropped the term "Registered Retirement Savings Plan" into a conversation about weightier matters of the era, whether it was the Vietnam war, music, or any other preoccupation of the times.

In the 1990s, the boomers have suddenly awakened to the fact that they must make up for lost time. Despite their equity focus and penchant for analytical tools to pick the best equity mutual funds, early retirement does not appear to be within reach of most of Canada's seven to eight million boomers and the 77 million more in the United States.

"The problem is that boomers are not financially prepared, and there is no evidence that they are boosting their savings and investments fast enough," noted Maureen Allyn, chief economist at Scudder Kemper Investments Inc., at a high-level talkfest it sponsored in New York early in 1998.

Boomer efforts to provide for the future were even described as "random acts of saving" by Horace Deets, executive director of the American Association for Retired Persons (AARP). The boomers are "pretty worried about retirement," according to Bambi Holzer, a Paine Webber investment strategist who has written another book on the topic: *Retire Rich: The Baby Boomer's Guide to a Secure Future* (John Wiley & Sons, New York, 1998). (As an aside, that book looks mostly at traditional retirement planning in the United States, plus stock investing and mutual funds. It doesn't address the "life after funds" and alternatives for the wealthy that this book does.)

## Size of Canadian High-Net-Worth Market

Number of Individuals with Over $1 Million of
Investable Financial Assets:

|  |  |  |
|---|---|---|
|  | 1996 | 225,000 |
| **Projected:** | 2000 | 365,000 |
|  | 2005 | 630,000 |

*Source: The Canadian High Net Worth Market, Ernst & Young, 1997*

Holzer cites a survey by the Municipal Bond Investors Assurance Corp., which states that 93% of baby boomers say financial security in retirement is "extremely important." But another one, by U.S. Trust Corp., showed that 69% are worried they won't get a comfortable retirement and 53% expect the U.S. Social Security system will go bust before they collect.

However, a survey by Scudder Canada Investor Services Inc. showed that Canadian boomers are more confident than their U.S. counterparts about their financial future. Forty-eight per cent of 1,500 Canadian boomers surveyed said they were saving or investing for retirement, compared with just 24% of U.S. boomers. About 59% of Canadians plan early retirement (before age 65), versus 47% of Americans. However, 38% of Canadian respondents do not believe that the Canada Pension Plan (CPP) will be part of their retirement nest egg, while 17% of Americans expect to rely to some extent on U.S. Social Security.

An earlier Dun & Bradstreet survey commissioned by Primerica Financial Services Canada found that neither boomers nor the younger "Generation Xers" are as financially savvy as they think they are. While that poll found 90% of Canadians earning more than $50,000 a year are saving for retirement, only 49% of those making less than $25,000 reported doing so. One astounding statistic was that 14% of non-savers between age 50 and 64 said they have not even thought about it. Far from having built up tidy retirement nest eggs, almost two-thirds of the 6,000 Canadian adults surveyed by Primerica reported that they are still in debt, and that the amount of indebtedness has increased or remained the same in the past two years. Nevertheless, they are optimistic that they will eventually be debt-free; one-half predict within three years, a belief that prompted Primerica to comment that many are wearing rose-colored glasses.

Boomers are "trying to squeeze some money for their future economic survival" at the same time as they are squeezed for time, meeting the demands of their children, and demands of downsizing employers, says Christopher Hayes, a retirement researcher at Long Island University. "They are caught in a money squeeze as they juggle debt, tuition drain, and mortgages."

Canadian boomers are headed down a similar path, according to Primerica Canada president Glenn Williams. Williams oversaw a survey for Primerica's U.S. parent two years ago. "Traditionally, Canadians have been better savers and handle debt better but the numbers are starting to converge," he says. "We're starting to pick up the bad habits of our neighbors to the south."

At the New York conference mentioned earlier, Scudder's Allyn warned that many boomers would have to work longer than they would like. "They won't be able to rely on the same level of replacement income as retirees have in the past since government benefits will be somewhat reduced," she said. "Other workers may end up having to pay a bit more in taxes than is fair."

That is precisely what is happening in Canada, where contributions to the Canada Pension Plan are legislated to almost double in the next five years. There is an emerging politics of intergenerational conflict, as programs such as the proposed (and now dead) Seniors' Benefit encourage middle-income earners to plunder their RRSPs to fund an early retirement and live off the government later.

It's arguable that the boomers' belated conversion to retirement planning will be a self-fulfilling prophecy, with their insatiable demand for stocks outstripping demand worldwide, thereby driving stock prices ever higher well into the second decade of the 21st century. In every market the boomers have touched—from music to housing—they have driven up prices. It is little wonder then that the 1990s have experienced significant "asset price inflation"—the boomers view stocks and bonds as just another scarce commodity and seem willing to pay ever-inflated prices to feather their retirement nests.

"Retirement is the new frontier for baby boomers," Scudder Kemper chief investment strategist Robert Froehlich told 1,000 people at the New York conference, "When hundreds of people do something, it's a trend; when thousands do it, it's a movement; and when 77 million do it, it's a revolution. Get ready for the *retirement* revolution."

Boomers have impacted a multitude of industries, from diapers to real estate, since the 1950s. But the focus going forward will not shift from decade to decade. "Their focus today, tomorrow, and the next is retirement," Froehlich said.

Two industries that will benefit from this trend will be pharmaceuticals and discount stores. A third is, of course, the wealth management business itself. Mutual fund investors have made financial services such an immense growth industry that mutual funds specializing in wealth management have knocked the socks off their more diversified stock-fund competitors.

The most spectacular example of this in Canada has been the AIC Advantage Fund, which has confounded the skeptics by churning out high double-digit growth year after year. However circular this phenomenon is—it's a bit like a snake eating its own tail—it has not gone unnoticed by bigger firms than AIC. In the past two years, C.I. Mutual Funds, Fidelity Investments Canada Ltd., and even some bank no-load funds have come out with AIC Advantage clones that have fared almost as well.

Scudder Kemper incorporates its views on boomer aging in its own fund investment philosophies. Its Scudder Global Fund has developed a "secure streams of income" theme, based on its perception that as boomers edge closer to retirement, they will search for income (or yield) over growth. According to Scudder, that, in turn, translates into a rising preference for bonds and utility stocks. Stocks such as "utility winners" are arising because it expects that the supply of such stocks will not keep up with the demand for them.

Until the extended stock honeymoon ran into stormy weather in 1998, boomers had been relatively accepting of some of the less attractive attributes of mutual funds. But one of the distinguishing characteristics of this generation is its determination to "have it all." Consequently, as stock returns slow to more modest historical levels, bargain-seeking boomers will start to seek value for their money management dollars. And make no mistake, mutual fund investors pay a high price for the admitted benefits of professional investment management, diversification, and record-keeping convenience.

If you don't believe this is the case, do the following quick calculation. Say you have $200,000 in mutual funds in your RRSP. Based on the average mutual fund management expense ratio (MER) of 2.1%, you are paying $4,200 a year in management fees. If your portfolio is triple that amount, your annual $13,500 RRSP contribution will be almost completely offset by $12,600 in fees. If stock markets stay flat, how will you break through to the next plateau? Chapter 3 looks in detail at the high cost of mutual funds.

New research reported by the *Wall Street Journal* in August 1998 demonstrates that mutual funds aren't always ideal. For U.S. portfolios of over $75,000, stocks are less costly to own than mutual funds, resulting in improved long-term performance. Reducing costs is one of the easiest ways for investors to enhance their returns. We analyze the implications of this research for high-net-worth investors in Chapter 11.

There are two main types of mutual fund investors, whether boomers or not: the do-it-yourselfers and the investors who want professional financial advisers. Many boomers are "do-it-yourselfers," who, if they're not already in the markets directly, like to pick their own no-load mutual funds, supported by personal computers and the Internet. Scudder says 78% of Canadian boomers believe they can select the right investments to meet their financial goals (versus 70% of American boomers).

But many other investors recognize that they need the advice and guidance of professional investment advisers, and pay for the privilege by buying "load" (commission-carrying) mutual funds from a financial planner or broker licensed to sell them.

As Chapter 4 shows, some of the advice available in Canadian load mutual fund channels has been tainted by self-serving considerations, if not outright conflicts of interest. There is no one standard to describe the necessary education or proficiency of the so-called "financial planner." A real qualified financial planner is a rare and valuable find in Canada. If one has the CFP (Certified Financial Planner) credential, however, you have some assurance that the individual has the requisite skills to bridge such varied disciplines as security selection, life insurance, estate planning, and taxation.

Unfortunately, many individuals have taken advantage of a regulatory black hole and, with no more qualification than a license to sell mutual funds, pass themselves off as the same "jack of all trades" financial planner. To them, a financial plan is nothing more than a tool to sell clients high-MER rear-load mutual funds that pay the salesperson 5% of the entire investment upfront. Some try to triple the haul by convincing the investor to use "leverage" by tapping the equity from their home to buy equity mutual funds.

This may be a valid approach, but only for sophisticated investors who can rebound from setbacks. Some so-called financial planners disregard the "Know Your Client" guidelines and sell inappropriate products, thereby giving their more legitimate confrères a bad name. As Chapter 4 shows, many financial planners have a greater talent for planning their own retirement than that of their clients.

The high-MER rear-load type of mutual fund investor is probably the most common species occupying the abused fund-investor landscape. Because of the complexities and expenses involved in the infamous declining redemption schedules associated with rear-load funds, it can take years to extricate oneself from these funds and the high annual expense ratios associated with them. Chapter 6 addresses some of the transition strategies for this type of investor.

The other major creature in the mutual funds wilderness is the bank no-load investor. Typically, this person was once a "GIC refugee," a term coined by Marketing Solutions president Dan Richards to describe the circa-1993 era conservative investor who was fleeing low-paying Guaranteed Investment Certificates (GICs) for mutual funds. Typically, this investor moved down a few meters from the GIC counter of his or her friendly local bank, only to be sold the no-load mutual funds of the same bank. While the load or broker-sold sales people often characterize the no-load alternatives as "no-load, no-advice," the bigger challenge for bank and trust company no-load groups has been generating comparable performance as the brand-name load groups.

For years, the banks were plagued by poor performance when measured against broker-sold funds such as Trimark, Templeton, Fidelity, and Mackenzie. The bank funds that did best, like TD GreenLine, wisely subcontracted much of their external fund management rather than doing it in-house. Yet the in-house approach is more profitable; banks are also addicted to the profits generated by high management fees. The banks don't have to pay trailer fees to independent brokers and dealers because they own their own distribution system—that is, their own huge network of branches. Although the banks could have used lower fees to entice investors away from the load fund groups, Canadian consumers appeared to be so fee-insensitive that the banks got away with fees comparable to the load channels. Eventually, however, again led by TD Greenline, the banks succumbed to investors' desires for brand-name mutual funds by providing "third-party" mutual funds that often compete with their own in-house products.

The Canadian banks recognize a major shift in the market when they see one. Just as they did in the 1980s when they embraced and validated mutual funds, the banks are about to validate the high-net-worth market in a big way, and are specifically targeting the baby boomers. The banks realize that fund investors are confused and need help choosing the right funds. The Scudder talkfest pointed out that "boomers will demand simplification—in their investments, lifestyles, and spending options." What could be simpler, or more convenient, than delegating not only security selection, but even the choice of mutual funds themselves? This is exactly what mutual fund "Wrap" programs are all about.

Unfortunately, at least in the "junior" versions of Wrap programs (aimed at investors with as little as $10,000) the banks' estimate of how much investors are willing to pay for fund selection appears to be a little high. CIBC and Scotiabank have made deals with independent mutual fund gurus, packaging up collections of third-party funds and adding fees on top of fees for the privilege. Paradoxically, other banks, including CIBC, have also embraced low-cost passively managed index funds. As Chapter 9 describes, passive investing appeals to fee-conscious investors who are also aware of the inability of many managed fund managers to beat the major stock indexes.

But these bank no-load innovations are at the low-end of the mass market. The real action is in the so-called "affluent mass market" or high-net-worth end of the market—one that many baby boomers are poised to enter, particularly when the assets of spouses are pooled together.

The banks, or their trust company units, have long been in the high-net-worth segment of the market, though they have never been as visible as their retail mutual fund arms. Some banks, such as Scotiabank, have an internal investment management team running segregated management (see Chapter 13) that is similar to their investment team running their retail no-load funds. They have lower fees, of course, and the service is generally packaged for the affluent, including certain minimum investment levels.

Boomers like to feel they are special or unique. In the end, any given mutual fund is primarily a "one-size-fits-all" investment. Alternative investment products customized to the individual investor's needs—which avoid the investor's dislikes or adapt to their moral or ethical stance—will find a ready market with boomers.

Others may throw up their hands in dismay at the immensity of choice that exists in the market and seek out a single individual or organization that can make all the investing decisions on their behalf. Just as this type of investor willingly forgoes 2% or more of a portfolio's yearly value in return for professional stock picking in, for example, Canadian or U.S. equity funds, so will some investors with enough money seek out "discretionary" management—handing over all the major decisions such as asset allocation and geographical distribution to the "discretion" of a single money manager or money management firm.

To see the future—what we call "Life After Mutual Funds" (or LAMF)—you need look no further than CIBC. Two years ago, its trust division, CIBC Trust, decided to target discretionary management to the baby-boom generation. Discretionary management means that individual investors withdraw from active decision-making on their investment portfolio. Instead they hand over their retirement savings to a professional manager who makes all investment decisions for them. They have, therefore, left the decisions "to the discretion" of the manager, once an initial client profile has been established and the usual investor objectives and risk tolerances are agreed upon. Discretionary management is discussed further in Chapter 12.

Until CIBC and other major players started redefining the landscape, discretionary investment management was the preserve of the truly wealthy ($500,000 and up). What's happening now is that this form of investing is moving downscale to include baby boomers on the cusp of achieving modest wealth ($100,000 or $150,000).

Discretionary management appeals to a certain type of individual—it's the opposite of the collegial process of bouncing individual stock ideas off a broker; instead, investors who don't have time or the skills to make such day-to-day decisions hand over the decision-making process to a professional, usually for a set annual fee of assets: typically 1% to 1.4%, after custodial and trading costs, in the products described in Part 3.

A CIBC Trust brochure nicely sums up the dilemma of successful but stressed-out boomers: it's difficult to have all three of time, money, and financial expertise. What's fascinating is CIBC's perception that the baby-boom generation is ready for discretionary management. In effect, CIBC is lowering the bar on discretionary investment management, which has traditionally required minimum investments of $500,000 for true segregated management (discretionary management using individually selected stocks and bonds).

But boomer couples are approaching such levels with their double RRSPs. The bank says it is seeing many baby boomers "who are looking for assistance in investing for retirement." They are demanding more personalized investment options. At the same time, the vast amount of investment options out there is also perceived as overwhelming. For those who find it difficult to make any investment decision at all, the best plan may be discretionary management—to delegate all your investment decisions to a professional.

Interestingly, there is some blending of these products and approaches. CIBC Trust also offers a series of different products, ranging from index no-load funds to discretionary wrap programs that actively manage the major asset classes with passive investing underlying each. These are described in Chapter 13.

Many affluent investors may even return to the old-fashioned stockbroker, buying and selling individual stocks. Many have already. However, *The Wealthy Boomer* is not primarily about researching and investing in individual stocks, although that may be the appropriate solution for a minority of our readers and is covered in Chapter 10. The book's primary focus is Managed Money, of which mutual funds are the most visible subset. That's because they are aimed at a mass market or what some call "the sub-affluent mass market."

These products are not usually advertised, which has the convenient allied benefit of reducing costs as well. Mutual funds, by contrast, are seemingly ubiquitous because they are heavily advertised, which of course adds to their costs, one way or the other. They are a mass-market product, marketed just like any other commodity: soap, automobiles, hamburgers.

Apart from their high profile, funds are also widely available and easily purchased, for as little as $500 for a one-time purchase or $50 a month. They are literally available at every major intersection in Canada, including most of the small towns, since the banks entered the business in a big way in the 1980s. Such convenience comes at a price, however.

Mutual funds can be likened to compact cars designed for the mass market. There are also mid-size and luxury products. These may offer greater access to managers, be tailored more to individual needs, or be more cost-effective.

The next level up is the affluent mass market featuring the products and services described in Part 3—Wrap accounts and pooled funds. In this book, we use the term "Wrap" to describe products and services that bundle all aspects and costs of the investment management process into a single fee.

At the top of the wealth market—the Cadillacs—are the separately managed or segregated accounts. They give you your own personal money manager: your portfolio is managed separately from other client accounts.

So mutual fund investors will eventually reach a point in their financial lives when the admitted advantages of funds are outweighed by such considerations as cost, "customizability," and other facets this book examines.

The crossover point is largely determined by the amount of money an investor has accumulated. It used to be that the high-net-worth market was defined as investors with at least $200,000 in investable financial assets. However, all financial institutions want to sell to this market, so to some extent the phrase "high net worth" has become somewhat devalued, just as the term "financial planner" has lost some panache because of overuse by people—some licensed to sell only mutual funds—who are not fully qualified to dispense full-blown financial planning advice.

As a result of these marketing considerations, the "high net worth" threshold is being lowered, so that some low-level Wrap programs are available for as little as $50,000, while costly selections of ordinary mutual funds—portfolio of funds or what we call "junior Wrap programs"—are available from some banks for as little as $10,000.

But before we examine the many alternatives in depth, let's look a little closer at some of the drawbacks to traditional, retail-level, open-end mutual funds. That's the subject of Part 1.

*Part One*

# Problems with Mutual Funds

## Chapter Two

# Mutual Funds Are Great, But . . .

Mutual funds are arguably the most brilliant financial innovation of all time. For nearly half of Canadian adults, mutual funds have been the centerpiece of their meager retirement savings plans. They have provided both professional management and stock picking that have allowed small investors to participate in one of the greatest bull markets ever. They are easily purchased and easily redeemed.

Among the many benefits of mutual funds cited by well-known American mutual-fund executive John Bogle in *Bogle on Mutual Funds* (Dell Publishing, New York, 1994), are their ability to reduce the risk of owning individual stocks and bonds through diversification; their enormous convenience in record keeping and ease of transaction; the hundreds of options that have been developed to suit the particular needs of a wide range of different investors; and, of course, professional investment management that achieves returns reflecting the markets chosen.

## Funds have democratized equity investing

Throughout the 1990s, chronically low interest rates drove Canadian savers, who had been comfortable investing in the banks' Guaranteed Investment Certificates (GICs), to explore higher-returning, stock market-based equity mutual funds. Such individuals were dubbed "GIC refugees," by Dan Richards, president of Toronto-based Marketing Solutions, whose clientele consists of many Canadian fund companies. Mutual funds popularized investing in the stock markets, Richards says. "They've really democratized equity investing, making it accessible to the average investor." So far, even with hiccups in 1994, October 1997, and most of 1998, these investors have been generally rewarded for the higher risk they've assumed.

As the 1990s close, the media have become infatuated with mutual funds. Regular cover stories on the topic appear in major Canadian news and business magazines. Several fund guide-books are available in the Canadian market, many of which are written by at least one mutual fund salesperson. The *Globe and Mail* (and soon *The National Post*) have launched mutual-fund web sites. During RRSP season, television advertising becomes so pervasive that, as one cartoon noted, "The RRSP ads are period-ically interrupted by hockey games."

With so many vested interests in the rich and powerful fund industry, only a few people are sufficiently objective to highlight the shortcomings of mutual funds. After all, mutual funds are the bread and butter of 60,000 salespeople in Canada. More than 80 mutual fund management firms employ thousands more invest-ment managers, administrators, and sales and marketing depart-ments. The media love to write about the fund industry, and their advertising departments welcome the revenue. And a sub-culture of experts checks up on the experts, including developers of fund-analysis software, popular speakers and professional fund gurus, authors, and newsletter pundits. Evidently, the mutual fund industry affects tens of thousands of Canadian workers.

Furthermore, with $320 billion of Canadians' retirement sav-ings committed to funds, it's obvious that big money is at stake. How big? Taking the average mutual fund management fee of 2% a year, the math is simple: 2% of $320 billion is $6.4 billion. That is, if Canadians did not invest another dime in mutual funds and the markets remain at their current levels, the people employed in the mutual fund industry would share $6.4 billion this year, another $6.4 billion next year, and so on. In short, it's hardly in anyone's best interest to kill, or even hobble, this golden goose.

## Funds' drawbacks can be substantial

But what about the seven million Canadian fund investors who pay out 2% of their retirement savings every year to this same industry? Are funds necessarily in their best interest at all stages of their financial lives? As *Money* magazine pointed out in an April 1998 cover story, "Our love affair with mutual funds has also tended to cloud our vision, allowing us to overlook funds' drawbacks, which can be substantial." Similarly, in the same month, the cover of *Barron's* was entitled "Beyond Mutual Funds," suggesting that "after piling into mutual funds for years, many investors are now opting to buy stocks directly and through privately managed accounts."

This book, subtitled *Life After Mutual Funds*, was conceived a year before that article appeared, but the concept is similar. *Barron's* noted that the United States now has 6,000 mutual funds, holding US$4.8 trillion. It predicted that by mid-1998, the amount of money invested in mutual funds would exceed total deposits in savings accounts in U.S. banks. Canadian banking executives expect the same occurrence here in the next few years: more money will be invested in our 1,700 or so mutual funds than in bank deposits.

But *Barron's* also warned that the mutual fund industry's explosive growth is slowing: the amount pouring into funds has stabilized in recent years at an annual rate of US$220 billion. In addition to more investors buying stocks directly, many are setting up individually managed accounts with private bankers or are considering lower-cost, passive index products.

As David Dreman explained in *Contrarian Investment Strategies: The Next Generation* (Simon & Schuster, New York, 1998), small investors have been more than willing to ascribe magical skills to professional money managers. Knowledgeable financial observers have played along, urging "the uninformed and emotional small investor to realize that he was ill equipped to deal with the complex modern market and to turn his money over to one of these seasoned pros."

## Fund managers rarely beat the indexes

However, as a group, these professional managers have failed to deliver the goods. They extract fees in both good markets and bad. Investors have been happy in the 1990s, but would have been equally happy being passively invested in the market indexes. Except in rare cases of fund outperformance, the markets, rather than the fund managers, have delivered the double-digit returns of equity funds. "The knowledge that professionals do not outperform the market has been widely known for a generation," Dreman observed, adding later that "fundamental research has been no more successful than technical analysis."

The two main reasons for investors' dawning disillusionment about mutual funds in the United States are performance and taxes. Most U.S. fund managers have seriously lagged the Standard & Poor's 500 (a broad index of U.S. stocks) while outside tax-sheltered plans, investors are grousing about taxes generated by funds that trade stocks actively. There is a growing concern about rising fees and expenses—even though U.S. fund expenses are about half of those in Canada.

None of these concerns is terribly new, although anyone who pointed them out in a raging bull market tended to be dismissed as a raving voice in the wilderness. Almost five years ago, American author Donald Christensen sounded a premature alarm with his book *Surviving the Coming Mutual Fund Crisis*, (Little, Brown & Co., New York, 1994) and appeared on CBC "Newsworld" to promote it. He conceded that the underlying premise of mutual funds was brilliant. As the "single most popular financial idea in world history, . . .[mutual funds have attracted] the greatest number of people, the widest range of categories of people, and the greatest amount of money" ($2 trillion in the United States). But, he noted, "As history proves to us over and over again, whenever a good financial idea becomes viewed by everybody as the only idea, it invariably turns into a bad idea."

## Diversification is all funds really promise

When all the implied promises of mutual fund promotional materials are removed, diversification is really the only concrete promise made by fund promoters.

Christensen summed up the GIC refugee idea perfectly. He notes that investors "chucked out one set of financial professionals (traditional bankers) because the stingy bums wouldn't pay out what people wanted. And another set of financial professionals (fee-paid money managers) was embraced even though that set didn't promise anything . . . except hope."

For their part, the banks have been delighted to shift from GICs to no-load mutual funds and their guaranteed 2% of assets a year. Unlike the GICs they have displaced, the risks are now borne by the fund unitholder, as disclosed in the fine print in the "risk factors" sections of fund prospectuses. The downside of risk was experienced by many fund investors for the first time when global markets went south in mid-1998.

A similar shift has been taking place in company pension plans: from the guaranteed future returns of the old-fashioned Defined Benefit pension plan to the variable market returns of Defined Contribution plans, which often contain—you guessed it—mutual funds.

Christensen also noted the creation of a sub-industry devoted to tracking and assessing the relative performance of mutual funds: "Speculative attention and expectation have moved from the underlying investment markets of funds to the funds themselves."

Today in Canada, several mutual-fund web sites make fund analysis as easy as pointing and clicking a computer mouse. For example, Portfolio Analytics Ltd., Bell Charts, and Southam's Source Disk offer monthly fund performance software, and Bell Charts president Rob Bell recently introduced his "five-bell" rating system, which is designed to be the Canadian equivalent of the American Morningstar. The *Globe and Mail*, Ranga Chand, Gordon Pape, Duff Young, the Croft/Kirzner index, *Investor's Digest* and even *The National Post*'s *Smart Funds* all, to some degree, attempt to rate mutual funds.

Such analysis has resulted in the curious phenomenon of the topic of mutual funds emerging as cocktail-party chatter. Suddenly, everyone is an expert, and they are by no means limited to the elite chattering classes. We have received "hot fund tips" from sources as diverse as taxi drivers and daycare workers. This sounds ominously similar to the apocryphal story in which Joseph Kennedy, patriarch of the Kennedy clan, decided to sell all his stocks before the 1929 Great Crash because the elevator boy offered him a stock tip.

"A mania becomes full blown when confidence in the object of the speculative focus is so strong that successful involvement in it is thought of as 'easy' and the end result certain," Christensen observed.

## Fund analysis now as complex as stock picking

Ironically, the act of comparing and contrasting mutual funds has become almost as complicated as analyzing the underlying stocks held by the funds. Anyone with the knowledge, time, and inclination to analyze and compare different mutual funds can do the same with individual securities, and avoid paying the mutual-fund management fees. Such investors can gain access to information through the Internet, and capitalize on the ease and affordability of trading stocks through discount brokers and online. But wasn't the purpose of mutual funds to delegate security analysis to professionals, albeit at a fee? People who spend hours a day analyzing mutual funds themselves are getting the worst of all possible worlds: they're paying for professional management, but aren't escaping the analysis duties they're already paying for.

Christensen was also prophetic when describing how superstar money manager Paul Tudor Jones earned US$60 million, even while admitting his performance was subpar because of the size of the fund he was managing. A similar trend is taking hold in Canada. In 1997, Canada's most celebrated fund manager, Frank Mersch, netted more than $30 million when Altamira Investment Services Inc. was sold to Boston's T.A. Associates. Meanwhile,

Mersch's flagship Altamira Equity Fund—a hot fund in its early days, often chalking up more than 30 per cent a year—had mushroomed past $2 billion in assets and regressed roughly to the performance of the TSE 300. In April 1998, Altamira unitholders were shocked to learn that Mersch was stepping down amid accusations by regulators of improprieties involving personal trades.

In June 1998, Mersch and the Ontario Securities Commission reached a settlement under which Mersch withdrew from managing money for a six-month period. Mersch admitted to the OSC that he had misled investigators about some of his personal investments, but asserted that he had not benefitted from his investment in Rutherford Ventures Corp., which later became Diamond Fields Resources Inc.

## Managers keep jumping ship

A month before this event, *Barron's* "Beyond Mutual Funds" supplement suggested that fund investors can no longer depend on a manager to stay with a particular fund for long before jumping ship. Although Mersch's departure involved Canada's best-known money manager, the pattern had already been established long before by Mersch's rivals. For example, Canadian investors who

followed Veronika Hirsch from Prudential to AGF to Fidelity to her own company could certainly sympathize with Altamira unitholders, as could the Elliott & Page enthusiasts who lost John Zechner to C.I. Mutual Funds, the Gerry Coleman fans forced to move from United Financial to Mackenzie's Ivy Canadian to C.I. Harbour Fund, or the Jonathan Baird supporters, who lost their man first from Dynamic Mutual Funds, and then C.I.

The earliest group seeking the greener pastures of "Life After Mutual Funds" are high-net-worth investors: those with at least $200,000 in assets, and usually much more. Private money managers can provide these investors with more tax efficiencies and a more tailored approach to their investments. Richard Bregman, a fee-based financial adviser with New York-based MJB Asset Management told *Barron's*, "There's a shift out there just waiting to happen. The typical adviser client is going to have more narrowly and clearly defined mutual-fund portfolios with a complement of individual securities." Fund industry consultant Neil Bathon of Boston-based Financial Research Corp. told *Barron's* that mutual funds are not going away but "they have to evolve to keep pace. I think the mutual fund industry is going to wake up to find it has to be more segmented and targeted and has to cater to niche groups rather than the mass market."

Similar trends are taking hold in Canada. While products such as Wrap accounts (see Chapter 13) are a few years behind the United States, Canadian sensitivity to high mutual-fund management fees may be more pronounced if only because of their relatively higher impact in Canada.

## Time for fund investors to take the next step?

Even one of the early champions of the Canadian mutual fund industry, Keith Douglas, once suggested in the *Investment Executive* trade newspaper that it may be time for mutual fund investors to "take the next step." For 15 years Douglas was president of the Investment Funds Institute of Canada (IFIC), the industry trade group promoting mutual funds in Canada. Granted, Douglas' comments must be taken with a grain of salt since he later became executive director of the Investment Counsel Association of Canada (ICAC) and has a vested interest in promoting a viable alternative to funds called "investment counseling." But his views are worth repeating. For first-time investors, he says, mutual funds may be the only way to go, but as portfolios grow, other options deserve attention. These options for "mutual-fund refugees" can begin with an investment of as little as $50,000 in some mutual fund Wrap programs, $150,000 and up for pooled funds, and $300,000 to $500,000 or more for segregated management or discretionary investment counsel. These terms are discussed further in Chapter 13.

Although Douglas singles out investment counseling (as does *The National Post*'s popular stock-market columnist, Patrick Bloomfield), he notes that he still owns some funds. Douglas remains "a mutual funds enthusiast" because they are "the only product likely to provide the diversification, rate of return, and peace of mind for most small investors. Someone who is an investment specialist is in charge and investors do not have to be involved in investment decisions."

But at some point, Douglas argues, more affluent investors may benefit from investment counseling, including such features as portfolios customized to individual needs. He contrasts this with the "collective" investment approach inherent in mutual funds—an approach that may become less satisfying "as the objectives of investors change with lifestyle, employment, age, and size of their portfolios."

## Save 1% a year on fees

Douglas observes that with investment counseling, investors can make another 100 basis points (1%) a year just on the basis of lower management fees. He explains that mutual fund investors "may have been well satisfied with their investment results from funds" but cites "other issues" that may cause investors to consider "a segregated investment portfolio which is specifically invested to suit their objectives and changed circumstances."

Even mutual fund industry leaders, such as Dan Richards, agree "there's no question that as people develop bigger portfo-

lios the notion of more customized management is appealing."
But he added that some of the bigger investment counselors
require a minimum investment of $1 million. Ironically, as IFIC
president Tom Hockin points out, mutual funds may be the vehicle that propels smaller investors to those high thresholds to
begin with. In that respect, the two modes of accessing professional money management are complementary. But the fastest
way to get a small mutual fund portfolio big enough to consider
the alternatives is to consider overcoming one of the biggest
impediments the average fund investor faces: high fees.

As Malcolm Hamilton notes in the Foreword, "fees are
important."

Canadians pay very high management expense ratios
(MERs), which is essentially what the companies charge to manage your money.

While the average MER of 2.1% may seem negligible, it is
deducted year after year, and can consume almost half of your
retirement savings over the 25 to 30 years normally taken when
saving in an RRSP.

How this happens, and how investors can minimize these
effects, are the subject of Chapter 3.

## Chapter Three

# The Cost of Convenience: High Management Expense Ratios (MERs)

Investors face two major obstacles on the road to retirement leisure: taxes and management fees. Preferential tax treatment and tax-efficient investing are discussed in Chapter 6 and later chapters. The alternative is to leave the country for less oppressive tax regimes.

But investors do have more control over the high tribute that most of us pay to the financial services industry, and especially the fees we pay to mutual fund companies and the intermediaries that sell them to us.

The main attraction of equity mutual funds is the perceived higher returns that these funds offer. But these returns are neither assured, nor as high as they could be. That's because a lot of money is siphoned off to pay the fund companies, the brokers who sell the funds, and the vast marketing machine involved.

## How fees started to rise

In order to understand this phenomenon, it is useful to understand the evolution of the fee structure of the industry. Actuary and pension consultant Malcolm Hamilton of William M. Mercer Ltd., author of our Foreword, explains that at a critical point in the development of the Canadian mutual fund industry, the major players decided that their businesses would best grow by paying high fees to the brokers and dealers who sell their funds, rather than by ensuring that the fees paid by consumers remained as low as possible.

Before the 1990s, investor attention on fees centered on the fixed 9% front loads normally charged to acquire a mutual fund.

The front load was not negotiable, as it is today. Like a stock-brokerage commission, the amount was deducted off the top, meaning that, in the case of the 9% front load, only 91% of your capital was "going to work for you" from day one.

Back then, the only way to get a lower sales charge was to buy large quantities of a fund: a $60,000 sale might get you a 4.5% commission, for example. Many investors disliked the 9% front load, which explains why buying individual stocks was the preferred mode of equity investing. Recognizing this, fund companies gradually backed off the 9% upfront commission. Front loads came down to about 5%, and today, whether through discount brokers or by strong negotiating with a full-service broker, it's normal to pay just 2, 1, or even 0% on a front load.

But the piper must still be paid somehow. The industry's solution was to create a less visible and more palatable alternative: it simply increased annual management fees. In the 1980s, the yearly management fee was usually one per cent or less so there was a little room to manoeuvre. Besides, Canadians happily pay large hidden costs in many types of investments—GICs, bonds, CSBs (Canada Savings Bonds)—so the idea of embedding costs was not too radical.

The big change occurred in 1987, when Mackenzie Financial Corp. introduced the Industrial Horizon Fund with a rear-load fund with declining redemption fee schedule. At the time, Mackenzie's flagship was the front-load Industrial Growth Fund. With the Horizon Fund, however, there was no front load at all. Investors paid only if they "redeemed" or cashed out, and the redemption charge declined, or fell, a little more each year. Brokers could now honestly tell their clients, "100% of your initial investment is going to work for you from day one."

Canadians flocked to the new rear-load funds, which now account for 80% of all load fund sales in Canada. But these funds were not without drawbacks. The first drawback was the redemption fee itself, often 6% early in the schedule, which applied if investors left the fund family, not if they switched to other funds in the same family. But the second drawback was more insidious—the yearly management fees were boosted closer to the current level of 2% or more. Before the rear-load innovation, Industrial Growth Fund had a management expense ratio (MER) of just 0.75%, which was raised soon after to 1.25%. The MER of Mackenzie's Industrial Horizon Fund today is about 2.4%. With few exceptions, such as Trimark, the MERs for front- or rear-load funds are roughly the same.

Evidently, regardless of the fee structure, brokers still had to be paid—even if consumers were no longer paying an upfront 9% sales charge. On a rear-load fund with no acquisition charges, brokers are still paid upfront: typically 4% to 5% of the amount invested. In these cases, however, the money does not come directly from consumers' initial investments, but from the fund companies themselves. To do this, the companies resorted to several complex mechanisms, the most popular being the mutual-fund limited partnership. Part of the resulting higher MERs goes to the limited partnership investors.

In these cases, unlike a one-time hit such as a front-load or stock commission, management fees kick in every year for the duration of the investment. Over the normal 30- or 40-year retirement time horizon it turns out that the front load, even at the stiff 9% level, would have been a better deal because of its lower yearly management fees. Of course, investors seldom hold funds that long: no-loads usually are held less than two years and load funds for about four years. By the same token, buying individual stocks and holding them is still a good deal if you hold them long enough. You pay the upfront sales charge only once, and then pay no other fees for all the years you hold the stock. That is, there's no equivalent to the yearly mutual fund management fee.

## Low returns will change MER consciousness

Given the strong returns of the markets and funds in recent years, Canadian investors have been understandably disinterested in the impact of high fees. But awareness started to heighten in 1997, when Malcolm Hamilton issued a sobering wake-up call at a pension conference. In a speech entitled "Why the Past Hasn't Prepared Us for the Future," he explained, "Demographically, the future looks nothing like the past. In a world with low returns, low retirement savings limits, large

mutual fund management fees, and large income-tested government benefits, we should not assume that retirement savings
will, for every person in every circumstance, be rewarded."

Using 2.1% as the average of Canadian management fees and
other fixed expenses, Hamilton showed that, assuming a marginal
tax rate of 50% pre- and post-retirement, after 25 years, management fees consume a hefty 39% of the total investment return.

Although the effect from fees seems negligible in the early
years, it gradually rises over 25 years. This happens because of the
compounding nature of the fees deducted. The first year, you lose
2.1%. The second year, you lose 2.1% of the remaining 97.9%, the
third year, 2.1% of the remaining 95.8%, and so on for 25 years.

"Canadians tend to look at a 2% MER over a one-year time
horizon and conclude it's a negligible cost. That's not the right
perspective for retirement savings," Hamilton explained. "If a
mutual-fund company said, 'We have no MER but we take 40%
of every $1 contributed,' no one would give them a nickel."
Instead, they have done "a very sensible marketing thing, which
is to push their fees into the MER, where it's underappreciated."
In the coming era of single-digit returns, Hamilton observes that
"the difference between 8% and 6% is a lot more important
than the difference between 15% and 13%."

Prominent fund executives don't dispute Hamilton's thesis. In
its submission to the FP's annual *Smart Funds* guide, Trimark
Investment Management Inc. wrote that "As competition inten-
sifies, we expect to see downward pressure on fees. Double-digit
returns the last several years have deflected attention from the
costs of investment management. However, fees now associated
with many funds will not be sustainable if returns revert to historical norms of 10 per cent or less."

John Cleghorn, chairman of the Royal Bank, reiterated this
point to a *Financial Post* editorial committee in the spring of 1998.
"Fees for automated banking machines (ABMs) in Canada are
lower than in the U.S., but not our mutual fund management
fees," he explained. "On the ABM side we can see a reduction
there and I think we'll see it over time in mutual funds. We will
see more North American pricing. While in traditional banking

it's cheaper to deal with Canadian banks, it's not cheaper to buy a mutual fund in Canada. It's got to come down."

Up until now, Canadians have tolerated high MERs because they believed they could find managers who could outperform the market. "But the average investment manager *is* the market," Hamilton says, "and if you're paying 2% to get the average investment manager you're going to get the market minus 2%."

The following table, condensed from *The Financial Post*'s mutual-fund report, shows average MERs of major mutual-fund categories.

| Fund Category | Industry Average MER (%) |
|---|---|
| International equity | 2.5 |
| Canadian equity funds | 2.4 |
| Canadian balanced funds | 2.2 |
| Canadian fixed-income funds | 1.6 |
| Canadian money market funds | 1.0 |

It is important to note that Canadian fund MERs are almost twice those of the United States. According to *Money* magazine, the average Canadian MER is 2.1%; whereas the average U.S. MER is 1.41%. In part, this can be explained because in the United States there is a preponderance of non-taxable municipal bond funds with low MERs. Americans also invest proportionately less in high-MER global equity funds than do Canadians.

But the main reason for the disparity is that Canadian fund dealers receive higher commissions than their American counterparts. A major component of the MER is the yearly service fee, or "trailer" fee, which accounts for 0.25 to 1% of the average 2.1% MER. We'll discuss trailer fees in Chapter 4.

We asked another actuary, Fred Thompson, to confirm Hamilton's analysis and show the impact of MERs ranging from 1 to 3.5%. As shown in the accompanying chart, over a 30-year period an MER of 3.5% will consume 65% of a fund's value in an RRSP. By contrast, an MER of just 1%—achievable in some no-load funds, pension pooled funds, or "segregated" management—gobbles up just over 20%, a more reasonable price to pay for the benefits of professional management and diversification.

## Percentage of Fund Lost to MER

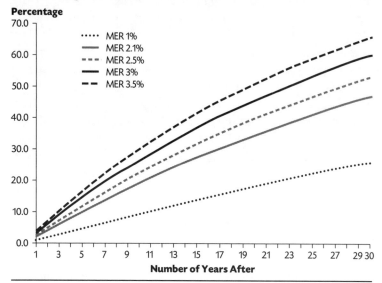

This graph shows how this effect accelerates over time at levels of 1%, 2.1%, 2.5%, 3%, and 3.5%. Even though 2.1% is the "average" MER of a Canadian mutual fund, plenty of funds weigh in at about 2.98%. With the recent trend to "Wrap" packages that impose fees on top of fees, MERs of 3% and 3.5% are becoming more, rather than less, common. Furthermore, most labor-sponsored venture capital funds have MERs in the stratosphere: 5% or more.

In recent years, knowledgeable industry insiders have become more critical about Canadian MERs. For example, Richard Croft, a private money manager and occasional *National Post* columnist, wrote an intriguing column in the April 1998 issue of *The FundLetter* newsletter. Entitled "The Price of Performance," Croft acknowledged Hamilton's thesis and summed up the fund industry's rebuttal "that performance numbers are by far the most important issue, and that performance numbers already reflect the costs of managing the funds."

These are valid points. That means the performance numbers you read in the newspapers are "net of fees." So when you see the XYZ Supercharged Growth Fund reporting a 40% return, despite a 2.95% MER, you know that it could have given you a 42.95% return before fees were deducted. Is management worth it? In this case, certainly. Stephen Kangas, co-author of *The National Post*'s *Smart Funds* books, argues that it's futile to be driven exclusively by MERs if you end up with fourth-quartile performance. Just as it is a mistake to let the taxation tail wag the investment dog, so too it is possible to throw out the high-performance baby with the high-fee bathwater. As Dan Richards notes, there will always be room for someone who has demonstrated the ability to truly add value. Thus, management fees on small-cap equity funds are higher than mainstream equity funds for good reason: it's more expensive to run small-cap funds and, over time, returns on small-cap funds have justified the higher fees. "So you shouldn't be blindly driven by management fees alone," suggests Richards, "You just have to be sure that if you're paying a premium that there's good reason for it."

But with so many funds out there, it *is* possible to find low-MER funds that are in the first quartile. In his *FundLetter* article, Croft acknowledged that the MER computations are "straightforward." He further noted that "some in the financial industry will argue that such calculations speak only to one side of the debate— that the MER is the cost of having your money professionally managed and that professional management adds value."

The best measure of how much value is added is determined by assessing whether you could achieve better results yourself. "Cost out the time it takes you to research investment decisions, then consider transactions costs, and you begin to get an idea of how much value a manager adds," advises Croft.

## Seek strong low-MER funds

After examining both sides of the argument, it's clear mutual funds can be a pretty good deal, *if* you find the few funds or fund families that combine both strong performance *and* low MERs. Croft concludes that MERs should not be the sole consideration and that a select handful of excellent money managers both add value and are worth the price of admission. But Croft also agrees with our premise that "the alternative to high-MER funds is not to become an independent trader; the alternative is finding well-performing funds that have lower MERs."

The marketing literature of one such company, no-load firm Phillips, Hager & North Ltd., states that "clients pay fees from only one place: their investments." The company says its fees are among the lowest in the industry "partly because we do not pay agents any portion of capital as commission or of returns as 'trailer' service fees." Interestingly, it adds that "low fees should not mean little advice or poor service."

Fundamentally, getting a top-performing fund means getting a low MER fund, which means no trailer or adviser compensation. This implies that investors must do more work themselves or find another way to pay the adviser—perhaps on a fee basis. The alternative is to accept the fact that mediocre or average-performing funds may be the price of getting service with no other visible charges.

Even such a passionate fund promoter as Duff Young recently wrote in a *Globe and Mail* column (April 25, 1998) that "Commissions aren't the problem. It's the high annual expenses that'll kill you. So saving a few dollars in commission is of little benefit if you end up buying expensive funds (those with high management expense ratios)."

Similarly, John Bogle, chairman of the Vanguard Group of Investment Companies in the United States, led the low-fee charge in the United States. In his book, *Bogle on Mutual Funds* (Bantam Doubleday Dell, 1994), he observed that "in no other section of the financial services field are cost and value more closely linked." Reversing the Oscar Wilde quotation that a cynic is someone "who knows the price of everything and the value of nothing," Bogle wrote that "in the case of mutual funds it might be said that knowing the price of everything reveals the value of everything, since each dollar of cost that you pay reduces your return by a precisely equal amount . . . other things being equal, lower costs mean higher returns."

In the early days of the U.S. fund industry, most funds had what Bogle described as "reasonably low" expense ratios of 0.6% to 1% of a fund's average net assets. Although Bogle acknowledged that cost is just one of three sides of the eternal triangle of investing (the other two being reward and risk), he urged investors not to underestimate the importance of cost.

To illustrate this point, Bogle scrutinized the "invisible cost" of executing portfolio transactions. Even though giant funds pay lower commissions to buy and sell stocks than do individual investors, brokerage costs can account for 0.5% to 2% of fund assets per year. (In Canada, these brokerage commissions are in addition to MERs.) Furthermore, smaller funds with high rates of portfolio turnover have even higher costs. Portfolio turnover in equity funds is almost double that of pension funds. When all visible costs are added up, Bogle found that the average cost of owning a U.S. mutual fund is 2.2% a year, with the highest-cost families of funds as high as 3.5%.

As a result, the expense ratio "represents the most significant cost you will incur in owning a mutual fund," Bogle explains. And he noted that the economies of scale from larger funds often are used to benefit fund management rather than unitholders. Bogle found that advisory fees to run a large government bond fund "cannot be justified by the costs incurred. They can be justified only by the principle that the fund's sponsor is entitled to amass most of the compelling economies of scale that exist in fund management to its own benefit, rather than sharing them with fund shareholders."

## Economies of scale haven't lowered fees

Bogle further notes that, based on the tremendous growth of fund-industry assets, "We might expect that fund expense ratios would have declined over the years. However, the reverse has proven true: expense ratios have risen." For example, for the average stock fund, the expense ratio rose from 0.7% of assets in 1961 to 1.5% in 1992, even while equity fund assets rose twentyfold from US$23 billion to US$463 billion. "What we are witnessing is not only the failure of managers to share economies of scale with fund shareholders but also their penchant to increase costs to fund investors at an even faster rate than fund asset growth," Bogle notes.

The trend in Canada has been similar. At $11 billion, Canada's largest mutual fund, Templeton Growth, now sports a considerably higher MER than when it was just a $1-billion fund. Templeton was the last major fund company to introduce trailer fees—an annual payment of 0.5% to 1% a year paid to brokers for "servicing" fund clients, and one of the biggest contributors to higher MERs. To justify this action, Templeton argued that the lack of trailers was hurting growth and fund performance.

The front-load Trimark Fund has assets of $3 billion and an MER of 1.52%. Trimark Select Growth, a virtual clone sold primarily with a rear load, has almost twice the assets at $5.8 billion, but a higher MER of 2.27%. Any alleged gains from greater economies of scale are overridden by sales considerations.

An MER analysis by CentrePost Mutual Funds showed MERs of Canada's largest funds are higher than the industry average. The 13 largest global equity funds averaged an MER of 2.42%, even though the industry average of 320 such funds was 2.28%. The top 10 Canadian equity funds averaged a 2.22% MER, even though the average of 271 funds was 2.00%.

Dan Richards still believes that the fund companies will have opportunities to cut margins as funds grow in size. He notes, "Normally you take a category, let's say computers or VCRs, and if you get an exponential increase in volume, prices come down because of economies of scale. As volume has grown from $30 billion to $330 billion, the price of mutual funds has stayed flat and in some cases moved up. Part of the reason they've gone up is because there is a significant distribution cost embedded in mutual funds that tends to be relatively fixed; but the other reason they haven't come down is there hasn't been a catalyst in the industry who really has taken it upon themselves as their mission to preach the gospel of lower management fees. We don't have anyone here in Canada, unlike the U.S., where they had Vanguard to be the champion."

Another illustration that fees can be higher because of sales charges comes from the life insurance industry's segregated funds (seg funds), which are mutual fund-like products with certain guarantees attached to them (more on this in Chapter 7). One of the biggest seg-fund groups is Great-West Life, which sells the funds in two ways: through a declining-redemption schedule or on a so-called "no-load" basis. But the no-load versions have management fees that are 0.24% higher than the rear version. High MER funds, load or not, are really nothing more than "buried-load funds."

## Sales structure keeps fees up

For all of the reasons discussed above, Richards argues that the current MER environment can't last much longer. The companies are locked into a compensation structure that has not caught up with the huge growth of the industry over the past five years. A 2% MER splits 1% to the fund company for investment management and 1% to the selling brokers. That 1% is the same as many alternatives presented in this book. It's not that the investment management provided by the large-load fund firms is more expensive, but that there's a big price to pay for the advice obtained from independent brokers and dealers. "It's a lot harder for a fund company to drop fees because they still have their embedded adviser-compensation costs," Richards says. "Whenever you have an industry that goes through hypergrowth the way the mutual-fund industry has, you have anomalies simply because the market reality is out of sync. Ultimately, market forces serve to correct those."

The good news is that investors can help to accelerate the arrival of these market forces. The starting point is to change the perception that 2.5 or 3% is a "little, inconsequential number." Thinking in "basis points" is a good start. A basis point is one-hundredth of a per cent. That is, 100 basis points is another way of saying 1%. When you see that a fund has an MER of, say, 2.75%, think of it as 275 basis points. Consider that some pension funds and U.S. index funds have MERs of just 20 basis points. A good analogy is to liken the MER to the price of a cup of coffee. Nowadays, consumers willingly plunk down $1.50 for a quality coffee. They also occasionally buy the upscale lattes and café au laits for $2.50 or $3, but they think about it first.

In your mind, $1 may a reasonable price to pay for a cup of coffee. As it happens, 1% is a low price for a mutual fund MER. For $2—or a 2% MER—you'd expect something above average. And a $3 coffee or a 3% MER had better be something special. You'd want an extra caffeine jolt from a $3 cup of coffee, and you'd expect a mega-return from a fund sporting an MER of 300 basis points!

Change your thinking that 2% is a reasonable MER. Two per cent, or 200 basis points, is below average for Canadian funds, but pricy compared to the 1% fees seen in the products described later in Part 3. Even 1.5%, or 150 basis points, is no bargain, although it is about the best you can expect in broker-sold equity funds in Canada. But 250 basis points is pricy; 275 basis points is expensive; 300 basis points is exorbitant. And 350 basis points borders on highway robbery.

When *The Financial Post* first published Hamilton's research in late 1997, it caused a stir both among consumers and the fund industry alike. Richards concedes, "The analysis . . . for the first time really put what management fees cost in a context people could relate to."

One reader asked whether high MERs would ultimately reduce an investment to zero. Hamilton explains, "It approaches zero but never gets there. If you put money in a mutual fund with a 2.1% MER and leave it there for four centuries, that doesn't mean you won't have any money. It means the vast majority of the returns the market provides for four centuries end up with people other than you."

Rather, the 39% "loss" cited by Hamilton (over 25 years) is the difference between what you *could* have generated from the market and what was left after the MER was deducted every year. (And remember, you can get almost a market return by investing in low-fee index products, which are discussed in Chapter 9.) Say you think the market will generate an 8% return, or 5.9% after a 2.1% MER is deducted. A dollar invested does not fall to 61 cents after 25 years. Rather, $1 grows to $6.85 over 25 years at 8%; but $1 invested in a fund levying a 2.1% MER would grow to just $4.19 over the same period: the $4.19

is 39% less than the $6.85 you could have had. Over 50 years, the $1 would grow to $46.90 in the market and $17.57 through the fund.

No one in the fund industry disputes these calculations, although some financial planners complain about how the figures can be interpreted. Essex Capital Management's Brian Forrest, for example, says, "Stating that with a 2.1% MER the investor is left with only 61% of the money after 25 years is verbal and mathematical slight of hand." He explains, "If you think that paying 2.1% for professional management is too much, try earning the same rates by trading your own stock portfolio. Small trades can cost as much as 3% going in and another 3% selling in brokerage commissions. You will also spend an enormous amount of time keeping track of your holdings, doing research, figuring out when to buy and when to sell, and you will probably make the odd huge error—further cutting into your yields."

## How to calculate the impact of MERs

Having discussed the impact of MERs, you are probably interested in understanding how they are affecting your investments. To do this, you need a good scientific calculator or spreadsheet.

Call the initial principal, P; the expected annual rate of return, R; the MER, M; and the number of years to retirement, N.

The formula to calculate the final value (FV) of the investment after deduction of the management expense ratio is

$$FV = P \times (1 + (R - M))^N$$

In the example below,

$$P = \$10,000$$
$$R = 10\%$$
$$M = 0, 1, 2.1, \text{ or } 3.5$$
$$N = 30$$

multiply the initial amount to be invested, in this case $10,000, by (1 + the market return minus fees) all raised to the power of N, which is the number of years invested.

## $10,000 Growing at 10% a Year

| MER | Value at 30 Years | % Loss to MER |
|-----|-------------------|---------------|
| 0% | $175,000 | 0 |
| 1% | $133,000 | 24% |
| 2.1% | $98,000 | 44% |
| 3.5% | $66,000 | 62% |

Note that if you could get 10% a year with no management fees, it would grow to $175,000 after 30 years, as it might tax-sheltered in an RRSP. In the early 1990s, you might have achieved this return with an ordinary bank GIC or strip bond.

Yet even those examples do not involve 0% management fees, since there are built-in commissions. These examples also might have yielded 10.5 or 11% before fees.

In the real world, of course, no one will invest your money for you without some payment for their efforts. However, this book examines many investment options that charge a more reasonable 1% a year of assets. In such cases, the above chart shows that over 30 years, what would otherwise have grown to $175,000 at a 10% rate of return grows only at 9% (10% a year minus the 1% annual management fee), resulting in a $133,000 nest egg, a loss of $42,000 or 24% of what you could have earned.

The chart also shows the impact of an average 2.1% MER over a 30-year period. What would in a perfect fee-less world have grown to $175,000 becomes only $98,000, a "loss" of 44%. Examples of popular funds with such an average 2.1% MER include Templeton Growth (2.0%), Ivy Growth & Income (2.12%), and Altamira Balanced Fund (2%).

Plenty of funds are more expensive than the average, such as AGF China Focus (3.5%), 20/20 India (3.49%), and the AIM Tiger Fund (3.36%). Those are MERs without any fees-on-fees overlays. If you add in the impact of programs such as CIBC Choices or the Manulife GIF (Guaranteed Investment Fund), many funds have 3.5% MERs.

What is the impact of a 3.5% MER on your retirement savings? As the chart shows, your money will compound at 6.5% (10%

minus 3.5%) a year for 30 years, meaning what would otherwise have grown to $175,000 becomes just $66,000: a whopping 62% less than it could have been with no costs.

A key element in this equation is the compounding effect of time. As Hamilton says, "If you're saving for something two years from now, the MER doesn't matter. If you're saving for retirement, it does matter."

Even with strip bonds and index products, you can't escape paying some commissions, so no one can eliminate intermediary costs altogether. But if you can move from funds with 2.5 or 3% MERs to ones with MERs of 1 or 1.5% with comparable performance, then the graph shows that the potential gains are significant.

## Charging what the traffic will bear

In the early years, when consumers were unaware of the MER's impact, fund companies charged as much as they believed consumers would tolerate. In fact, that was the explanation offered by Memorial University finance professor Dale Domian in an interview with *Canadian Business* magazine: "It's just a case of charging what the market will bear." The article cited simple greed as the motivating factor, using as evidence the fact that in Canada investors pay an average MER of 1.6% to buy a fund that tracks the S&P 500 index. In the United States, a similar fund is available at an MER of as little as 0.2%—eight times cheaper than the Canadian equivalent. As discussed in Chapter 9, the mutual-fund versions of indexing solutions are considerably more expensive than other passive investing choices.

Fortunately, more Canadians now get the message. They understand that the mutual fund industry's "ugly secret" is, as *Canadian Business* put it, "The more you pay, the less you are likely to get." However, the magazine also presented the flip-side—the usual fund-industry argument on MERs: that no one objects to paying high fees for high performance. The companies argue that they have earned those fees and, indeed, as long as they delivered 20 to 30% a year in investment returns, who could begrudge them those fees when we were in turn enjoying 18 to 28% returns?

But the magazine's writer, Jonathan Harris, rebutted this argument when he also noted that "the problem is that many funds charge high fees for lacklustre performance." Harris concluded that MERs are "breathtakingly high in Canada—far higher than in the U.S. Canadian MERs are, in fact, far higher than any objective analysis of the industry would support" (*Canadian Business*, September 1997). The magazine commissioned Toronto-based FundScope, a mutual-fund research firm, to analyze funds that were three years or older. It found that, all other things being equal, funds with the lowest fees were most likely to outperform the market. Several other studies support this finding. For example, in the 1997 self-published *The Money Management Game: What They Don't Tell You About Mutual Funds*, Toronto broker Andy Filipiuk cites a Morningstar analysis of U.S. equity funds over 10 years, ending November 30, 1995. It revealed that funds with expense ratios under 1.36% returned an average of 13.1% a year, while funds with MERs above 1.36% yielded just 11.1%. He also cited Princeton University and Securities and Exchange Commission (SEC) studies showing that between 1971 and 1993, for every 1% spent by an average equity fund on expenses, returns dropped 1.9%.

Furthermore, in March 1998, *Consumer Reports* demonstrated its premise that "most stock funds charge investors too much and return too little." Of the 2,029 domestic (U.S.) equity funds available since 1995, it found that fewer than 6% had matched or outperformed the returns of the S&P 500 index.

As a result, *Canadian Business*'s Harris concluded that the mutual fund industry "thrives on ignorance." Other studies have revealed that "financial illiteracy" in Canada has reached distressingly high levels. For example, almost half of 2,000 Canadians polled in May 1997 didn't even know they were charged fees. Furthermore, Richards' Marketing Solutions showed that a significant minority of Canadians believe that "no-load funds" means they're paying no sales charges or any management fees whatsoever.

Granted, the fund companies don't always go out of their way to clarify these matters for consumers. For example, when Canada Trust unveiled its "zero commissions" campaign on front-load funds purchased through its discount arm, Dynamic Mutual Funds accused it of misleading advertising. Dynamic ran ads pointing out that Canada Trust still received annual trailer fees, often of 1%, which can be considered to be a deferred commission. Further, many front-load funds have trailer fees that are twice as high as rear-load funds, so all Canada Trust really proved was that there is no such thing as a free lunch.

## Good advice is worth something

In its challenge leveled at Canada Trust, Dynamic pointed out that at least the visible commissions associated with load funds buy advice and service. This distinction is important because there are two types of mutual fund consumers and two main ways of selling to them. First, the load funds sold by advisers will argue that an adviser is necessary because they keep investors invested during market downturns. Second, the "no-load, no-advice" funds are aimed at do-it-yourselfers, many of whom are computer-literate and cost-conscious.

Good advice should at least direct investors to funds that beat the indexes and justify their fees, however high. Former AGF vice president Allen Clarke argues there's nothing wrong with taking an extra 1% a year out of the pie if the fund managers and advisers add 5% or 6% a year in extra performance. Clarke explains that the biggest component of MERs are commissions, which can come down, as so-called "back-office" administration becomes more efficient. In theory, as funds become larger, accounting and legal fees should decrease. Even so, he warns, "If you drill down into MERs, there's a limit to what you can do there. The two biggest components are the profitability for the mutual fund companies and the commission structures."

Clarke compares do-it-yourself investors to people who save money by changing their own oil at Canadian Tire. There is always a minority of the population who is willing to take the trouble, but most people are happy to pay a little more than the cost of the oil to get someone else to do it for them. "Sure you can do it cheaper. But you have to go out and find the right money manager, then you have to buy an asset allocation product, find the other managers in other styles, assemble the whole thing, you have to do performance measurement; Mercer is going to charge you $10,000 a year to do performance measurement on a single account. So you can save money and change your own oil or you can pay a little more and have it done by professionals."

In the United States, 30% of the population is willing to go direct, bypassing some of these intermediaries. But only 20% of Canadian fund buyers deal with direct firms such as Scudder or Altamira. "The Canadian market wants to deal through the advice channel and quite frankly appears to be willing to pay for the advice process," Clarke notes.

He argues that more interesting than MERs is how value is added to the broker/customer relationship. Historically, value was added through transactions by stock picking or market timing or recommendations such as investing in U.S. stocks. Now, there's a different understanding in how money should be managed. The big Canadian brokerages are training brokers about asset class selection and how to construct portfolios.

"What's evolving is a new way. They meet with the client, figure out what the need is, then get into selection of asset classes, which modern portfolio theory says is more important than the money manager. Then you have to get into construction of portfolios. Quite frankly, if all they do is call the client up every six months to tell them not to do anything, just leave it alone, then he's earned that 100 basis points that's added to the MER."

Clarke's view is similar to that of many load-fund investment advisers who swear by U.S. adviser/author Nick Murray and his philosophy, outlined in his 1996 self-published book, *The Excellent Investment Advisor*. Both Clarke and Murray point out that the average client is predisposed to trying to do something with the account, even though most activities end up negating performance. However, if an adviser can talk the investor out of destructive portfolio activity, it can add 600 to 700 basis points to performance. "Is it worth it to pay that extra 100 basis points? I think it is," Clarke says, "The market has become so confusing, the advice channel is secure. I think people are getting good value. But that doesn't mean I don't think MERs are not going to come down in the future."

Yet, investors with 20-fund portfolios holding $100,000 complain that their portfolios aren't growing. "You blame it on the MER," Clarke says. "I say if a portfolio isn't growing it is most likely because it isn't getting proper advice, and [the investors are] transaction oriented and stepping out of the market and stepping back into the market, going into the U.S., timing various subsections of the market, figuring it's time to jump in or out of small caps. That's the activity that all the research shows damages portfolio performance. Obviously the pure math tells you that if you charge an extra 50 basis points in the long run it reduces performance, but would you pay 50 basis points to add 600 basis points? People don't understand that. The point is if you pay the extra money, you get more."

Clarke says he'll pay $1 to get $8. "If you're really knowledgeable and willing to do it yourself, you can save the $1. It comes down to whether or not you want to change your own oil. You can go out and buy a book on how to change oil, you can go out and buy all the things you need to change your own oil, and you can crawl under the car and change oil. Then there are people driving along and they don't even know they need to change their oil. Someone comes along and tells them they're going to blow their engine if they don't change the oil. I should be paid for informing you of the impending disaster and now I have a solution. I'll change your oil professionally. They're adding to the relationship. They deserve to get paid for it."

But who will lead the charge to lower MERs? When Scudder is suggested, Clarke questions whether "people are beating a path to Scudder's door. And maybe Canadian Tire should be crowded with guys crawling under cars changing their oil on Saturday morning, but it isn't happening." There seems to be no definitive resolution to this debate. The load camp usually cites the 1996 study by Boston's Dalbar Inc., which showed that actual investor

returns depend more on investor behavior than on fund performance. It found that investors who were advised by a sales force
outperformed no-load do-it-yourselfers by 16% in equity funds
and 30% in fixed income funds, and that a simple "buy-and-
hold" strategy was three times better than frequent switching.

Slightly different conclusions were reached in a March 1998
*Consumer Reports* study of actual fund returns (as opposed to
investor returns studied by Dalbar). This study showed that in the
United States, over a three-year period no-load funds were nearly
twice as likely to outperform the S&P 500 index as load funds. On
average, no-loads outperformed by more than 1% a year over the
period studied. These aren't contrary findings, says The Rogers
Group's chairman, Jim Rogers. "The Dalbar load funds didn't
likely do better in absolute terms but, because of (likely) adviser-
driven strategies, the investors in such funds did better."

No-load funds eliminate the intermediary and the costs associated with them. No-load firms generally sell directly to the
public and may charge less because they don't have to pay the
high costs of distributing load funds through the independent
networks of brokers and dealers. Scudder and Altamira are classic
"direct sellers" who find their customers through advertising,
and then deal directly with them without intermediaries. Both also
work through various bank discount brokers and pay modest
trailer fees.

The bank no-load groups differ slightly from the Altamira/
Scudder variety of direct sellers, since the banks own their network of branches. In theory, this should make it somewhat easier
for them to drive down fees than independent broker-dependent
firms. Ironically, older Canadian fund companies such as United
and Guardian once had their own dealer networks. One holdover
continues to be Canada's largest fund company, Winnipeg-based
Investors Group, which sells its own proprietary funds and a few
third-party funds through a 3,000-strong "captive" sales force.

But neither Investors Group nor the banks have lowered their
management fees. Both appear to charge what the traffic will
bear, which happens to be fees comparable to their broker-sold
rivals. In fact, the only bank to give wealthier investors a break on

fees as mutual funds assets rise is the Bank of Montreal's First Canadian Funds.

Dan Richards says the problem for load companies is that their embedded distribution costs are variable, not fixed, unlike the fixed costs of the banks' no-load groups. As a result, it doesn't cost more for a bank to sell another $10 million of a fund. For the average broker-sold load fund, however, distribution costs run between 0.75 and 1.25%. On a front-load equity fund, the fund companies pay brokers and dealers 1% a year in trailer fees; on DSC or rear-load funds, it's 50 basis points. These distribution costs establish a minimum standard, which can't be lowered, according to Richards, "unless a fund company does some pretty creative things. It's tough to run a business at a 1.5% MER."

One could argue that the AGFs, Fidelitys, Mackenzies, and Trimarks have a distribution structure that made more sense five years ago than it does now. When you have a smaller amount of money to manage, it makes more sense to have low fixed and high variable costs. As the companies have become huge, however, it makes less sense to have high variable costs. Increasingly, the Investors Group's strategy of owning its own network may make sense.

At this point it is important to acknowledge that if the fund companies did lower costs quickly, the alternatives outlined in this book would be much less attractive. But, given that the number of existing fund investors is now so huge and the steady stream of newcomers coming into funds so attractive, it's understandable that fees won't be coming down fast enough to accommodate boomers whose wealth is becoming substantial. After all, the mass market is a volume business and too much money is being made to kill the golden goose—or even put it on a diet.

For these reasons, we expect most retail-level mutual funds will continue to take over 2% of your investment right off the top, each and every year. When you consider that most fund managers fail to beat the major indexes they are measured against over the long run, you're likely to get a return that underperforms the index. The truth is, the mutual fund industry has now *become* the market.

The sheer momentum of one of history's greatest manias will certainly propel fund assets under management to even higher levels in the early years of the next century. But gradually, as retirement portfolios grow to serious levels, boomers will grow increasingly critical about high fees and the failure of so many fund managers to outperform the market benchmarks.

The fund companies may pay lip service to the notion of lowering MERs. Some may even introduce a dual-fee system, giving affluent investors MER breaks once assets hit, say, the $100,000 level. They'll eventually be forced to do so once the "Life After Mutual Funds" phenomenon starts to make headway in the early 21st century.

## When is it time to make the change?

But don't hold your breath waiting for the fund companies to lower their costs. It's up to individuals to decide whether their net worth has reached the point where mutual funds no longer meet their needs.

Investors move up from mutual funds when they decide they want something different, says AGF's Clarke. "As people get closer to the crest of the hill to retirement, it becomes more real to clients. What happens in the broker's mind is that as the accounts get bigger, the broker and planner realize there are other alternatives. They can go to discretionary money management, or a Wrap product, and often the broker or planner will pre-empt the process and say to the client 'at this stage in your life we should look at something where the fee is tax deductible, where we look at performance measurement, or the account is fully diversified.' The amount of the money is less the trigger than the life-positioning realization that the whole thing has to be treated more seriously."

An investor who has been lucky enough to find an excellent investment adviser may indeed be informed when the transition point has been reached. But as the next chapter shows, not all advisers in Canada put their clients' interests ahead of their own. Just as no one rings a bell when the stock market tops out, not all brokers living off the trailer fees of hundreds of clients will ring a bell and notify them that it's time to find cheaper alternatives. That's the purpose of this book: we're making the wake-up call!

## Why fees may get higher before they get lower

Despite the pressure for lower MERs, the industry appears headed in the opposite direction. In spite of the entry of low-MER foreign newcomers such as Scudder, there is a disturbing trend wherein fees are being layered on top of fees in the already-high MERs of the average broker-sold fund.

At least three trends are responsible for taking MERs in Canada higher rather than lower. The first is the trend to miniature "Wrap" programs that choose a group of mutual funds for naive investors and impose a 1% fee on top of the funds' underlying fees for the privilege. Two bank fund groups, Scotiabank and CIBC Securities, offer such programs.

The second trend stems from Canadians' desire to have the best of both worlds—by participating in rising stock markets while also insulating their portfolios from loss. This trick is accomplished by the banks' popular index-linked GICs, which pay bonus interest in proportion to gains in the Canadian or U.S. stock market, and guarantee the initial principal (but often no interest) if markets fall. The fund industry is responding by aligning with life insurance companies, which have always performed this trick with their segregated, or "seg" funds. What the seg funds lacked is the glamor of the more popular mutual funds. The nervous and volatile stock markets that have been the norm in the late 1990s have spawned a new generation of mutual funds masquerading as seg funds, with additional MERs of anywhere from 0.3% to 1%. Manulife Financial has sold almost $3 billion of its new Guaranteed Investment Funds (GIFs) after just a year. The GIFs package up popular brand-name funds but the effective MER is often a full percentage point higher. BPI, C.I. Mutual Funds, Trimark, and Templeton have all announced seg-fund versions of their underlying funds. This phenomenon is explored in more detail in Chapter 7 on "guaranteed alternatives" to mutual funds.

A third force that may push MERs higher is, ironically, the cost of regulation. The Canadian fund industry has long attributed some of the cost pressures to an antiquated and cumbersome regulatory framework with separate securities commissions in 10 provinces, not to mention the costs of bilingualism.

As a case in point, the Ontario Securities Commission's Glorianne Stromberg told Ottawa policymakers in 1998 that it is "probably true" that the costs of implementing some of her proposals for investment funds reform will be passed on to consumers. At the same time she questioned whether there is enough scrutiny on allocation of fund costs and expenses between the managers and their funds. "It appears that the tendency is simply to pass on costs rather than to take a good hard look at one's operations to see if it is appropriate to do so or to see if there are not more efficient ways of doing things for less cost." These amounts all appear in the MER of the funds and reduce the amount of the investor's return, Stromberg said. More of her work is explored in the next chapter.

## Trailer fee rebate a good sign

On a more optimistic note, there are signs that the brokers themselves may open up the MER floodgates where the manufacturers have failed. For example, in March 1998, newcomer Priority Brokerage, led by chairman Paul Bates, announced that investors holding $25,000 in any fund will receive a 0.25% rebate of the trailer fee if the funds are held for three months or more. Industry observers such as Dan Richards hailed the announcement as the opening salvo in the MER wars. Soon after, elite no-load outfit GBC Asset Management Inc. announced that investors with more than $500,000 in the GBC Canadian Bond Fund will receive an annual 0.25% rebate of the management fee.

The banks are also becoming aggressive with low-fee index funds. By comparison with U.S. index funds, Canadian index funds are still costly. But CIBC Securities Inc. is coming close to the Vanguard model by setting the MER on several new index funds at an aggressive 90 basis points (0.9% a year). TD GreenLine

Funds has committed to establishing a similar 90 basis-point MER threshold for its international index funds and an even more aggressive 80 basis points for its North American index funds. Chapter 9 looks at how investors can forget about expensive actively managed funds and rely on low-cost "passive" investing.

Royal Mutual Funds' new Strategic Indexing Funds have MERs that are roughly between fully managed funds and pure index funds. Dan Richards believes Royal's impact on MERs could be significant. Royal is the largest no-load firm in the country. "This is the first shot fired in the management expense war. It's the first time that a mainstream player has competed explicitly on price," says Richards. The door has been opened for further downward pressure on fees. If this is successful for the Royal Bank, inevitably other banks will be looking for alternatives.

The proposed megabank mergers could also help to lower mutual fund MERs. Royal's proposed merger partner, the Bank of Montreal, sells First Canadian no-load funds that already ratchet MERs down as you buy more funds. And, as we note above, it looks like a combined CIBC–TD would be the equivalent of Canada's Vanguard in indexing, albeit with an index-fund MER target of 0.8% to 0.9%.

"Life After Mutual Funds" will not truly begin, however, until the great bull market of the 1990s finally peters out. By 1998, the bull was showing signs of pawing sideways. The U.S. market had "corrected" 13% from its year high by August, while the Canadian stock market was down 25%—technically a bear market. If we are entering a new era of single-digit returns of 8% or 9%, investors will be left with 6% or 7% after fees of 2%, which is not much better than the risk-free 6% generated with long-term bonds. As for bond funds, these funds manage to hold their own as long as interest rates decline, since such an occurrence provides a capital gain that masks the performance losses from management fees. But once interest rates bottom, it becomes much harder for fixed-income fund managers to beat the indexes. Most bond funds are stable filler products that allow the banks and planners licensed only to sell funds to compete with full-service advisers who can sell bonds directly.

As with all investment products, there is a time and a place for mutual funds, depending on the investor's stage of the investment life cycle. For those just starting out in their investment lives, mutual funds may yet be the only game in town. For many more, mutual funds will allow investors to reach the next stage, the stage of "serious money," which can be variously defined as $50,000, $150,000, $500,000, or $1 million or more. In some cases, while mutual funds may not be the optimum product, other types of investment funds may be, such as pooled funds, closed-end funds, segregated funds, or offshore funds. Chapter 8 is devoted to these mutual-fund lookalike products.

Our main concern with traditional open-end mutual funds is the high-MER, often rear-load versions, so often forced upon newcomers by financial planners and brokers who have more interest in seeing their own net worth rise than their clients'. These are the type of sales practices condemned by Glorianne Stromberg in her provocative *Stromberg Report*. "When you read the numbers it makes one wonder whether financial advisors who recommend high-MER funds are in breach of their fiduciary obligations to their clients," Stromberg told the authors. We'll discuss Stromberg, fiduciary duty, and conflicts of interest in more detail in Chapter 4.

What, then, are consumers to do? The *Money* magazine cover story alluded to earlier highlights the fact that fund expenses erode returns. "To the extent [that] you invest in funds, it's wise to seek out portfolios that keep their expenses below the average for their peers."

Since MERs cut into performance, it is logical to seek consistent, strong-performing fund groups that have both low MERs and low volatility. Chapter 6 looks at how investors who are still committed to mutual funds can minimize the damage.

## Consumers will vote with their wallets

As the 1990s close, there is evidence that consumers are responding to the fee message and are starting to vote with their wallets for the families that give them the best deal. "Someone has to conclude they can get a leg up on the competition by having lower fees," Hamilton says, "If enough money follows low fees, then it starts to snowball. Then there's a business reason to cut fees, and also [consolidate]. If you compete on low fees, you need economies of scale. . . . Entrepreneurs are driven by profit."

All it will take is a major player to exploit these trends as a point of difference. Trimark chairman Robert Krembil predicts that at some point fees may be unbundled, with separate charges for investment management, distribution, and advice.

There are two arguments about how MER considerations should influence decisions for mutual fund investors. One is that the MER is important in the long run, i.e., Canadian RRSP investing. Second, you're unlikely to find a manager who can make up for the high MERs by providing consistently above-average performance. "If you could find a manager who could add 400 basis points (4%) to annual returns, there would be less of a problem with a 200 basis point (2%) MER," Hamilton says. "The question is where can you find management that adds enough value to compensate for the MER loss. It's virtually certain that when you get to well-developed efficient markets like the U.S. large-cap stocks or Canadian large-cap stocks, there's such a wealth of information publicly available to managers pursuing those returns. If they get efficient markets it's very hard for even a capable manager to add enough value to overdo even 100 basis points." For this reason, CIBC Securities Inc. dropped its actively managed U.S. large-cap equity fund altogether, replacing it with a lower-MER index version.

It's harder for a bond fund manager to add even 25 basis points' value. "Overcoming almost any MER in the bond markets in North America is extremely difficult," says Hamilton, "When you get to Emerging Markets or non-North American equities (EAFE), small caps, or venture capital, it's more plausible that a manager can add value. If you're in a niche where there are not as many players and pricing isn't as efficient, there's more of an opportunity for a level-headed manager with discipline to actually beat the markets. People should be more inclined in those areas to accept the idea of paying something. Obviously they should never pay more than they have to but don't be close minded about whether the managers can add value. The odds of someone adding value on a U.S. or Canadian bond fund is pretty small. It's hard to do."

It's no casual matter for the average investor to make such determinations, however. When it comes to deciding where mutual fund managers can justify their fees, and where they may not, most investors need some professional advice.

Unfortunately, as the next chapter covers, the advice dispensed by mutual-fund salespeople, some of them unqualified but posing as "financial planners," is all too often suspect. Because the field is so competitive, some inferior funds may pay salespeople more than superior funds. While the fund industry has started to address the more blatant conflicts of interest, it is still very much a "buyer beware" situation.

## Chapter Four

# Tainted Advice: Conflicts of Interest by Fund Salespeople

For years, the Canadian mutual fund industry enjoyed a pristine reputation, a happy circumstance that supported its arguments for self-regulation.

There were few scandals comparable to such international brouhahas as the Investors Overseas Services scam perpetrated by Bernie Cornfield in the early 1970s. But something as huge as the mutual fund business—industry assets have now passed $300 billion in Canada and a few trillion dollars in the United States—must inevitably attract a few questionable practitioners.

By 1998, the Canadian mutual fund industry was no longer quite as squeaky clean as its supporters once maintained. Irregularities on both the distribution and manufacturing ends of the business were starting to emerge. The most dramatic revelation came when Frank Mersch, the heart and soul of the stock-picking operation at troubled no-load firm Altamira Investment Services, Inc., left the firm in May 1998 amid a blaze of negative publicity.

A month later, the OSC effectively barred Mersch from the industry for six months for making misleading statements about his personal investments.

## Personal trading by fund managers

So ended the Altamira phase of Canada's mutual fund king, following the humbling of the queen two years earlier, when Veronika Hirsch ran afoul of regulators in two provinces over a personal purchase of a junior gold stock. Hirsch had built her name, in part, by playing Bre-X early both in her funds at

Prudential and later at AGF. But it was the lesser-known Oliver Gold that embarrassed Hirsch and the industry. The media fallout caused the entire fund industry including, ironically, Altamira, to review and in some cases tighten up internal ethical guidelines and personal trading policies.

Hirsch had labored in relative obscurity for more than a decade at Prudential Fund Management (now Maxxum Funds) before moving to a high-profile job as lead Canadian equity manager at AGF Management Ltd. AGF highlighted its new star in saturation advertising campaigns, including prominent television spots, but in less than a year Hirsch was hired away by rival Fidelity Investments Canada Ltd. to head up the new Fidelity True North fund. Within months, Hirsch left Fidelity, too, after widespread media reports alleging personal trading irregularities with Oliver Gold.

The Hirsch case appeared to be largely one of jurisdictional confusion between Ontario and British Columbia and perhaps some sloppy paperwork on Hirsch's part. An OSC hearing ultimately found no evidence Hirsch purchased shares in Oliver Gold Corp. on her own account in advance of purchases in the stock for the portfolio she managed while at AGF. The settlement agreements with the two principal regulators stated Hirsch broke

the rules when she did not check whether the private placement in Oliver Gold was open to residents of Ontario, where Hirsch lived. She also made a false statement when she gave the Vancouver address of her stockbroker in order to make the purchase. Hirsch paid $140,000 to regulators in late 1997 to resolve the issue. The furor died down and at her new firm, Hirsch Asset Management Corp., where she is a money manager and 50% owner, Hirsch has adopted a ban on personal trading.

But personal trading was only one of 14 examples of possible problems in the Canadian fund industry cited by Stephen Erlichman, a former partner at the Toronto law firm Davies, Ward & Beck, in a mid-1990s paper to the Insight Conference about fiduciary duties and conflicts of interest in the industry. Erlichman cited a *Globe and Mail* column written by Wendy Brodkin, a principal with Towers Perrin, in which Brodkin raised eyebrows in the investment industry when she referred to the Hirsch and Mersch cases as "hardly isolated incidents." She continued, "It's been going on forever and it may continue to go on forever, given the current standards. The investment industry is fraught with questionable practices and even more questionable ethics . . . a lot of people are getting away with a lot of things." Among other things, Brodkin mentioned front running (buying a stock for your own account, and later for the fund), questionable priority of transactions and allocation of securities, and unauthorized trading and allocation of securities after price changes. She warned investors that "the only person you can really count on to look out for your best interests is you."

Traditionally, the Canadian mutual fund industry has been subject to minimal regulation. Even now, the industry is arguing that it can regulate itself by transforming lobby groups such as the Investment Funds Institute of Canada (IFIC) into so-called self-regulatory organizations (SROs).

## The Stromberg Report

But an industry so massive that its total worth will soon eclipse bank deposits invites further government and regulatory scrutiny.

As a case in point, in 1994, the Ontario Securities Commission's then-chairman Ed Waitzer commissioned Glorianne Stromberg, a semi-retired lawyer with extensive experience in the financial services industry, to take a broad look at investment funds. This examination involved interviewing virtually all the key leaders of the Canadian mutual fund industry, with the intention of identifying industry vulnerabilities.

As Stromberg reported to the Standing Senate Committee on Banking, Trade, and Commerce in 1998, current regulatory requirements "contain few requirements respecting the establishment and structuring of these funds. There is no requirement for the investment fund manager to be registered with any securities authority in order to establish and operate investment funds. In addition, there is no requirement for the investment fund manager to have 'outside directors.' There are no requirements with respect to minimum regulatory capital, insurance and bonding coverage, management resources, competency and proficiency of personnel, adequacy of internal systems, controls, and procedures, or procedures for monitoring the same. In addition, there is no requirement in the case of investment funds sponsored by the investment fund manager for the sponsored investment funds to have independent boards."

Furthermore, the manager and trustees of the funds are usually the same entity or affiliates. For tax reasons, most mutual funds in Canada are structured as trusts. Their terms are set by the manager-trustees. Because of this, there is really no one who is considering fairness and the transactions "from the perspective of what is in the best interests of the investment fund and its investors," Stromberg said. "It is no wonder that there are questions about who is looking out for the interests of investors."

By the end of 1998, however, the fund industry will have implemented a new mandatory code of ethics to restrict how fund managers invest their own money—one that will prohibit the sort of private placements that got Hirsch and Mersch unwanted media attention. The IFIC's Model Code for Personal Investing insists that a compliance officer at the fund company pre-clear all trades, with the exception of mutual fund units and some government bonds. Such a code should help investors to regain trust in the integrity of the fund managers responsible for their life savings. But the humbling of the fund managers is only one part of the story. Fund managers make good press, but only a few hundred of them are plying their trade in Canada, and individual investors rarely interact with the managers who are running their funds.

## Financial planners under scrutiny

By late 1997, abuses of trust were being revealed on the distribution end of the business. Almost all investors come into intimate personal contact with brokers and financial planners, more than 60,000 of whom were selling mutual funds by 1998. Inevitably, some of these individuals have been more interested in financing their own retirement than their clients'. One such example involved the case of London-based mutual fund salesperson Dino DeLellis, which was widely reported after the OSC revoked his Ontario securities license for selling unsuitable but lucrative (for him) limited partnerships to conservative investors.

One of DeLellis's former employers was Fortune Financial, which has encountered some legal difficulties involving former fund salesman Paul Tindall. Tindall is being investigated by the OSC, and Tindall and Fortune Financial have been sued for losses in high-risk real estate limited partnerships (LPs) by 24 investors who claim they had clearly expressed their need for conservative investments. A statement of claim filed by the investors in February 1998 against Tindall and Fortune alleged he was negligent and misrepresented investments to them. Tindall and Fortune deny the allegations, and Fortune Financial chairman David Singh said the company and Tindall will vigorously defend the action and provide evidence investors knew the risks and were seeking investments with above-average returns and tax advantages, that Tindall took extraordinary actions to keep the LP from floundering, and that he never took undisclosed fees from the promoter of the LP, or commissions from the banks that loaned investors the money to invest in the LP. While Tindall says he did nothing improper and had advised the clients of the risks, he nevertheless resigned from Fortune in March 1998. He handed his client base to his wife, Anne Louise, who also works at Fortune. Fortune founder David Singh told *Canadian Business* magazine that Tindall was "the first adviser in nine years who has been accused by a few clients of recommending unsuitable investments." In May 1998, Fortune said it was settling the lawsuits out of court.

Such cases are not aberrations. In 1997, Stromberg noted that the OSC audited 23 mutual fund dealers and uncovered "widespread regulatory lapses" and, in some cases, "abuses that clearly must be addressed." Names such as DeLellis and Tindall are, of course, less recognizable than the Mersches and Hirsches running the funds. They would be familiar primarily to the several hundred clients "serviced" by these brokers.

But the abuses that have come to light should have been no great surprise. These types of breaches of trust were predicted in January 1995, when the *Stromberg Report* was released.

One implication of the report was that the Canadian mutual fund industry was rife with actual or potential conflicts of interest. The media jumped on the sales practices abuses that Stromberg uncovered, and that was the area the industry decided to clean up first. On May 1, 1998, a new Sales Practices Rule came into effect for fund salespeople, with the industry declaring that it was adopting a tough new "zero tolerance" stance on improper sales practices. Although this constitutes mere self-regulation by the industry—arguably the fox is still in charge of the chicken coop— it nevertheless was viewed as addressing many of the ills identified by Stromberg.

In an attempt to give the industry its fair due, however, former AGF vice-chairman Allen Clarke says Stromberg fails to explain the benefits that have been bestowed upon the Canadian public by having well-run mutual funds made available to them. He points to the billions of dollars that Canadian investors have made through equity mutual funds, where previously they would have had paltry returns from bank GICs. He notes, "If you want to have quality products in the marketplace, people have to be paid: the salespeople and the brokerage firms and the planners and the manufacturers of funds take some piece of the action."

The lapses of trust are most apparent in the dealer channels that sell "load" mutual funds. The conflict is like the classic one described decades earlier in *Where Are the Customers' Yachts?* (by Fred Schwed, Jr., Wiley Investment Classics, New York, 1940, 1995). Schwed recounts the tale of an out-of-town visitor being shown the wonders of New York's financial district. A guide indicates some handsome ships anchored near the shore, saying, "Look, those are the bankers' and brokers' yachts." To which the naive visitor replies, "Where are the customers' yachts?"

Where indeed? We hasten to add here that we are talking only about a small minority of salespeople. No one really knows what percentage of brokers, financial planners, or fund salespeople are bad apples. But the fact remains that some investors are unfortunate enough to encounter financial services salespeople whose advice is chiefly designed to maximize their own wealth rather than their clients'. Some products—frequently the more questionable ones—pay a salesperson better than other, perhaps more appropriate, investments.

And herein lies the conflict: good dealers—and most are—will disregard their personal gain in such circumstances, but bad dealers may recommend a particular stock or fund not because they believe it may be a good investment for their client, but because they know it will generate lucrative commissions.

## Fund salespeople to have fiduciary obligations

Erlichman predicted that the Canadian mutual fund industry is "ripe for increased legal proceedings alleging breaches of fiduciary obligations" to clients. According to *Webster's Dictionary*, the term "fiduciary" relates to confidence and trust. It cites as an example *fiat* money, which depends on public confidence for value or currency. When it comes to investment management, clients or investors trust that their life savings will be prudently managed on their behalf by their investment manager. While the term has no specific legal definition, securities lawyer Neil Gross of Toronto-based Carson, Gross & McPherson says, "The most common statement in the law is that a fiduciary owes a duty of utmost good faith and loyalty."

Historically, the legal use of the term goes back to the fiduciary relationship between trustees and beneficiaries (more on trusts in Chapter 15). Although the legal aspects become complex, Erlichman cites Section 116 of the *Ontario Securities Act* in concluding that "trustees of mutual fund trusts, directors of mutual fund corporations, managers, and possibly investment advisers are implicitly fiduciaries." He added that "Canadian courts have held that the relationship between financial advisers and their clients are not, as a matter of law, fiduciary in nature but that, in certain circumstances, a fiduciary relationship can arise."

For mutual fund investors, the most heartening aspect of the new Mutual Fund Sales Practices Rule, which was put in place on May 1, 1998, was its declaration that both mutual fund dealers and sales representatives have a fiduciary obligation when an investor relies on them for expertise or advice. That was by no means an obvious or explicitly stated obligation before that time. In fact, the fund industry had shied away from using what Gross refers to as "the F word." The purpose of the Mutual Fund Sales Practices Rule, developed by the Canadian Securities Administrators (CSA, a national body of securities regulators) is laid out in a booklet issued by the IFIC. At the heart of the Rule are provisions designed to prevent the kind of conflicts of interest revealed by Stromberg. The exact wording is, "Dealers and sales representatives have a fiduciary obligation where an investor relies on them for expertise and advice."

John Mountain, the IFIC's vice-president of regulation, concedes that the industry agonized over whether to use the term "fiduciary" and the precise wording it would use. It considered a blanket statement that all fund salespeople have a fiduciary obligation to their clients, but were persuaded by IFIC lawyers to add the qualifier "where an investor relies on them for expertise and advice." That means that a person who puts through a transaction from do-it-yourself investors buying no-load funds or load funds at discount brokers would not bear a fiduciary responsibility.

The Rule's preamble makes it clear that fund dealers who give advice are considered by clients to be experts and that with that perception come weighty responsibilities. "Ours is an industry where the concept of *caveat emptor*, or 'buyer beware,' must be tempered by the fact that many investors depend exclusively on the advice of sales representatives," the Rule states. "The people sitting across from a sales representative or on the other end of the telephone consider that sales representative to be the expert who is making recommendations to them that are in their best interests."

Given that a third of a trillion dollars of Canadian savings are now invested in mutual funds, it is astonishing that IFIC members had not clarified this point to their sales forces before. One would have assumed that a salesperson giving advice on someone's life savings or retirement nest egg would automatically have a fiduciary obligation. But stockbrokers have argued that they do not necessarily have a fiduciary obligation in all situations including the fiasco over Bre-X Minerals Ltd. In the high-net-worth realm of discretionary investment management, managers have always understood and acted in a manner consistent with owing a fiduciary obligation to their clients.

The full implications of this now-clarified fiduciary obligation to small investors will not be apparent until the bull market ends as it appeared to by August 1998. If the legal floodgates open against the industry, the timing will likely be in the wake of a major—and protracted—stock-market decline. Senior OSC officials told a *Financial Post* editorial briefing in late 1997 that complaints about stock losses generally quintuple in bear markets. The OSC said it was bracing itself for an onslaught of consumer complaints from mutual fund investors if and when the bear market starts.

In early 1998, Stromberg was compiling a follow-up report on the industry, designed to find out how much the consumer/investor is adequately protected. One aspect of that follow-up was to identify which of her recommendations had been adopted and which ones had been ignored. Even before the new Rule, the industry had eliminated some of the more egregious potentials for conflicts such as bonus commissions that paid salespeople extra money for recommending particular funds or all-expenses-paid trips to sales conferences in exotic places like Hawaii.

Compared to the previous regime, which in retrospect may become viewed as the "Wild West" frontier days of the Canadian mutual fund industry, the post-1997 era may prove to be one of intense scrupulousness. Previously, the industry largely relied on a legal document—the prospectus—to disclose sales practices.

The fund industry developed a code of conduct in 1991. This early attempt at self-regulation limited the use of sales conferences and cooperative marketing, and emphasized greater disclosure of trailer commissions. Following Stromberg's report, IFIC revised the 1991 Code and prohibited such sales practices as bonus commissions.

## The battle for shelf space

When Stromberg catalogued the sales practices of the mid-1990s, she cited the main cause of conflict as the intense battle for "shelf space." This is a battle involving more than 75 different fund companies to gain "mind share" with the individual independent sales representatives who typically sell six or seven mutual fund families.

The battle to be on fund-family short lists often resulted in a flow of money directly or indirectly between the fund companies and the sales representatives, whether in the form of "bonus commissions" for selling a particular fund, in higher trailer commissions if a certain level of sales of a fund were maintained, or in less tangible assistance such as in paying for client seminars or other events.

The essence of the new Rule is to insert a wedge between the fund companies and the representatives when it comes to money flows. That wedge comprises the dealer firms that employ the salespeople and that are in a position to control money flows that might otherwise distort an individual rep's advice. No longer can fund companies make payments to salespeople that are conditional on sales or a certain level of assets. While commissions and trailer fees are still permitted, dealers cannot adjust the commission grid to offer incentives to representatives to sell one fund over another.

The Rule also cracks down on educational events such as seminars or conferences, and other so-called "cooperative marketing" events. Fund companies can still pay some of the direct costs of dealer seminars, but no more than 50% of such direct expenses. Fund companies can no longer subsidize client-appreciation events such as dinners or golf tournaments, general client mailings, and general sales communications.

## The financial planner credentials issue

Another related issue concerns the granting of credentials for financial planners. The Financial Planning Standards Council of Canada (FPSCC) was created in 1995 to develop a new regime in which only individuals who have earned the Certified Financial Planner (CFP) designation would be able to call themselves a financial planner.

At this point it is important to clarify that the authors have the utmost respect for "real" financial planners. Done properly, financial planning involves far more than simply setting up a portfolio of mutual funds. It should also encompass estate planning, taxation, and a host of other issues that often require the integrated cooperation of an accountant, a lawyer, a trusts expert, an insurance agent, and a financial planner.

Unfortunately, in the late 1990s, a virulent subspecies of financial planner has emerged—someone qualified only to sell mutual funds but who nevertheless passes him- or herself off as a full-fledged financial planner. To paraphrase Lucien Bouchard's comment, "Canada is not a real country," such unqualified fund salespeople are "not real financial planners." Rather, they are fund floggers, pure and simple.

This chain of events has, to some extent, led to a devaluation of the term "financial planner," and in some minds the phrase "financial plan" has become synonymous with "mutual fund sales." The FPSCC is trying to reverse this devaluation of a formerly prestigious job description, with the help of associations from the accounting, insurance, mutual fund, and financial planning worlds. Unfortunately, the educational arms of the banks and brokerage companies pulled out of the Standards Council in early 1998.

With guidance from people like Stromberg, the mutual fund industry is trying to regulate itself. Pure mutual funds salespeople sell a far more restricted product line than full-service stockbrokers, who are regulated by the Investment Dealers Association (IDA). By the spring of 1999, a new Mutual Fund Dealers Association (MFDA)—a spin-off of the IDA and IFIC— should be operational.

Few of the abuses identified by Stromberg have come from brokers registered with the IDA, which has been tightening the regulatory framework for years. Since the early 1990s, no IDA adviser has been allowed to go on a junket without paying their own costs. IDA members can sell a much broader array of products, including funds and stocks, and are subject to greater supervision than the funds-only dealers and planners.

Everyone who sells mutual funds will have to join the MFDA unless they are a member of the IDA. But Stromberg questions whether the financial landscape is changing too quickly for something like the MFDA to help consumers in time to forestall an extensive catastrophe. Stromberg says the new Rule applies universally to all members of a mutual fund organization, whether or not they are members of a stock exchange or the IDA. But these are only minimum standards. Stromberg points out that it "is open to each mutual fund organization and dealer to impose higher standards."

Two-thirds of individuals who sell mutual funds (about 60,000 dealers and salespeople) are not members of the IDA and are therefore not subject to the self-regulatory rules imposed upon IDA member firms. Consequently, two-thirds of the people who sell mutual funds are not supervised. This has resulted in what the MFDA's new president Joe Oliver calls a "serious regulatory gap." Oliver, who is also the IDA president, says the situation has resulted in "an uncertain level of investor protection and a concern about the integrity of the distribution process."

Stromberg further warns that it could take two or three years before the MFDA gets up to speed on regulating itself and "the playing field is level in terms of protection of the public interest. Leaving aside the consequences of a severe, prolonged market correction, a major insolvency or a major fraud, the revolutionary changes that are occurring in the whole financial industry sector call into question whether the MFDA, by the time it is operational, will be relevant."

## The blurring of products and advice

It is important to note that mutual funds are a subset of a much broader financial landscape. As Stromberg puts it, "We are increasingly seeing a blurring of product and advice and a blurring of the distribution of product and advice. Few people now deal only in conventional mutual funds. Most people are now dealing, directly or indirectly, with a much broader range of products such as GICs, insurance contracts, labor-sponsored investment funds, limited partnerships, and so on. Some of these products have mutual fund characteristics; others do not."

This blurring is most evident in the debate raging over financial planning education and proficiency standards. "To understand mutual funds and other related products, there is a need to understand issues relating to the underlying securities of the mutual funds and of the other products and to understand how these underlying securities and considerations affect an overall financial plan," Stromberg says.

The nebulous concept of "advice" has become the core activity of people who portray themselves to consumers as "financial planners." As Stromberg points out, to the extent that advice has become the central function, the sale of the product has become secondary to the advice. "People want to be able to deal in the broadest range of products possible and they want to be remunerated both for their advisory services in the selection and ongoing monitoring of product and for the acquisition of the product. This has become the basis on which people justify the need for and their entitlement to trailer fees."

She worries that the MFDA has been created for "yesterday's world," where legions of people were confined only to the sale of "plain-vanilla" mutual funds. In the future, Stromberg says, mutual fund dealers will not want to be so constrained, hence their desire to sell other securities under the IDA umbrella or to gain registration to sell life insurance, segregated funds and other products. It is now easier for mutual fund dealers to become IDA members because of a recent OSC decision that lets investment dealers hire individuals whose registration is limited to mutual funds.

The blurring of function is why Stromberg continues to call for the creation of a single, national, self-regulated organization in which membership will be mandatory for all those who sell securities, including mutual funds. She sees a need for a common set of rules and standards for selling all investment fund securities, whether mutual funds, segregated funds, index-linked GICs, labor-sponsored funds, or other funds pooled for investment purposes. Those rules should apply to all who sell them regardless of the pillar of the financial services industry the seller belongs to, Stromberg says. "An unacceptable sales practice for an IDA member should be an unacceptable sales practice for an MFDA member and vice-versa."

In a speech in April 1998, MFDA and IDA president Joe Oliver said proficiency requirements for investment advisers "are broader and more stringent than for fund distributors." The historical reason for having less onerous requirements for people who sell only funds was that the early funds were, as Oliver put it, "relatively simple securities. Funds were few and balanced, and the risk of loss was relatively low."

Today, however, the rise of funds specialized by sector, country, or security has considerably raised the risk of owning certain mutual funds. Any investor who was overweight in gold funds or Asian equity funds in 1997 knows the unpleasant feeling of losing nearly half of one's capital. Since funds are, in effect, securities, regulators have come to recognize that the pure-fund salesperson needs to have a broad understanding of investing, alternative investment opportunities, capital markets, and the regulatory environment.

Oliver says public pressure is building for regulatory authorities to "crack down" on non-qualified planners. "Many distributors use the term 'financial planner' because it resonates with the public," he notes. An IDA poll revealed that only 4% of investors who purchased mutual funds believed that they were buying them from fund salespersons. Many distributors who call themselves financial planners "have no special qualifications at all, and others appear to be minimally qualified," Oliver said. "We have a serious issue of investor protection." He adds that some fund dealers maintain "only minimal" accounting records, with many relying on the fund companies to record transactions or provide clients with activity confirmations.

The financial planning credentials issue crosses the lines of mutual fund dealers, full-service investment dealers, banks, insurance dealers, and credit and other intermediaries. In addition to common standards for financial planners, Stromberg would like to see the introduction of a common exam and marking system, and in-house apprenticeships to ensure that theory is applied properly to practice.

Unfortunately, many of the financial planning firms seem quite willing to take in other firms' recent rejects. At one point, DeLellis (the mutual fund salesperson discussed earlier, whose license was revoked by the OSC), had five jobs in five years, some with other well-known financial planning firms, none of which was an IDA member.

Brenda Eprile, who recently moved from the OSC to Deloitte & Touche, says one answer to these problems would be to screen new sales hires thoroughly and supervise them effectively. "Some firms are willing to hire sales representatives with a history of disciplinary actions or customer complaints because they are 'big producers,'" Eprile told a conference in 1998. "Many firms use only minimum hiring procedures particularly in the area of scrutinizing an applicant's background."

An OSC review of 23 fund distributors uncovered "a host of problems in the area of supervision," Eprile reported. There was often no linking of trading reviews to "know your client" information. Policies were often inadequate for trades involving leverage (borrowing money). Eprile described the "many serious problems" that can stem from failure to supervise salespeople who sell "inappropriate securities" to their clients, and who sometimes put "clients at risk of losing critically important assets such as their principal residence due to excessive leveraging."

## Trailer fees

One of Stromberg's early targets was the trailer fee, which was introduced in Canada in the mid-1980s. The little-understood trailer fee, or "service fee," is a quarterly payment that dealers receive from fund companies for "servicing" consumers invested in their funds. The trailer is also one of the biggest components of management expense ratios (MERs): trailers on load funds are typically 0.5 to 1%, comprising as much as half the MER. Trailers are lower on bond and money market funds, higher on equity funds.

Stromberg uncovered instances of trailers as high as 1.5%. In her report, she noted, "This percentage is virtually the same percentage charged by highly trained portfolio managers for providing investment advisory and portfolio management services to the investment fund. There would appear to be an imbalance in such compensation both on an overall basis and relative to the level of services that are being provided."

Noting the trend for managers to pay ever-higher trailers, Stromberg summed up the situation that faced Templeton Growth Fund from 1987 to 1992, before it was forced to cave in to broker demands for trailers: "If a manager does not agree to increase the amount that it will pay by way of trailer or service fees to what a competitor is prepared to pay, the manager can expect that the sales representative will cause his or her clients to switch their investments to an investment fund group that will pay the higher amount regardless of whether this benefits the client or has tax consequences for the client. The payment of high trailer or service fees by an investment fund manager may also be a factor in a sales representative not recommending a change in the client's portfolio when it would be in the client's interests to make such a change." Stromberg also noted that no standards exist to outline the exact services provided for the trailer fee. "In effect, investors are paying twice for services."

Even so-called "no load" funds are building trailer fees into their management fees, which are, in effect, a sales charge. The major concern is that despite reference to these fees in prospectuses, investors are often unaware that the fees are being paid to the broker by the fund manager and that "the cost of these fees is being passed on to investors through higher management fees that are being charged by the investment fund manager to the investment funds."

In a statement foreshadowing Hamilton's analysis, Stromberg

noted, "Investors are unaware of the impact that trailer or service fees have on their total return both on an annual basis and on a compound basis over the length of time of their investment in the investment fund."

Large trailers are a major reason that MERs are higher in Canada than in the United States. The average trailer in Canada is 65 basis points versus 30 basis points in the United States. And more of the "good deal" low-MER fund companies are converting to the high-MER, trailer-fee model. For example, Prudential Funds of Canada used to have strong low-MER Canadian natural resources and precious metals funds—managed by Veronika Hirsch before she became widely known. Prudential was later acquired by London Fund Management, which was in turn acquired by Great-West Life Assurance Co. Today, renamed the MAXXUM Group of Funds, the company has jacked up MERs to average load fund levels and implemented trailer fees. The MAXXUM funds are far more widely available, and brokers are more likely to sell them. But what was formerly a great deal for the intelligent consumer who sought out the family is now considerably less of a deal. Not surprisingly, performance of the specialty funds that made Hirsch famous has dropped off.

Stromberg likened trailers to "lifetime annuities" for the selling brokers and flagged their potential conflicts of interest. Let's look at a current example, given the penchant for many brokers to recommend switches out of Trimark Funds in 1997–98. Who benefits when a broker recommends switching out of Trimark Fund, with a 1.52% MER and paying a 30 basis points trailer, to a 2.5% MER fund paying a 1% trailer? (In fairness, those assets now being switched out were originally put in by brokers and dealers, despite having lower payouts than average.)

Still, the potential is there for less scrupulous brokers to triple their annual trailer commissions by recommending higher-trailer funds that cost the investor an extra 1% a year. Fund salespeople justify the trailer as compensating them for "advice." But of what value is advice if it costs the client money? The issue is, whose retirement are these financial planners really concerned about—their own or their clients'? If there were a true "fiduciary" relationship, it would be scandalous to recommend a fund so blatantly in the broker's interest but hurting the client's investment returns. But until Stromberg came along, this type of situation was common.

This is why Stromberg called for the fund industry to voluntarily end trailers, a stance that made her unpopular with financial planners and brokers. Stromberg hails the Bates break—the 0.25% trailer fee rebate described in Chapter 3—as "generally a step in the right direction for investors."

Investor advocate Joe Killoran calls trailer fees "the most sophisticated form of tied selling," because there's little disclosure of their role. "The annual MER amount deducted and trailer fees paid never appear on client statements," Killoran says. "Investors never see and don't know about these independent advice-skewing details."

Many dealers argue that trailer fees are justified when large amounts of service are performed for clients. Stromberg took issue with the service fees paid automatically even when brokers ignored clients. As this book was being finished, Stromberg's second report was also nearing completion. Prepared for Industry Canada's Office of Consumer Affairs, the report reviews how well protected retail consumer-investors are who are relying on investment funds for retirement income. The government wants to know what has been done to benefit consumers, the role it can play to help them, and how consumers can better identify and achieve their goals and assess risk.

Shortly before sequestering herself for her follow-up report, Stromberg summed up the situation in the following e-mail to *The Financial Post*:

1. There is basically a 1% distribution component built into the management fee of most of the Canadian mutual funds.

2. People who think they are buying mutual funds at a discount because they are using a discount broker are often deluding themselves. The reality is that you are often paying more than you would if you were buying on a zero front-end load basis or on a deferred-sales-charge basis by reason of there being an account opening fee or transaction fee charged for the transaction or an exit fee charged if you withdraw assets in certain circumstances or close the account.

3. Beware of dealers who generate additional fees for themselves by switching your account from a deferred-sales-charge basis (once the DSC period expires) to a zero front-end charge basis. This results in the dealers receiving a higher trailer fee than they would receive if the switch weren't made. It may also trigger tax liabilities for the investor.
4. Be aware that built into the management fee for most of the so-called "no-load" funds is a component for trailer fees and that these funds, in reality, are "level-load" funds.

Duff Young, in a *Globe and Mail* column in April 1998, warned investors to be wary of the "no-commission" hyperbole that abounded when Canada Trust launched a major marketing campaign that emphasized zero front loads but neglected to inform investors of the higher trailer fees. "The loads are small potatoes to investors," Young wrote. "The average fund in Canada charges well over 2% in annual expenses. So the real money is in the annual management fees clipped off the top. That's where the trailers come from, which are typically 0.5%. On most funds, there's a way for discount brokers to double that trailer without even having to give advice. If they sell a fund without that rear-load burden, they'll earn twice the trailer, because the fund company doesn't have to pay them the deferred commission. Thus they earn a fat 1% trailer every year."

## High-profile seminar "shills"

Another issue addressed by Stromberg years earlier was that of the "educational seminar"—a thinly disguised sales prospecting device. DeLellis—and many others—hired big-name speakers to attract potential customers and benefitted from the apparent transference of credibility from the speakers to himself.

DeLellis may have left a legacy by placing the spotlight on what Killoran first described as "mutual fund shills." In April 1998, securities regulators were considering a clamp-down on mutual fund educational seminars. Jack Geller, acting chairman of the OSC, told a fund industry group that a new review of seminars and other types of fund industry-sponsored education was under way.

Geller said he realized the potential for abuse while acting as chairman at the OSC hearing that examined the conduct of DeLellis. "DeLellis really brought home to me what seems to be an abuse of sales seminars. We have to come to a decision whether [new] regulation is necessary," Geller said. Currently, speakers are not required to be licensed to sell investments or have any professional training or education.

Still to come under scrutiny are the potential conflicts among mutual fund distributors who in some cases are integrated vertically and are becoming manufacturers of their own in-house products as well as selling other groups' funds. A prime example are the Infinity Funds, 60% of which are sold by the same Fortune Financial we encountered earlier. Fifty per cent of Infinity is owned by Fortune chairman David Singh and one of Fortune's leading salespeople, Richard Charlton. A senior OSC lawyer, Rebecca Cowdery, told *Canadian Business* magazine that the Commission views the Infinity/Fortune arrangement as "a big conflict of interest."

Nor is Fortune alone in this practice. The Toronto-based Equion Group also sells its own proprietary Optima Strategy Funds. And the Financial Concepts Group plans to sell both third-party mutual funds and its own proprietary funds through a new mutual fund subsidiary, Alpha Strategic Partners.

## Full disclosure the best remedy for abuses

The obvious remedy for conflicts of interest is full disclosure. Depending on strict legal interpretations, upholding fiduciary relationships can be a dicey proposition. In the end, investors need to rely on common sense and a "buyer beware" stance to all investments, broker-mediated or otherwise. Stromberg's recommendations in her first report could be summed up by such simple concepts as "fairness and integrity" and "information and knowledge."

The explosion in media coverage of the fund industry has increased the amount of such information, although it's questionable whether this translates into knowledge. Information is abundant; arguably knowledge is a scarcer, more precious commodity.

When the fund industry talks about the need for advice and the need to compensate the distribution networks, it is referring to this intangible of human knowledge conveyed between the knowledgeable broker/dealer and the unsophisticated client.

Even so, disclosure is a powerful tool. Stromberg recommended three sets of disclosure documents, including a one-page point-of-sale document that would alert investors to the full extent of broker motivations. A one-page disclosure document for mutual funds became the personal crusade of Joe Killoran, publisher of the now-defunct *Frugal Bugle* newsletter. Killoran, a self-styled "lone-ranger" consumer advocate whose battle cry is, "Sunshine is the greatest disinfectant," has attempted to turn himself into the Ralph Nader of Canadian mutual funds. But, perhaps owing to his uncompromising tactics, Killoran has faced an uphill battle in getting the fund industry and media to go along with his suggestions.

Of course, the mutual fund industry has always had a disclosure document. It's called the prospectus, a legal document that has become transformed not so much into a document of disclosure as a document of liability. As Donald Christensen wrote in *Surviving the Coming Mutual Fund Crisis*, "The prospectuses became mired in so much indecipherable, self-protecting legalese as to effectively transform them into documents of non disclosure."

Jim Rogers, chairman of Vancouver-based The Rogers Group Financial Advisors Ltd., doesn't agree with Stromberg and her supporters that trailer fees need to be jettisoned altogether. The key is full disclosure on the part of the financial adviser. Rogers argues it's impossible for the fund companies to sort out the differing MERs and trailer fees that might be accorded to brokers who do dispense full service. With so many distribution channels, it would be impractical to decide who deserves a continuous service fee. Instead, Rogers suggests that trailers need to be made consistent, perhaps set at a uniform 0.5% across the board. That would remove the bias for unscrupulous planners to recommend switches from low-MER funds paying 0.30% to high-MER funds paying 1% trailers. Together with uniform trailers, Rogers suggests full upfront and ongoing disclosure (shown on client statements) of all fees paid, including the trailer and how much of the MER it is responsible for. That way the customer would be in the best position to judge whether an appropriate level of service was provided. Where service is minimal, it should be up to the salesperson, not the manufacturers, to refund some or all of the trailer fee.

So far, we have looked at two major shortcomings of mutual funds: high MERs and a murky advice-dispensing sales structure. The pressure on MERs will continue and eventually high MERs may become less of an issue; regulators and the fund industry are well on the way to resolving the conflicts of interest that abound in the sales channel. But there are a host of smaller drawbacks to mutual funds. They are inefficient in a number of ways. The ways they are invested are affected by how much money they hold, which in turn may force them to own primarily large, liquid stocks.

There are also significant tax problems with funds, especially for investors outside registered plans.

These drawbacks are examined in the following chapter.

*Chapter Five*

# Inefficiencies and Other Problems

Regardless of how good your fund manager may be or how cost-effective is the particular fund you own, several major problems are associated with the pooled structure used by all mutual funds, pooled funds, closed-end funds, and segregated funds. The pooled structure, after all, is simply a method to allow investors to gain access to money managers who would not take their accounts by themselves. The inefficiency of the pool is part of the price that has to be paid for reaching these top-level managers.

Not only is the pool inefficient, but it also has additional costs above money management and regular accounting. Every day, within two hours of market closing, accountants for every fund must tabulate the total value of the fund's investments and the number of shares outstanding after that day's purchases and redemptions. These extra costs are part of the MER charged to all investors.

## The need for cash reserves

All pools—and especially mutual-fund pools—place an extra burden on the money manager. They may not want this burden, but they must accept it along with the management of the fund's portfolio. The manager is compelled to manage a cash reserve within the fund. This cash reserve is an unavoidable by-product of new money flowing into the fund, proceeds from sale of stocks, and the result of dividends paid. The cash reserve in every pool will hamper its performance in a rising market because the pool cannot be fully invested.

When markets move in the opposite direction, the cash reserve would ideally become a buying reserve, but that is often not the case. It is at this point, when markets are down, that cash management becomes a major burden. When markets go down, most funds experience an increase in redemptions. This means that after the value of the portfolio has dropped, the managers are often forced to sell at what may be the bottom, when they would prefer to buy.

This is a good way to compare a pooled investment with a "segregated" investment portfolio. In a segregated investment, stocks and bonds are owned directly by an individual, not through units in a pool. Both may be managed by the same person and invested in exactly the same securities. (See Chapters 12 and 13 for more on segregated investment or "seg" management.)

After a market decline, managers who have both pooled and segregated accounts need to sell stocks in their pooled accounts to raise money for redemptions. The managers may be simultaneously buying the same stocks at the same price for the segregated accounts. "Bottom fishing" (snapping up stocks at bargain prices) is more difficult with a pool.

When a pool sells an investment in the underlying portfolio—hopefully at a high rather than a low point in the market—all current investors in the pool are taxed on the entire amount of the gain, whether they have received it or not. This means that many investors have been taxed on returns they have not earned. For this reason, it is essential that investors avoid all pools, particularly mutual funds, that have significant accrued but unrealized capital gains in their underlying portfolios. For tax purposes, mutual funds, and other pools normally pay out all

gains and income for the entire year to shareholders of record at year-end. This means that if you own the fund at the end of December, but did not own it for much of the year, you will pay tax on gains that others received earlier in the year. This is why investors should avoid buying funds late in the year.

## Problems with large funds

One of the most awkward problems for fund managers occurs when they are too successful. Because they collect fees on every dollar in the fund, the fund companies want as much money in the fund as possible. But while it may be reasonably easy to manage a $200-million fund, it is much harder to manage a $2-billion fund. The ideal number of stocks for diversification purposes is between 30 and 40. If a fund has $200 million in it, an average of $6 million would be invested in each underlying stock. Government regulations prevent mutual funds from owning more than 10% of any one company's stock. At $6 million per company, few companies would be above the 10% threshold. However, when the fund reaches $1 billion, it will have to put approximately $30 million into each stock in order to keep within the target of 40 companies. They are effectively prevented from investing in companies with less than $300 million in market capitalization. If the fund has $2 billion, as many Canadian funds do, the maximum of 10% per company would mean investing only in companies with over $600 million in market cap.

Although nothing prevents a fund from investing less than 10% in a target company, the compromise that this entails is a rapid increase in the total number of companies held in the fund. Large funds are either large-cap funds or "deworsified" funds (over-diversified funds create mediocre returns) with 100 or more holdings. With 100 holdings, many positions will be less than 1% of the fund. No matter how good the stock selection is, if the fund owns only 1% in a stock, any given "killing" or spectacular rise in the price of a particular stock will have a limited impact on the overall fund value. Eventually, if you have a big enough fund and buy enough stocks, the contents of your fund looks like the index, both in number of securities and in weighting.

Holding large blocks of stock also poses a problem when it comes time to sell. It can be difficult for the market to absorb a block of $30 million from one fund, and fund companies rarely hold the stock in only one fund.

Fund managers understand these problems, but typically don't control the fund company, which places them in a potential conflict situation. Fund managers want to do the best they can for clients investing in their fund, which helps their own careers, while the fund company cares about getting the fund as large as possible. Managers know that funds tend to underperform as they become larger. This gives managers an incentive to leave a fund after it becomes too large, but before the size has eroded its performance. Investors are best served by investing for the long run, but it is quite possible that the manager will not be there as long as the fund unitholder. An individual investor's "long run" of 30 years to retirement is likely to be longer than the tenure of a hot fund manager at any given fund company, judging by the careers of such prominent Canadian managers as John Zechner, Gerry Coleman, Jonathan Baird, Veronika Hirsch, Frank Mersch, and Will Sutherland, to name six of the more publicized cases of manager departures in recent years.

Manager turnover is a problem with all mutual fund investing. The best money managers are like free-agent professional athletes: here today, gone tomorrow. Not only do managers move around, with surprising regularity, but the mandates of the funds themselves also change. Mutual-fund companies routinely merge funds with each other, change fund objectives, and change fund style. Sometimes all these changes, from individual manager to style and objective, can occur with little or no change in branding and little awareness of investors.

## Trading costs

The high MERs discussed in Chapter 3 and the load charges of which many fund investors are well aware are not the only costs associated with mutual funds. Excluded from the MERs are the portfolio's trading costs. In some cases, the most active mutual funds can deduct commissions of over 1% per year above the quoted MER from the portfolio.

With so many problems, fund investors are faced with two unpleasant options. Although they know that mutual funds are best held, like all growth investments, for the long run, it is rare for most funds to go without some significant change for more than two or three years. Investors are faced with either trying to "manage the managers," and unavoidably doing some closet market timing at the same time, or paying someone else to manage the managers for them. This approach is addressed in Chapter 13.

Mutual funds also present a legal problem for those investing on behalf of estates, charities, and foundations. Mutual funds are prohibited investments in many such situations because of the trustee relationship, though in practice it is common to use them. This legal structure prevents a trustee from delegating decision making to a mutual fund or similar pooled structure. In theory, should losses occur on a mutual fund or other unapproved investment, the person who made the decision to invest in the fund—the trustee—could well be required to make up the difference out of his or her own pocket.

## The transfer of risk to the individual

Another point that Glorianne Stromberg made is that individual investors are assuming more risk as they move from GICs and other vehicles insured by the Canadian Deposit Insurance Corp. into the markets, whether directly or indirectly through mutual funds. The average self-directed RRSP is full of stocks and equity mutual funds, neither of which is guaranteed against stunning market setbacks. Indeed, as the bull market started to change to a bear in 1998, the phrase "self-worked RRSP" may have been a more apt description of the self-directed RRSP.

At the Scudder Kemper talkfest mentioned in the Introduction, Scudder economist Maureen Allyn warned that "it's possible that boomers are being lulled by three years of 20% to 30% returns in the stock market. If that changes, the economy and the markets could be at risk, especially since actual savings rates are lower."

The scary part is what happens when the large-cap stocks and indexes fail to deliver such returns. If history is any guide, funds will try to give unitholders what they want by taking more risks in the funds. Author Donald Christensen quoted a *Business Week* article from 1973 that recapped what had happened to mutual funds in the 1960s: "A safe place for small investors became a playground for speculators." Christensen added that since the funds had sold themselves to shareholders based on hot performance and touted their managers as special beings to achieve it, "The funds had to keep running, so they took greater and greater risks in a frantic chase after performance: half-baked franchising stocks, flaky computer leasing and software companies, letter stock that could only be sold when and if it was registered."

The pressure on managers to change style or make other compromises must be massive when performance lags and redemptions increase. For example, 18 balanced mutual funds—not the more aggressive equity funds—owned shares in Bre-X Minerals Ltd. Investors could legitimately ask why supposedly conservative money managers were buying stocks that brokerage firms such as Nesbitt Burns carefully described as "speculative" in every published opinion. Knowing that their careers hang in the balance, all fund managers, for all types of funds, are under immense pressure to do whatever it takes to achieve consistently top performance.

Mutual funds are a big part of the Canadian RRSP, but this trend extends well beyond registered plans. Increasingly, the traditional big corporate benefit pension plan—the defined benefit plan—is being replaced by market-oriented defined contribution (DC) plans or group RRSPs. Furthermore, the main investment vehicle in DC plans is equity or balanced mutual funds. Allied to this trend is that of securitization: providers of financial services are, as Stromberg puts it, "structuring their activities and products to reduce or eliminate their market risk."

Stromberg says the secular shift in household savings that has occurred in the last 10 years from deposit-type instruments and life insurance to products such as mutual funds has resulted in the increasing "retailization" of the marketplace. "It is no longer appropriate to think of the marketplace as being divided simply into the 'retail market' and the 'institutional market.' The marketplace has become an '*instividual*' marketplace," Stromberg told the Standing Senate Committee on Banking, Trade, and Commerce in 1998. She warned it is important that regulators not favor institutional investors over individual retail consumers.

As Chapter 7 on guaranteed investments (such as "seg" funds and index-linked GICs) points out, as the bull market extended into previously uncharted territory, individual investors were increasingly hedging their bets.

There are arguments that the combination of aging demographics, globalization of markets, and the continuing technology revolution will keep the markets soaring well into the next century. Such is the view of Harry S. Dent, Jr., in *The Great Boom Ahead* (Hyperion, New York, 1993), and his new *The Roaring 2000s* (Simon & Schuster, New York, 1998), Patrick McKeough in *Riding the Bull: How You Can Profit from the Coming Stock Market Boom* (Key Porter, Toronto, 1993), and, indeed, of much of Wall Street. There are still many superbulls who believe that the combination of 5% interest rates and 12% to 15% annual stock returns means houses should be remortgaged so the otherwise idle equity in them can be put to better use in the stock markets.

The arguments in favor of an ever-raging bull were well articulated in the Scudder Kemper boomer conference. While a few anxious questions were posed about what might happen when the boomers finally retire and start to cash in their chips, the U.S. experts were generally agreed that the boomers would retain their faith in stocks well past retirement. Indeed, some would continue to work past the age of retirement for the simple joy of it. There was even an argument that the generation following the boomers would have less wealth, and that the boomers' desire to pass their wealth on to the next generation would keep them invested in stocks for their entire lives.

At press time, the law of gravity had not yet been repealed. The business cycle and the statistical certainty of "regression to the mean" are as important and valid today as ever. As one insightful adviser puts it, "If everyone's thinking the same, then no one is thinking at all."

Investors may want to compare North American valuations at their early-1998 highs to Japanese valuations in 1986. Nothing says they can't go higher—in Japan, they did for three more stellar years. But since the 1989 fall, they've been down nine long and painful years.

## Can funds defend against bear markets?

*The Wealthy Boomer* is not about whether a stock-market correction will occur in the near future. Indeed, shortly before press time, the U.S. stock market was down almost 15% from its highs earlier in the year. The Canadian market, encumbered by a plummeting Canadian dollar, was down 25%—arguably an official bear market. For strategies to cope with full-bore bear markets, we refer interested readers to another Key Porter book published in 1997—the late Andrew Sarlos's *Fear, Greed and the End of the Rainbow: Guarding Your Assets in the Coming Bear Market* (Key Porter, Toronto, 1997). Or, if you really want to be frightened into running to cash, read Robert Prechter, Jr.'s *At the Crest of the Tidal Wave: A Forecast for the Great Bear Market* (New Classic Library, Gainsville, Georgia, 1995), or, more recently, John Rothchild's *The Bear Book: Survive and Profit in Ferocious Markets* (Wiley, New York, 1998).

In the event of such a financial catastrophe, the meaning of our subtitle would be slightly different than our main thesis that "Life After Mutual Funds" is a life-cycle phenomenon correlated with an individual's level of wealth: because of the fund boom's emphasis on equity funds, it's likely that any post-crash flight out of funds would tar all funds with the same brush. As happened in the 1960s and at other times when mutual funds as a broad product category fell out of favor, the odds are that investor disillusionment with equity funds would spread to fixed income and balanced funds, throwing the fund baby out with the stocks' bath water.

There have been numerous predictions since the mid-1990s of an impending stock reversal, and most have been wrong. The highest-profile case of premature pessimistic punditry was that of Elaine Garzarelli, who correctly called the 1987 crash a few weeks before the event. However, Garzarelli issued a general alert to "sell all stocks and equity mutual funds now!" in 1996, only to return to the markets in the funds she managed in 1997 (in Canada, through the O'Donnell Group).

There is also a thriving business among newsletters in taking the gloomy, "sky is falling" pessimistic role. They serve a function in providing a counter view to the eternally optimistic prognostications found on financial television shows, such as CNBC, better known by its critics as "Bubblevision." For a more objective view of the U.S. market, investors would be well served by finding a non-American perspective. Few periodicals enjoy a better reputation than the British-written *Economist*, a weekly newsmagazine that provides a unique European perspective on world and North American markets and economies.

Its April 18, 1998, cover story warned that America's economy had reached the bubble stage. Coupled with the deflation/depression in Japan and the broader Asian crisis, the magazine warned that the United States was experiencing massive "asset inflation," i.e., soaring prices for stocks. As evidence, it cited the merger mania, particularly involving major North American (including Canadian) banks. U.S. stocks had soared 65% between spring 1996 and spring 1998. The magazine warned that, "ominously, merger mania is usually associated with the final stages of a bull market." And it warned that, having missed the chance to ease such asset price inflation by raising interest rates in 1996, the Federal Reserve "needs to raise interest rates now." By August, the *Economist* declared a bear market on its cover, and deemed it a good thing, since investors still building their nest eggs could do so at more reasonable prices. But bulls like Pat McKeough think the bull will regain its horns for one more run in 1999–2000.

Timing markets is extremely difficult even for investment professionals, which is why most of the world's finest investors believe in being "fully invested" at all times. The prolonged bull market was associated primarily with equity mutual funds, for obvious reasons. If and when the stock-price asset inflation ends definitively, or worse, reverses, those overexposed to equity mutual funds will learn a hard lesson about diversification of asset classes. Many already had by press time.

In advising individuals on how to play out the last stages of a bull market, Sarlos said that mutual funds are "playing the game on your behalf." But they "are in the market to the end and they make extremely good money in the final phase of a bull. But be clear that mutual funds are downgrading their holdings at this point. It's the old formula: increased reward equals increased risk." He noted that mutual fund managers "have very little choice about staying in the market until it turns," and that fund investors who are nervous should think about switching to a fund with more leeway in keeping a large proportion of the fund in cash. This might be that great underrated fund type, the humble balanced fund. Sarlos conceded that younger investors who are decades from retirement can get a measure of protection from a bear market simply by dollar cost averaging—buying monthly year in and year out. For older investors who are near or at retirement, he advocated a significant retrenchment of stocks and equity funds—to as little as 20 or 25%.

Not even the *Economist* ventures to say when the asset bubble will be pricked for sure, although the same issue that featured a bubble surrounding the Statue of Liberty also featured a segue into an examination of what it termed "post-bubble Japan." Several noted bears have long viewed any collapse of the Japanese economy as the final indicator of the end of the Wall Street run. Sarlos suggested that a bear market could start when the Japanese stop buying U.S. government bonds and suggested "that's when you should sell your stocks."

A similar line of thought was developed by two more Europeans: James Davidson and Lord Rees Mogg in *The Great Reckoning* (Simon & Schuster, New York, 1993). Reviewing the Japanese bubble stock market of the late 1980s, Davidson and Rees Mogg noted that "even after assets reach extreme valuations, they go on to still greater extremes. . . . In the classic assets mania, markets outrun any rational valuation based on yield or cash return."

Many of Davidson and Rees Mogg's 1993 predictions about Japan were materializing by early 1998, notably as reviewed in the *Economist* in the April 11 to 17, 1998, edition. In "Japan on the Brink," the eminent British magazine wrote that reports of Japan's "imminent demise are now coming thick and fast," and noted that "unexpectedly bad news from Japan might just be the event that brings investors back to reality and so causes a crash."

While the *Economist* downplayed the potential worldwide ramifications of a full-scale crack-up of the world's second-largest economy (Japan), Davidson and Rees Mogg warned five years earlier that the liquidation in Japan "is a tremendous deflationary event, bound to have far-reaching consequences. When the world's largest creditor suffers losses of the magnitude now being endured, they are inevitably felt right around the globe." And four years before the "Asian flu" of 1997, the same authors warned that "if the rest of the world, particularly Japan, goes into a slump, deflationary pressures will be felt throughout the Pacific."

We'll leave the final word to Nesbitt Burns' Dr. Sherry Cooper and Harris Investment Management's Donald Coxe. The title of a presentation they gave late in May 1998 was "Asia: As Bad as It Gets; North America: As Good as It Gets."

## Investment management subservient to marketing

Mutual funds are as much about marketing as investing in the 1990s, which is why the hoary cliché "Mutual funds are sold, not bought" is as true as ever. As Glorianne Stromberg once told *Canadian Business* magazine, the fund business may have started out in the portfolio management, investment counseling, and advice business, but "somewhere along the line, the marketers got a hold of it, and the advisory function has been almost superseded by the sales function."

Mutual funds are sold with mega-marketing budgets and by building mind share with the 60,000-plus brokers and dealers who sell funds to some seven million Canadian consumers. Every RRSP campaign features a barrage of mutual fund commercials. Trimark, one of the more cost-conscious fund companies while still a large firm, is reported to have spent $70 million on advertising for the 1998 RRSP season. The money comes from consumers' pockets, either directly or indirectly. Marketing expenses are not usually billed directly to funds but consumers do pay much of the freight in paying fees that wind up in the advisers' pockets. The brand-name "load" mutual funds rely heavily on independent brokers and planners, and there's a major battle for "shelf space," a place on the list of the half dozen fund families sold by the typical adviser.

The current trend to sell mutual funds with television advertising bears out Stromberg's prophetic mid-decade comment that funds are being marketed just like soap, coffee, or any other mass-market consumer product. In a widely reported October 1995 speech to Bishop University, Stromberg said that investment funds are often "viewed simply as a commodity to be sold in the same way that laundry soap or coffee is sold. The name of the game is to gain shelf space with distributors and to offer whatever incentives and engage in whatever practices it takes to gain such shelf space . . . regardless of whether these incentives and practices result in the interests of industry participants being in conflict with the interests of investors and regardless of what the impact of these incentives may be on the inherent integrity of the investment funds."

The fund marketing managers' penchant for launching "new and improved" products manifests itself in the never-ending blitz of new fund launches. Seldom does a week pass without at least one new fund announcement in Canada. Even though an all-global equity fund such as Templeton Growth is arguably all the average RRSP investor will need in his or her foreign content, that has not stopped the blitz of higher-MER Asian funds, European funds, Latin American funds, emerging markets, and other variants.

The latest "flavor of the month" has been to divide world equity markets up not by geographical region but by industry sectors such as telecommunications, health sciences, financial services, and even—this from a bank (CIBC)—demographics.

Many fund families now boast between 30 and 50 funds, a figure that borders on the ludicrous. The idea, of course, is the old strategy of throwing mud against a wall to see what will stick. With 40 funds, a few will inevitably be good performers, and those are the funds that will be featured in the next crop of performance-oriented advertisements. Bad funds can be closed or merged, which results in a phenomenon called "survivorship bias." The rules have been skewed so that when two funds merge, the track record of the superior fund is used for the newly named fund.

Specialized equity funds are, of course, far more volatile than broadly based funds. Unusually volatile families such as Sagit Investment Management Ltd.'s Cambridge Funds often wind up with hot funds initially on the top-10 lists and a year or two later on the worst performer's list. There are investors who avoid the top-10 lists for this reason.

The March 1998 issue of *Consumer Reports* criticized the practice of trying to predict next year's top-performing funds. "The investment industry and the financial media that report on it (and profit handsomely from the huge amounts of advertising the industry buys) tout the latest top funds and make celebrities out of this year's hot-shot fund managers. The commercial hype turns the sober business of weighing the market's substantial risks into a casino game—with investors' money at stake."

But for every person who avoids top-10 fund lists, there are several more than ready to "chase last year's winner." And the biggest winner of them all in the Canadian market has long been the AIC Advantage Fund. So far, everyone associated with this fund, which essentially invests in the mutual fund companies themselves, has made out like bandits.

Funds like this don't need to be advertised. They're powered by free publicity. But the average fund needs extensive marketing support to get noticed. The marketing blitz far transcends 30-second television commercials or even advertising in the usual sense of the word. As more mutual fund firms engage public relations professionals to help them, the power of the legitimate press has not gone unnoticed. The problem with a traditional advertisement is that the reader knows in advance the nature of the beast: it's a sales pitch. But what journalists like to call "pure editorial" is more powerful, provided it's legitimate and contained in a credible, wide-circulation vehicle.

From the fund marketer's point of view, the perfect vehicle would be "advertorial," an advertisement disguised as an editorial. The major newspapers regularly oblige on this point, and IFIC regularly distributes a paid, multi-page "supplement" that allows it to preach the gospel of fund investing without having it sullied by some scurrilous but objective journalist.

Still, such supplements are generally perceived as just another form of advertisement, which defeats the objective. Fortunately, the newspapers are sufficiently obsessed with mutual fund coverage to give the companies plenty of legitimate "free" publicity. The profiles of particular funds sometimes backfire but generally do an admirable job of providing big-weight media credibility on particular funds.

For some people, sadly the older, more conservative investors, bank sponsorship of mutual funds has helped legitimize the positioning of mutual funds as both conservative investments and investments appropriate for everyone.

The mutual fund industry's penetration of most facets of the media can also be more subtle, often disguised as "educational" seminars or objective, third-party newsletters. Many of the mutual fund guides are written, in whole or in part, by people whose main job is to sell mutual funds. Several financial planners have resorted to the vanity press to self-publish ostensibly objective financial books that give them credibility in the public eye. In fact, one of the many practices that the DeLellis case uncovered was that DeLellis and another writer "co-authored" a book on financial planning. The only problem is that the names of at least 18 other financial planners appear on different versions of the same book.

Financial newsletters are also a popular "adjunct service" for prospect-hungry fund salespeople. Some credible organizations are preparing boiler-plate copy for newsletters, upon which the local financial planner can slap his or her own logo. Much of this pseudo-editorial is not badly written, although the messages are predictable: invest in stocks or equity funds for the long run, maximize your RRSP contributions, "dollar-cost" average to smooth out the ride along the way, diversify and allocate assets, and so on.

The pseudo-media marketing machine extends even beyond this. Financial planners can distribute audiocassettes that make it look like Sir John Templeton himself is their investing mentor.

Although a few nuggets of investing wisdom are contained in this multi-media blitz, it's pretty clear the main objective is to help brokers and planners sell more mutual funds.

## "Di-worseification" and other flawed fund portfolio types

When it comes to building a fund portfolio, the combined flaws of individual investors and sometimes-misguided investment advisers conspire to create some weird collections of mutual funds. Perhaps you can recognize yourself in some of the following typical fund portfolios that the authors have spied in actual client portfolios, along with typical funds found in each.

The common sins tend to be overdiversification, duplication, too many fund families, forgetting about asset allocation, or just too many funds.

### The Dog's Breakfast
- $50,000 spread among 17 funds, originally sold by a rookie fund salesperson, then some do-it-yourself no-loads, finally consolidated in a self-directed RRSP at a discount broker.
- Ten different fund families, with duplicates of some funds sold with front- and back-end loads.
- Five large-cap Canadian equity funds with an 85% overlap of the TSE 300.
- Balanced funds that vie with bond and money market funds to make total asset allocation almost impossible to determine.

### The Sector Savant
- The Sector Savant knows he can't choose individual stocks, preferring instead to lose money choosing the wrong industrial sector funds or regional equity funds.
- Portfolio is packed full of technology and health sciences funds.
- AIC Advantage, gold funds, energy funds.
- Isn't quite sure what all the fuss is about regarding asset allocation and is 100% in equity funds.

### The Bonus Commission Portfolio
- Victim of unscrupulous fund salesperson during the heyday of bonus commissions.
- Portfolio chock-full of high-MER, rear-load funds that paid salesperson an extra commission for selling it.
- Close relative of Dog's Breakfast.

### The New Fund Junkie
- This investor never saw a new fund launch she didn't like.
- Total disregard for limiting the number of fund families, oblivious to MERs.

- A collector of funds, even if each one takes up just a 1% position in total portfolio.
- Avid reader of newspaper fund profiles, but can't resist buying immediately after.

## Last Year's Winners
- Always in search of the next hot fund, tends to sell previously held dogs just as they're set to recover.
- Buys last year's winners as they hit number 1 on the one-year radar screens.
- Constantly incurring redemption fees; oblivious to the need to have a limited number of load fund families.

## Just Show Me the Numbers Portfolio
- Close cousin of Last Year's Winners, this investor has never examined the actual holdings of any fund or investigated the manager behind it.
- "Just show me the numbers," is his cry. Portfolio concentrated on a few big past winners, always including the AIC Advantage Fund.

## The "Just in Case" 50-Fund Portfolio
- Treats every fund like a stock, and therefore tries to diversify with no more than 2% weighting per fund just in case she misses out on a triple in India or a quick double in Latin America.

## The "Been Asleep Five Years" Portfolio
- Buy-and-holder combined with no adviser or an indifferent adviser content with trailer fees.
- Asset allocation a bit out of whack but probably better off than many of the other portfolios.

## The "I Don't Know What I Own" Portfolio
- "I think I own the Mackenzie Fund or is it Trimark True North? Something like that. I don't know what it invests in: in mutual funds I think. Stocks are too risky for me."

### The Global Equity Junkie
- Emerging Markets. Asia. Latin America. U.S. small caps. Global resources. So many countries, so little foreign content room.
- Gets upset when people say derivatives are dangerous.
- Has boring day job and is too old to bungie jump, so gets his thrills playing fund roulette with his, and his wife's, RRSPs.

### The "I Thought Mutual Funds Always Hold Stocks" Portfolio
- Investor is 83 and portfolio is 100% equity funds.
- Doesn't know the difference between a stock and a bond.
- Thinks asset allocation is too complicated.
- Sometimes worries about a stock-market crash.

### The "I Let the Gurus Pick 'Em" Portfolio
- Not content with delegating stock picking to the pros, this investor even lets the gurus pick the funds, but forgets about the 1% fees on top of fees that entails.
- Has great faith in Canadian banks, but not enough to invest in bank stocks.

### The "Have My Cake and Eat It Too" Portfolio
- Torn between greed, envy, and fear, investor is happy to double her fees in order to guarantee her principal against a stock decline and still make money if the bull market continues.
- Might have been better off in life insurance industry segregated funds, but would rather pay high fees for the "glamour" of mutual funds. See also Chapter 7.

## Chapter Six

# If You Must Be in Funds, How to Minimize the Damage

Many fund investors with modest amounts of wealth will have to stay in funds for some time. This chapter addresses how they can minimize the damage, and grow their nest eggs to the point when they can consider the other alternatives surveyed in this book. Typically, the investment industry doesn't regard you as having "serious money" until you reach $500,000 or $1 million in assets, depending on the firm. But anyone with more than $250,000 has many options beyond mutual funds. Even investors with as little as $50,000 can probably get away from the trap that conventional mutual funds often represent.

If you have less than this, mutual funds, ironically, may be one of the best ways to grow your assets to the point when you can take advantage of lower-cost alternatives.

What, then, should a smart investor do while building up to these levels? Some may already have the necessary $200,000 or $300,000 but are trapped in back-end load mutual funds and redeeming them would be too costly at this stage in the declining schedule. Some people are quite happy with the security of brand-name mutual funds and do not mind drawbacks like high MERs.

For all these types of investors, remaining with mutual funds appears to be in the cards for the time being. There are various transition strategies for investors who, for whatever reason, are temporarily committed to funds. By proper selection of particular fund families, you can get many of the advantages—chiefly, lower costs—of the alternatives to funds examined later in this book. We close this chapter by showing how to optimize any mutual fund portfolio.

## Before getting started

Long before choosing any specific investment, whether stocks, mutual funds, or anything else, it is essential to have a comprehensive plan. In spite of the importance of this critical first step in the investment process, few people take the time to do one—let alone do it well. After all, a plan—not your spouse, neighbors, or even your adviser—should determine what you want your investments to achieve. It should consider projected rate of return, the investment time frame, and, most importantly, what level of risk the investor is comfortable taking to reach the objectives. Once the plan is complete, the investor must then determine the appropriate asset mix—the most important decision for every investor. The asset mix is the key to controlling risk and is the essential factor in determining total return. Historically, almost all investors, and certainly all prudent and more conservatively minded investors, have been well served with balanced portfolios that contain a mix of at least two or three types of assets. The most common asset classes are equities (stocks and stock mutual funds), fixed-income investments (bonds, mortgages, GICs, and so on), cash (bank deposits, T-bills, money market instruments, and savings bonds), and real estate and managed futures.

In the long term, there is little doubt that equities have proven to be the asset class that has made the most money. This fact is supported by the well-known asset growth charts of Chicago-based Ibbitson & Associates and by several academic studies. For example, Chris Robinson of York University has shown that a portfolio of 100% stocks gives investors the best shot at not outliving their money. Jeremy Siegel's *Stocks for the Long Run: A Guide to Selecting Markets for Long-Term Growth* (Irwin Professional Publishing, Illinois, 1994) presents a similar argument.

Such attractive returns come at a price, however. In the occasional, unavoidable bad years—like 1998—when equity portfolios drop 25% or more, it is essential to have other ingredients in a portfolio, just as an omelet needs more than just eggs. In such horrifying times it is the fixed-income and, to a lesser degree, cash portions of portfolios that allow investors to sleep at night. More importantly, such diversified portfolios prevent investors from panicking and cashing out everything at the bottom of the market.

Granted, mutual fund managers do their best to reduce risk, and usually they can prevent catastrophic losses. After all, all mutual funds have professionally managed portfolios, and are more diversified than small investors can normally achieve by investing directly in stocks. The ability of funds to reduce risk while enhancing returns is one of their most attractive attributes. Unfortunately, the only way to reduce the risk significantly in any portfolio is to invest a portion in fixed-income investments. As typically happens at least once every decade, equity markets will drop 20 to 30%, whether over the course of many months (a bear market) or in a single day, such as occurred in October 1987. In this unavoidable market environment all-stock portfolios and all equity mutual funds will experience significant, even horrifying, losses. Until 1998, investors in broadly based equity funds were spared such losses, but investors in specialty funds regularly experience comparable losses in regional equity funds or narrow industry-sector funds. To hear more about such experiences, just ask anyone who was overexposed to Asian or gold mutual funds in 1997.

Just as there are no secure stocks, there is no such thing as a secure stock mutual fund. Some may be more conservative and some more aggressive, but all equity funds have good return potential and therefore carry significant risk. Risk control for a portfolio depends almost entirely upon diversifying among different asset classes. To a lesser degree it depends on diversification among complementary sub-classes of each type of investment. Examples are Canadian small-cap equity or global large-cap equity. Risk management by individual fund managers is inconsequential to the big picture or to the investor's long-term success.

## Bond funds versus laddered bond portfolio

Several compelling factors suggest that investors will typically be better served by buying bonds or bank GICs, rather than bond mutual funds. Once an individual's asset mix has been established, the portion that is to be safe and secure—fixed-income products—is often best invested in a portfolio of laddered bonds, strip bonds, or GICs.

In a laddered portfolio, the investor simply ensures that equal amounts of bonds mature in each of several years. While it may be tempting to try and guess when interest rates will go back up, and perhaps invest only for 90 days or six months, prudent investors know that longer-term interest rates are almost always higher than short-term interest rates. Because of this, investors are usually best served by investing in longer-term instruments.

Once the ladder has been set up, no further action is necessary by the investor. For example, consider someone investing $100,000 who wants half the portfolio in secure investments and a maximum term of five years. With $50,000 for five years, this person would initially invest $10,000 for one year, $10,000 for two years, and so on. Initially he or she will earn the average interest for each of those years, but in future years as the short-term money comes due, it will always be "rolled over" to a five-year term. The ladder has been "re-extended" so no single bond investment is reinvested for less than five years. This way the investor gets the return of long-term interest rates and has the added bonus of never having to choose, predict, or worry about where interest rates are going next. There will also be the added security of knowing that some money will always be close to coming due.

The decision whether to buy bonds, GICs, strip bonds, or similar vehicles depends on whether the investor needs ongoing cash flow or prefers compounding. It also depends on which products offer the best relative interest rates on the day some money comes up for reinvestment.

## Style diversification

Advisers and investors can classify stocks or equity funds as growth or value investments; one manager—John Di Tomasso— has described the two styles as "opposite sides of the same coin." A good value manager will not buy a cheaply valued stock that has no earnings prospects, just as a good growth manager doesn't want to overpay for that growth.

Value investors look for undervalued companies based on

criteria such as relatively low price-to-earnings or price-to-book-value ratios. Alternatively, growth investments are companies expected to grow earnings rapidly, beyond the premium the market has priced into the stock's price. Value stocks often include banks and utilities, while growth stocks may include software and computer companies.

Neither style is better or worse in the long term. Both generate virtually identical returns and have similar risk. Unfortunately, as the chart shows, value and growth styles perform better at different times. In some years, value stocks (and value mutual funds) earn tremendous returns, while growth investors investing in equally well-run companies may lose money. In other years, the opposite is true. Ideally, of course, it would be nice to predict the future and choose which type would perform best each year, and simply switch back and forth accordingly. But timing is almost impossible, and is certainly not necessary for average investors. Instead, smart investors will divide an equal amount of money

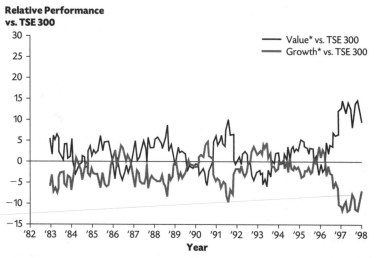

## Canadian Value Stocks vs. Growth Stocks

**Relative Performance vs. TSE 300**

*TSE 300 Total Return Index/Barra Value and Growth Indices: 12 month rolling returns relative to the TSE 300 Index.

*Source: Northern Trust Global Advisors*

between both value and growth, and will earn good returns while reducing the swings in their portfolios.

For example, both the Spectrum United Canadian Equity and Ivy Canadian Funds are value funds. The managers are independent of each other, but have a similar outlook and philosophy on managing money. A review of the top 10 holdings of each shows considerable overlap. Beyond the top 10, there is considerable overlap in the sectors of the market they invest in. Value funds typically do not own many resource stocks, but hold larger weightings in the interest-sensitive financial services and utilities groups. Because these two funds provide little real diversification, only one needs to be held in a portfolio. Investors who own both these funds and who want to diversify their holdings would be better off with a growth fund, such as Mackenzie's Universal Canadian Growth Fund.

One of our major concerns with mutual funds is the constraint that the relatively small Canadian stock market will inevitably result in overlap. Also, the standard is more gray than black and white, and value and growth investors can own the same companies, such as Bell Canada and Shell.

In addition to growth or value investing, a third style, often called market-driven investing, includes sector rotation and momentum investing. With this approach, the managers make significant bets on sectors and stocks given short-term market factors. A manager may decide, for example, that interest rates are likely to go down, which favors the "interest-sensitive" group of stocks. The manager then substantially overweights those stocks in the portfolio. Another manager may decide nickel prices are going to go up and will add large positions in companies such as Inco and Falconbridge to the portfolio.

Unlike growth or value investing, rather than spending much time researching individual companies, this management style reacts to the market and adopts a short-term perspective. While it is not inherently a bad strategy, it involves more active trading, which means higher levels of risk. It also means less tax efficiency because little is held for the long term and there is little tax deferral.

We conclude our discussion of management style by looking at the group of fund professionals who call themselves "blend managers." Again, there is no particular problem with blend managers, except that this approach makes it more difficult to assess whether the manager is actually doing what she says she is doing. A major problem underlying many managers' poor performance is a lack of style consistency, or style drift. It is tempting for managers to change their style over time. The best managers know what they are good at and stick to what they are doing, even when that style is temporarily out of favor.

## Manager orientation

Having addressed the issue of management style, it is now important to examine the manager's focus on company research.

Investors will occasionally see the phrases "top-down" and "bottom-up" in the marketing materials from fund companies. Similar to value and growth investing, top-down and bottom-up styles are opposite sides of the same coin.

Bottom-up managers focus on individual company research, while top-down managers conduct larger macroeconomic research. Bottom-up managers look more at company-specific factors such as profitability and the competition, while top-down managers look at interest rates, economic growth, and currency rates. Bottom-up managers focus on stock selection, while top-down managers generally focus on sector selection, looking to choose which sectors of the economy should prosper the most given their economic assumptions. Most value and growth managers are bottom-up, while most market-driven managers are top-down in orientation.

While there is little conclusive evidence, globalization in the 1990s seems to be undermining top-down Canadian portfolio management. The situation has arisen partly because of free trade and the increasing mobility of capital. In the second half of 1997 when Asian markets experienced their so-called "melt down," economic pressures from Asia dramatically reduced virtually all commodity prices. Prices that Canadian companies received for oil and gas, forest products, and metals dropped because of the perception of a substantial drop in demand from Asia. As a result, resource stocks suffered sizable drops in late 1997.

A portfolio manager looking at Canadian industrial production, Canadian interest rates, the Canadian dollar, or even North American economic indicators alone, would have completely missed the gathering storm in Asia. The 40% decline in oil and gas stocks in 1997–98 was also partly due to politics in the Middle East and the potential for more exports from Iraq, as well as the unseasonably warm winter and the expectation of a drop in demand in Asia. Similarly, in recent years the country-allocation decision in European funds has been the key to good returns. If the manager were overweight in the United Kingdom, the fund did well. If Italy were overweight, the fund did poorly. But 10 years from now European country allocation may become meaningless because of the European Union, and the resulting common currency and monetary policy. As the world gets smaller, making intelligent decisions on macroeconomic issues becomes more complex and perhaps of less importance. Arguably, investors will be better served by bottom-up managers than by top-down managers in the years ahead.

## Market capitalization diversification

Similar to the contrast between the value and growth management styles, stocks can also be divided into categories based on size or market capitalization. We can generalize and divide all companies into either large or small, based on market capitalization (large cap or small cap). As with the two principal management styles, returns on market capitalization are often quite different in any short-term period. For example, in 1997, the Canadian economy grew strongly and the TSE 300, which is heavily weighted in the largest companies in Canada, gained 15%. At the same time, small-cap stocks grew by only 7%, even though most economic growth was taking place in those smaller companies. As with style diversification, it is difficult to predict what size companies will fare better in the near future. Prudent

## Canadian Large Stocks vs. Small Stocks*

**Relative Performance
vs. TSE 300**

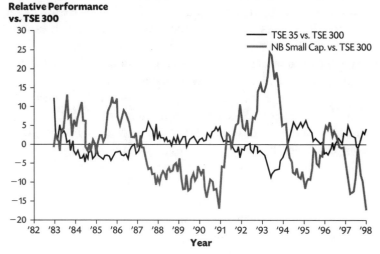

*Large Stocks represented by TSE 35, Small Stocks represented by Nesbitt Burns
Small Cap Index: 12 month rolling returns relative to the TSE 300 Index.

*Source: Northern Trust Global Advisors*

investors who are as concerned about risk as return will instead divide their equity assets between both types at all times.

## Global investing

Alert readers will probably notice a theme here, which also applies to international investing. While the fund industry has created hundreds of specialized regional and country-specific funds in recent years, ultimately no one knows which part of the world will yield the best returns in any given year. In 1994, most investors were surprised when Latin American funds were crushed, dropping an average 15% on the year. In 1997, it was Asia's turn to surprise, with Asian funds down an average of 27%. It's always tempting to try and choose the best regions, but no one has been able to do this consistently, and the attempt always poses large risks.

There is a superficially compelling argument that some regions, such as Asia, will grow faster than others, and that therefore only those high-growth regions should be owned for the long term. But does that necessarily mean that local companies will reap the benefits of this tremendous growth? Or will the companies that make the most money in the developing economies indeed be the existing world leaders? It could be that the companies that make the most money in the developing economies will be the dominant world leaders. Shareholders of companies such as Intel, Northern Telecom, Seagram, Bombardier, Microsoft, and Coca-Cola are all significant beneficiaries of the growth in these developing markets. Indeed, even though these economies have led the world in economic growth in the past decade, the U.S. stock market has led the world markets. It is possible that with globalization, older Western companies may indeed have the best returns while having significantly less risk than those offshore.

Investors then face two questions. First, which regions will have the most growth? Second, is it better to own funds that own shares in local companies or should you own global industry leaders directly? To further complicate matters, prudent investors will look for a growth fund and a value fund, and perhaps a large-cap and a small-cap fund as well. If you are going to invest in regional funds, you should own several funds from each region. But is it reasonable to have four Asian funds, four emerging market funds, four European funds, four American funds, and four Japanese funds?

Arguably, if an investor has less than 16 regional or country funds, to some degree he or she is trying to time that portion of his or her portfolio—trying to identify the "hot" region or style. Compounding the problems with regional or country-specific funds, the people that buy them will inevitably have to stomach shockingly large volatility when something goes wrong in a particular part of the world. For example, anyone who owned Latin American funds in 1994 or Asian funds in 1997 understands the almost irresistible temptation to try and time their investments in and out of those regions. Because of the complications of diversifying by style and size, and because of the potential to regress to some form of market timing, we believe there's a better way.

Instead, investors are better served by dealing exclusively in global funds. In a global fund, the manager, rather than the investor, decides which part of the world to be in. And the decision will be, in most parts of the world most of the time. This means investors can meet all their foreign investing needs with as few as two funds—global value and global growth—or perhaps four funds if you further diversify by market capitalization: global large-cap value, global large-cap growth, global small-cap value, global small-cap growth.

Although this is a simpler approach to foreign investing, it certainly will give you less to talk about over the barbecue or at cocktail parties. It will give you no reason to stay awake worrying in the middle of the night. It gives all investors both the enhanced return of foreign investing and the enhanced safety from diversifying internationally. This approach has a zero requirement for crystal-ball decision making or market timing. For example, while Asian funds plummeted 27% in 1997, global funds averaged returns of 13%. When Latin America had problems and the funds were down 15%, global funds returned 9%. Over the past 10 years, the average global fund has earned a respectable 11%, while their harder-to-stomach Asian funds have lost money (−.5%). There is not yet a 10-year record for Latin American funds. In the last five years, Latin funds have earned 9%, while global funds have earned 15% and Asian funds a paltry 2%. This highlights the value of owning only two to four complementary global funds. Not only should you expect to earn excellent returns, but you will also have less risk, and are less likely to degenerate into market timing.

## Mutual fund review criteria

As our discussion clearly indicates, investors must consider many issues before ever worrying whether fund A is better than fund B. Investors and many advisers spend too much time on fund selection and too little time on portfolio structure.

Once proper planning has been done, a clear set of objectives established, and an asset mix selected, choosing individual funds should be simple. It is important to remember that while mutual funds will be discussed for the equity portion of a portfolio, other vehicles should be used for the other portions. Within the equity portion, funds should be diversified several ways, by geography (Canadian and foreign), by market capitalization (large and small cap), and by manager style (growth and value). No manager can do all things but it is important to avoid needless duplication. Before considering any individual funds, decide exactly how many you should own—perhaps four or six, but rarely more than eight. The following items should be considered when reviewing mutual funds, and when building your short list of potential candidates.

To obtain an initial overview of a workable number of funds in each category, screen your funds based on five-year, risk-adjusted returns. As shown in the chart, all funds can be objectively ranked for absolute risk-adjusted return. Compound annual returns, as reported daily in every newspaper in the land, are almost meaningless for assessing a fund manager's ability. Instead, it is important to examine returns relative to risks taken. Comparisons of at least

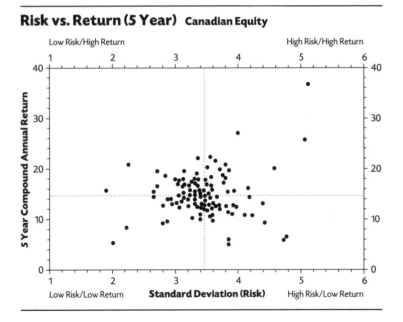

**Risk vs. Return (5 Year)** Canadian Equity

five years are needed to negate the occasional exceptionally good or exceptionally bad year, and style-based performance distortions.

Next, investors should review the individual fund manager, considering both tenure and consistency. Past performance is not as important as a consistent discipline. Every manager can be consistent, and every manager can be hot, but none can be consistently hot. As discussed earlier, fund managers tend to be like pro athletes with free-agent status—here today, gone tomorrow. Many of the biggest names in Canadian funds are no longer with the same firm at which they built their reputation.

To be objective in the assessment, investors must look only at funds for which the manager has been in place, or can be assessed elsewhere, for at least a five-year period. It is also important to assess the stability of and relationship with the management company. For example, if the fund manager is an employee of the fund company, he or she could be packing his or her desk as you are signing the cheque to invest money into the fund. Conversely, if the manager has a long-term employment contract or is a shareholder in the management company, you can be assured that they will be there to manage that portion of your portfolio for some time.

Another important element in assessing the fund manager is style consistency. After all, managers are only human. If what they are doing doesn't work in one particular year, there is always the temptation to try something different. Similarly, a surprising number of funds have changed objective or style in recent years. For example, large-cap, blue-chip Canadian equity funds have been transformed into resource funds or small-cap funds, with no change in title or marketing materials, and consequently no notification to investors. If a fund that looks attractive based on risk/reward comparisons has experienced a change in manager or style or objectives, the return numbers have been rendered meaningless, and the fund should be discarded from your list. Similarly, a manager who specialized five years ago in small-cap resource stocks, and today is running a blue-chip growth fund should automatically be disqualified, regardless of performance, because he or she has been proven to lack the necessary discipline.

When you have developed a short list based on risk/return and the managers themselves, the next thing to consider is relative performance in good and bad years. A fund that has even an occasional extremely bad year does a poor job of preserving capital, regardless of total return. Average returns can be misleading, even in a risk-adjusted return comparison. If a fund, for example, goes down 25%, it must go up 33% to break even. If it does go up 33% in the year after going down 25%, the average return will be shown in the paper as 4% per year, but the investor has only broken even. In this case, investors would have earned a greater return if they had earned a consistent 1% rather than a volatile 4%.

Many people will not get back to the break-even point. Instead, they will yield to human nature and sell after losing 25%. Because of the impact of consistency and capital preservation on long-term return, many superficially mediocre funds can be the best ones to own. Do not be concerned if a fund is never on a top 10 list because it also will be unlikely to ever show up on a bottom 10 list. In fact, choosing a fund from a top 10 list, certainly those with less than five-year records, is a sure route to ruin.

It is also important to consider the funds' underlying portfolios. Look at industry concentration and concentration in individual companies, and the nature of the individual stocks themselves. Generally, the relative weighting that a manager places in a particular industry is a good indicator of risk. For example, gold stocks comprise 5.3% of the TSE. If a fund is 10% in golds, regardless of style, size, and so on, there is significant risk and, of course, return potential in that fund. Similarly, a fund that holds 100 stocks is more diversified and safer than one with only 30 stocks. It is important to acknowledge that a statistically ideal portfolio, in terms of diversification, is somewhere around 40 companies. Beyond that point, any additional companies may be an example of the famous "di-worseification." Also, if a fund owns individual stocks that you would not be comfortable owning directly, such as Vancouver penny stocks, that may be your signal to avoid the whole fund, regardless of other criteria.

Another important part of the assessment is to look at recent cash flow in and out of the fund. A fund that has had large amounts of cash coming in may have less volatility, not because of the fund manager's ability but rather because of a lag in getting the cash invested. Ivy Canadian, for example, which is among the best in terms of risk/return, and is well managed, owes part of the credit for its seemingly low risk to the one-third it has been keeping in cash.

There is also cause for concern when a fund becomes too large. While it may be relatively easy to run a $200-million fund, it is much tougher to manage $2 billion in the Canadian market (as Frank Mersch may be able to attest before leaving the giant Altamira Equity Fund). Thankfully, we have seen an increased willingness of managers to close, or cap, small-cap funds in recent years when they reach an unwieldy size.

When investing outside an RRSP or RRIF, the tax efficiency of a fund is also of great importance. Chapter 5 discussed the tax efficiency problem of mutual funds generally. Funds that buy and hold realize significantly less in taxable gains than do more actively managed funds. This means investors have a significant tax advantage in lower turnover funds. Although taxes must be paid eventually, the longer they can be deferred, the greater the real benefit to investors.

There is also a downside to this efficiency. Many of these tax-efficient (tax-deferral) funds often come with significant accrued tax liabilities. This means the fund has significant, often enormous, unrealized capital gains built into the portfolio. Earlier investors received the benefit of these gains, but those that buy the fund later, with this liability still present, will pay tax on these gains as if they received them, even though they did not. Also investors who are seeking ongoing income from a fund need to consider how it will be taxed. Some income funds pay income that is taxed much like GIC interest, while some funds pay almost exclusively dividend income, which is taxed at a much lower rate.

Mutual fund management expense ratios (MERs), which were discussed in detail in Chapter 3, are an essential part of reviewing every fund.

A significant part of most MERs is the compensation for the investment advice that is also being received (hopefully). If an investor buys a load fund, then typically, in addition to load charges, one-third of the annual MER will go to the adviser every year to compensate for ongoing advice and service. This is perhaps more of an issue for those who deal with discount brokers, where the investor saves nothing on the MER while receiving less service. In fact, the perceived great saving of using a discount broker is one of the great unsupportable myths of the 1990s. If an investor holds a fund for five years and pays an average MER of 2.25%, the total hidden fees collected are 11.25%. In that same five years, the advising company (full service or discount) will likely have received 4% to 5% of the initial investment in trailer fees. Whether the investor saved 1% or 2% of loads is almost inconsequential, because loads are a minor part of the total fees. Even sadder, some investors buy backload funds through a discount firm, which results not only in a significantly lower level of service, but in this case not even saving 1%.

Whether investors buy front-end or back-end load, full service or discount, they are paying significant annual expenses for investment advice. If they invest with true no-load companies, such as Bissett & Associates or Phillips, Hager & North Ltd., which have significantly lower management fees, the investor is receiving real benefits in terms of cost savings. The substantially lower MER is due to having no trailer fees or other compensation to advisers working with investors and their portfolios. Therefore, few advisers can afford to, or will, recommend them, apart from "fee-only" planners.

## Seek lower-MER fund families

Fee-conscious fund investors, particularly those with less than $50,000 and who can't get access to the products and services described in Part 3, can stay in mutual funds for the time being, but should gradually switch to lower-MER fund families.

Smart investors should look for funds that not only generate above-average performance but also have below-average MERs. From a selection of more than 1,700 funds, that is quite possible. No-load groups with below-average MERs of 1% or so but strong performance include Bissett, PH&N, Saxon Funds, Sceptre Investment Counsel Ltd., and Scudder Canada Investor Services Ltd. Three others that can't be categorized as consistently strong performers, but which have below-average MERs, are CentrePost Funds, GBC Asset Management Inc., and Mawer Investment Management. Promising but not yet proven are Royal Mutual Funds Inc.'s new strategic index funds, and low-MER index funds from CIBC Securities Inc. and TD GreenLine Funds. (See also Chapter 9 on passive investing.)

Load-family MERs tend to be higher than no-loads because they factor in the cost of sales. Fund families tend to be high-MER or low-MER across the board. Among broker-sold funds, Trimark continues to lead the load-fund pack on MERs, particularly in its three original front-load funds: the global flagship Trimark Fund has an MER of just 1.52%; the balanced fund, Trimark Income Growth, has a 1.59% MER; and its domestic equity fund, Trimark Canadian, just 1.52% MER. Other load firms with below-average MERs include Elliott & Page, Guardian Group, and Templeton Management Ltd.

"Those low MERs will really pay off in the long run," says Warren Baldwin, vice-president of Toronto-based T.E. Financial Consultants Ltd., a fee-based financial planning firm. "This is the reason why, in spite of the fact that we are easily able to get load funds for zero front end, we still recommend inclusion of some of the excellent no-loads in the portfolio."

While equity (especially global) funds tend to have high, 2.5%-plus MERs, fees also act as a significant drag on bond funds, particularly in a world of 6% fixed-income returns.

## MERs especially important for bond funds

In his self-published *The Money Management Game: What They Don't Tell You About Mutual Funds*, broker Andy Filipiuk calculates that someone who invests $50,000 in a 20-year bond at 7% winds up with $193,484. He notes, however, that "The same bond, held in a bond fund with a 1.7% management fee would have $139,127, for a difference of $54,357."

Bond fund MERs need to come down because bond managers are unlikely to be able to make capital gains from interest rate declines. The average Canadian bond fund still sports a hefty 1.65% MER, while no-load funds PH&N Bond and Bissett Canadian Bond have MERs of just 0.57% and 0.75% respectively.

The actively managed no-load funds from the banks and trust companies are no cheaper in terms of MER than many of the more glamorous brand-name load funds. The banks justify their uncompetitive MERs by claiming that they pay for the investment advice that clients receive at the counter in their local branch—a questionable claim.

While there is little doubt that investors are better served by low-MER funds, there is evidence that good advice is worth paying for. If an investor does not have the time, interest, or energy to do the work suggested in this chapter, or if it's apparent that a professional is needed to monitor a portfolio on an ongoing basis, then the investor probably needs advice. Those who recognize this fact should realize that their worst choice of action would be to try to get advice without paying for it by buying no-load (no advice) funds through a full-service adviser. Remember that in the past few years, with one of the strongest and longest bull markets in history, there has been little real need for advice. Virtually everyone has made money regardless of what they have done. Advisers really show their worth when markets are at their worst. The 1998 "correction" should give you an opportunity to assess your own advisor's worth.

As documented in a well-known study by Boston-based Dalbar Inc., which examined how real investors actually did over 12 years in the United States, the key to making money was not the performance of the mutual funds themselves, but rather human behavior involved in moving in and out of equity mutual funds. The performance, and even such considerations as MERs, were of little consequence in determining long-term success. The key determinant of success was whether an investor worked with an adviser.

Surprisingly, this finding is not because the advisers had necessarily chosen better funds. Rather, it is because investors who are working with advisers are less likely to buy high and sell low, or try and time the market. Those investors without an adviser (no load) on average held their mutual funds only 17 months, while those receiving advice (load) were able to hold for an average of 48 months. A separate study by Morningstar of those investing in 219 funds over five years found that while the average fund returned 12.5% per year, the average investor lost 2.2% per year for the same reason.

But that was then. This is now. Are Canadian mutual fund investors smarter than their American counterparts? If anything, the opposite is true. A review comparing mutual fund performance with mutual fund cash flow (new investments into the funds) shows that after a period of strong returns (when stock prices are high), no-advice funds receive an inordinate amount of new cash. When times are tough, and securities are cheap and should be bought rather than sold, the no-advice funds tend to experience net redemptions. Knowing this, investors faced with two different funds, a higher-MER lower-performing fund that comes with advice, or a top performer sold with no advice, may be better off with the worse-performing fund.

Of course, adviser-distributed mutual funds can also be top performers. Arguably they are subject to more stringent scrutiny and accountability from the advisers who sell them than the direct sellers receive from no-load investors. For those who want service and personal accountability, or simply one person with whom to deal directly, then an adviser-sold (load) fund may be the more attractive choice.

If this seems too complicated, or if you have less than the few dollars required to achieve the diversification discussed here, or you cannot find the right adviser to do this work for you, there is a simple alternative. Readers of *The Financial Post* in 1997 will be familiar with this approach: the Rip Van Winkle two-fund portfolio. And it happens to use two adviser-sold funds.

## Keep it simple: the Rip Van Winkle two-fund portfolio

This simple approach to investing first appeared in *The Financial Post* in the summer of 1997. The premise is that all you really need are two funds: a balanced fund and global equity fund. The simplicity of this concept struck a chord with average readers/ investors, who want mutual funds as they were originally envisaged—something a professional takes care of on your behalf so you can concern yourself with other things.

Rip Van Winkle is a fictional bearded character created by American author Washington Irving. The character is a ne'er-do-well who sleeps for 20 years and awakes to a very different world. The idea of the portfolio is to choose two funds that run on "automatic pilot": if you leave the country for 30 years, or fall into a long coma, you should awaken to an investment portfolio that has grown considerably. No need for rebalancing, switching or even paying close attention to daily market changes.

Both you and your financial planner do nothing. That doesn't mean the portfolio is static, however; at least two fund managers are continually engaged in stock picking, moving in and out of geographical regions and modifying asset allocation on your behalf.

In this scenario, we're assuming an average RRSP/RRIF investor who wants a balance of stocks, bonds, and cash and maximum foreign content—growth with a little income. Both funds are from proven, credible fund families, both with below-average management fees.

Fund No. 1 is Trimark Income Growth, a basic low-fee Canadian balanced fund with an MER of 1.6%. This constitutes 80% of the Rip Van Winkle portfolio. There's a good cross-section of mid- to large-capitalization Canadian stocks, some bonds, cash, and mortgage securities. The asset mix is the classic 60% equity to 40% bonds, but was closer to 50/50 as 1998 progressed. The fund maximizes its permitted 20% foreign content with mostly U.S., and some European and Japanese, stocks. Average compound annual growth rate for the five years ended March 31, 1998, is 14.7%.

Since this portfolio was developed, Trimark has come under criticism for its underperforming Canadian equity funds. In the case of this particular fund, we're not overly concerned, since there is 20% foreign stocks and 40% fixed income. The Canadian portion is a mix of mid- to large-cap, blue-chip Canadian stocks, and Trimark has proven it can manage for the long term and not be shaken by short-term fads. In any case, Rip is still asleep and unconcerned about such short-term controversies!

Fund No. 2 is Templeton Growth Fund, the classic global equity fund created in 1954 by the legendary Sir John Templeton. Again, this fund has a lower than average MER of 2%, a long-term performance track record unmatched by any mutual fund (18.2% average compound annual growth rate for the five years ended May 31, 1998), and a good value-oriented geographical mix that buys bargains around the world at the time of maximum pessimism.

If you use Templeton for the 20% foreign-content portion of a registered plan, coupled with the 20% of the 80% from Trimark Income Growth, you'd have effective 36% foreign content. The combined asset allocation of these funds is skewed slightly to equities. That should be fine for any young investor. Older investors could bring the total portfolio into a traditional asset mix by substituting Templeton Global Balanced Fund.

Trimark fans could also substitute the Trimark Fund for Templeton Growth. The Trimark Fund has a lower MER than Templeton Growth—just 1.52% versus 2%—and has a stellar first-quartile record over 15 years.

On the other hand, purists who say Trimark is overweighted in North America could substitute Templeton International stock for Templeton Growth. Similarly, you could use Templeton International Balanced Fund instead of Templeton Global Balanced. Those already in particular families could substitute for the balanced fund: CentrePost Balanced, Dynamic Partners, Sceptre Balanced, Saxon Balanced, PH&N Balanced, and so on.

Granted, this portfolio takes the fun out of the fund tracking and switching game, but it's doubtful that all the energy spent on these pursuits will add to performance. One financial planner who liked the Rip approach noted, "One of the major hurdles I encountered was the clients' will to diversify into several different funds. They have ascribed to the 'don't put all your eggs in one basket' theory and simply see a mutual fund as only one egg. Some clients get very suspicious if you try to concentrate their assets into two or three funds."

Warren Baldwin agrees that the Rip portfolio makes sense for portfolios between $30,000 and $50,000. Beyond that, he'd like to see more diversification of management. With $75,000 or more, Baldwin says he "would use a couple more funds immediately. In both cases, I would consider an appropriate fund from PH&N or Bissett."

Baldwin puts even more stress on low MERs. "Mr. Van Winkle's 'Dream Portfolio' is 54 basis points below the MER for the same portfolio using 'average' MERs for the fund categories selected. Assume we are starting with zero in the RRSP portfolio and adding $12,000 per year over the next 25 years. Assume also the portfolio grows at a compound rate of 10% per year. Assuming that an alternative 'average' fund portfolio only grows at an annual rate of 9.46% (reduced due to the additional MER costs), the difference in accumulation after 25 years is almost $100,000. The MER on both PH&N and Bissett would further reduce the average MER for Mr. Van Winkle."

The Rip Van Winkle approach is only appropriate for investors who are willing to "park" money and not look at it for many years. Most investors have a tough time resisting the temptation to fiddle and refine, and will always run the risk of selling at the bottom of the next bear market. Ironically, most well-constituted mutual fund portfolios should require about as many changes as Rip's, hopefully not much more than the occasional, perhaps yearly, rebalancing among asset classes, and the occasional rolling over of a maturing bond in a laddered structure. When you do your homework upfront and own good funds in a sound structure, the average holding period should be many years. Indeed, other than accounting for major changes in management style or philosophy, or long-term deteriorating risk-adjusted return, there is little reason to sell any fund that was bought correctly.

## How to fix the flawed portfolio

Depending on what problems a portfolio has, the solution may be simple or complex. The problem with many fund portfolios is lack of liquidity, making it hard to make portfolio changes because of punishing rear-load loads. Fortunately, most funds have hidden in their prospectuses an option to withdraw 10% from each fund per year with no redemption charge—even if the fund is still in the six- or seven-year declining-redemption schedule. This feature was originally intended to allow people to live on their investments, for example, RRIF investors, but also allows investors to withdraw money each calendar year for rebalancing.

In addition, funds must pay out all capital gains and dividends received each year. Although this dividend is normally reinvested in additional shares, they can be paid in cash instead. With these two options investors could, in theory, withdraw 10% in December, get the year-end distribution in cash (perhaps another 10%), and in January withdraw yet another 10%, for a total 30%. This newfound liquidity can then be reinvested as is most appropriate, given the needs of the larger portfolio structure.

A second method for rebalancing a portfolio is to take advantage of free switching within funds at the same fund company. Most companies offer at least a dozen funds, with several having more than 30 alternatives. For example, if you find yourself lacking global exposure, and are overweight in an excellent Canadian fund, the fund company almost certainly has a global fund. You are better served to partially switch out of that excellent Canadian fund into even a mediocre global fund, rather than simply stay unbalanced because of the load charge.

Because the highest rear-load charges are well under 10%, it can make sense to pay the charge to get out of a bad fund in a bad fund company that does not fit within the appropriate structure of your total portfolio.

## Common mutual fund portfolio flaws

Most flawed mutual fund portfolios can be divided into five groups. These mistakes are the ones that cause investors to lose sleep, miss opportunities, and fail to meet their objectives, whether saving for a rainy day or for retirement. Also, sometimes what was once a reasonable portfolio may face these problems simply because it has been ignored for too long.

- Lacks a comprehensive plan
- Inappropriate asset mix
- Inadequate fund diversification
- Excessive fund diversification
- Excessive concentration in an individual fund or fund company

## The role of an adviser

Many investors today are confused about the role of an adviser in this process. They should expect at least an element of financial and estate planning before proceeding with any discussion of investment portfolios or individual investment selections. An individual's tax situation, for example, should be factored in to all investment decisions.

An adviser should help develop a comprehensive plan and determine an appropriate asset mix and portfolio structure. Typically, he or she will also recommend a short list of investments appropriate for each segment of the portfolio. The adviser normally takes care of implementation of the fund selections, provides ongoing monitoring, and ideally formal quarterly or semi-annual reviews. The adviser should also coordinate servicing and administration of the portfolio. Above all, the adviser builds a long-term relationship with the investor to work together effectively when the market sours. This is when advisers really earn their keep. For example, when a portfolio is down 25%, the adviser illuminates the cause and recommends actions based on whether it's a problem with individual investments, which may need replacement, or if it is simply a case of unavoidable market turbulence. The underappreciated value of an adviser emerges in this situation, which all investors must occasionally face. A great adviser supports the client, allowing the individual to resist the temptation to time out of the market at what may be the bottom. Perhaps this is why 85% of all investors with portfolios over $50,000 use a professional adviser.

Many people believe that with a book like this, and perhaps by doing some homework and using the Internet, they can skip using an adviser and save substantial dollars. There is compelling evidence this is wrong. Whether or not you pay load charges, the ongoing management fees are a much bigger issue. The impact of a 2% load is relatively small, and given the effort involved and the proven need for advice, it is probably money well spent. Or, as Red Adair once said, "If you think a professional is expensive, you should try an amateur."

Instead of hoping their adviser can choose the next best fund or group of funds, or worse, thinking they can do better themselves, investors should instead hope that their adviser truly understands them and their needs, and ensures that the portfolio precisely matches their objectives. Individual investment selection, which is of relatively little long-term importance, is a relatively small part of an adviser's role. Ultimately that is not their role, but more accurately that of their clients. Because individual investment decisions are almost trivial to the achievement of long-term goals, investors who find an adviser whose role is primarily to select investments should run, not walk, from the office. Similarly, if the phrase, "This should be good for the next year or two," comes up, the investor can be sure that this adviser's main talent is polishing his or her crystal ball, rather than helping investors meet their objectives.

While the best individual funds often attract the most attention, they do not merit the importance that many people place on them. Successful portfolio management is more about human nature than about investment performance or risk or fees, so investors need two other things to ensure their success. To make the most money, investors need an adviser to help them keep perspective, and a portfolio plan and structure that matches their long-term goals and objectives. Nothing is more important.

## Should you be in funds at all?

Mutual funds will be around a long, long time. Their benefits of professional management, diversification, low-cost of entry, and the multitude of easily accessed markets will continue to attract millions of investors worldwide. Barring a 1960s-style collapse of faith in the product, they may well be the best single type of investment product for the beginning investor, the small investor, the unsophisticated investor, and even experienced investors who have weighed the tradeoffs and decided they're still worth it.

With competition and the growing awareness of the potential drawbacks, it's also likely that the mutual fund industry will start to make funds more attractive on the cost front. As our MER analysis shows, once funds reach an MER of about 1% a year, it will be hard to choose funds over the other products discussed in this book solely on the basis of costs.

As we have said throughout this book, we are not against mutual funds per se. We merely believe that investors should not allow television commercials, seminars, and broker sales pitches to blind them from some of their deficiencies.

It's even arguable that beginning investors with, say, a total $5,000 or $10,000 in funds, are getting a greater deal than is warranted by the fees and service charges they're paying, relative to the costs of administering such small accounts. After all, it's doubtful that someone with $250,000 requires 10 times the service of someone with just $25,000.

At the same time, a broker that lets a client with $600,000 stay in high-MER load funds is feathering his or her own nest more than the client's. Thus far, the fund industry hasn't worked too hard at providing quantity discounts to large investors, although these do exist: First Canadian Funds have a declining MER once you hit significant assets; Trimark has a similar mechanism and Investors Group rebates their 50 basis points trailer fee at $50,000 in assets.

Market forces being what they are, the fund industry will be forced to adapt to the perception that fees are too high. The very fact that successful fund investing brings an investor's assets into the range of more efficient competitors means the industry will likely have to start unbundling investment management and broker advice, or set up a two-tiered system based on asset size. Dan Richards predicts that financial advisers will eventually have two mutual fund product lines: the first will be a line as currently constituted, with management fees where they are now, and a second line for someone with a minimum of $150,000 or $250,000, a different product with a lower management fee with lower compensation level.

Perhaps that day will come sooner, if individual investors insist upon it. In the meantime, the alternatives beckon. In Part 2, we look at a number of other fund products that aren't technically "mutual" funds, including some with a feature noticeably absent from traditional mutual funds—a guarantee of initial principal. We survey passive or "index" investing; the old standby of investing directly in stocks and bonds; and some hybrid strategies that combine mutual funds with some or all of these alternatives.

*Part Two*

# Alternatives to Mutual Funds

## Chapter Seven

# Guaranteed Alternatives that Provide Equity Exposure

In the public mind, mutual funds are mostly associated with the stock market. While it's true that funds provide exposure to all asset classes, including bonds, cash, real estate, gold, and managed futures, the mutual fund boom has, for the most part, been an equity fund boom, equities being a synonym for stocks.

As the bull market of the 1990s proceeded, the big returns posted in the performance charts came from equity funds, notably U.S. and specialized funds such as technology funds, which are usually overweight U.S. small-cap and mid-cap stocks.

The baby-boom generation, in particular, has embraced the notion of "stocks for the long run." (That phrase is the title of a book by an academic, Jeremy Siegel [Irwin Professional Publishing, New York, 1994].)

The people working on Wall Street, Bay Street, and in the rest of the global investment community are, for the most part, professional optimists. Many believe the party will continue at least until 2010 or 2015. Patrick McKeough, author of *Riding the Bull* (Key Porter, Toronto, 1993) and editor of *The Successful Investor* newsletter, has long articulated three reasons for the ongoing bull market: baby-boom demographics, the trend to globalization, and the communications/information revolution. McKeough thinks the mid-1998 correction will continue, or the market will go "sideways" till the end of 1998, and then be followed by another surge of the bull market.

If you want to understand the mindset of the average equity-oriented investment adviser, check out Nick Murray's 1996 self-published bestseller, *The Excellent Investment Advisor*. This kind of thinking, which has been well rewarded, is responsible for the "buy-the-dips" behavior that has smoothed out every stock-market swoon of recent years. When the market goes down, the professional investment adviser declares, "We're having a sale," and urges investors to snap up the bargains.

The typical investor, especially a Canadian one, is worried about losing capital in a bear market. There are plenty of bears out there, as well as media pundits willing to parrot them, who tell investors things like "what's important when going forward is not the return on capital, but the return *of* capital."

But high-cost equity mutual funds are by no means the only way to get equity exposure, assuming you are as optimistic as Murray. Other chapters explore some of the alternatives to equity mutual funds. In this chapter, we look at hybrid equity funds that also provide some bear market protection, albeit at a cost.

In the past two years, Canadians have been subjected to a barrage of new products that profess to provide what investors really want: the participation in the up-side of the stock market that equity fund investors have long enjoyed, along with some guarantees against stock-market declines.

As the markets soar ever higher, these new hybrid investment products have been big sellers. They capitalize on the fact that Canadians love to have their cake and eat it too.

## Index-linked GICs

The first of these products came from the big banks: index-linked GICs or equity-linked GICs. These have been hot sellers for the banks or, more to the point, have helped to stem the outflow of traditional GICs into mutual funds.

Index-linked GICs pay interest just like regular GICs. The difference is that the amount of interest paid varies with the gains made in the stock-market index to which it is linked. You can buy index-linked GICs based on the TSE 300, others based on the S&P 500, and still others based on a variety of global stock indexes. If the stock market to which the GIC is pegged goes up, you are paid interest in some proportion to the rise. If the stock market goes down—and this is the kicker for those afraid of losing their capital—then no interest is paid but your initial capital is preserved.

But index-linked GICs have a number of disadvantages compared to regular mutual funds, which perhaps explains why their critics disparagingly refer to them as "mutual funds with training wheels." Many index-linked GICs put a limit—or "cap"—on the growth: some may give you only 20% growth over two years or 30% over three—even if the market to which they are linked soars by 70% or 80%. With a regular equity fund, you'd get most of those gains.

Second, index-linked GICs do not pass along dividends, as do equity mutual funds, index funds, or TIPS (Toronto Index Participation Shares: see Chapter 9). Dividends can amount to a significant income stream in themselves.

And third, on the taxation side, index-linked GICs are taxed like interest, which is taxed punitively compared to dividends or capital gains. This makes the stock-market gains from index-linked GICs highly taxable outside registered investment plans such as RRSPs or RRIFs.

## Guaranteed Investment Funds (GIFs)

But while the banks were refining these products to protect their GIC base, the mutual fund companies were looking to the life insurance industry to develop a far more innovative product. It even sounds like a GIC: the GIF, or Guaranteed Investment Fund, created in 1996 by Manulife Financial's John Vivash. Vivash was the founding president of Fidelity Canada and came up with a brilliant marketing alternative to a similar product sold for decades by the staid life insurance industry.

Manulife refers to the GIF as a new product category. But the GIF is not much different from the life insurance industry's segregated funds (seg funds). These half-cousins of mutual funds have been on the scene for at least three decades but are still virtually unknown, according to a recent study.

Segregated funds are investment funds quite similar to open-end mutual funds. They involve the same pooling of money from small investors with a professional, diversified selection of stocks, bonds, and other securities. But they can only be offered by an insurance company and are subject to insurance-industry regulations. The assets of the seg funds are kept and managed separately from the general assets of a life insurance company: hence the name segregated (not to be confused with segregated management as defined in Chapters 12 and 13).

But seg funds also possess a few attractive characteristics that mutual funds do not. One that gets attention in the type of volatile equity markets we've experienced since October 1997 are certain return-of-capital guarantees. In the unlikely event that markets are under water for an entire decade, the old-time seg funds normally guarantee you will get 75% of the initial principal back, while many of the new mutual fund/seg fund hybrids such as the Manulife GIF, offer the full 100% back—after 10 years, of course.

The GIF is a segregated fund that puts several brand-name mutual funds under an insurance umbrella or "wrapper." Inside are funds from AGF Management Ltd., C.I. Mutual Funds, Fidelity Investments Canada Ltd., GT Global, Trimark Investment Management Inc., and others. They are identical to the underlying funds, but have higher MERs to pay for the insurance industry add-on benefits and guarantees.

So far, investors do not seem to be bothered by the extra MERs. Since its January 1997 launch, more than 40,000 individuals have invested $3 billion into the GIF program.

According to Angus Reid, a startling 94% of 300 Canadian investors polled had never heard of seg funds, or if they had, could not explain what they are. The survey showed that once investors understood these benefits, fully 44% of them concluded that seg funds were "just as good" as mutual funds, while 26% decided seg funds were better than mutual funds. And once they understood the benefits, 38% of those polled said they'd be interested in buying seg funds.

C.I. Mutual Funds has also unveiled its own group of C.I. Segregated Funds, using a Toronto life insurance company as its partner. Relative to the mutual fund industry, the life insurance industry has undermarketed seg funds. C.I. has one of the slickest mutual fund marketing machines around. Its chief operating officer, Bill Holland, expects seg-fund sales to grow faster than regular mutual funds, and if C.I. has decided there's a future in seg funds, you can be sure many other mutual fund-industry executives are thinking along the same lines.

The first major to follow C.I.'s lead was BPI Mutual Funds, which showed its hand in February 1998. BPI, which is not part of the Manulife GIF, announced its BPI Legacy Funds with TransAmerica Life. Soon after, Trimark and Templeton announced their entry.

"You can be confident that every fund company out there is looking at how you provide a product for nervous investors," agrees Dan Richards, president of Toronto-based Marketing Solutions.

Each of these hybrid products occupies a different place on the risk/return curve. A traditional GIC has the least risk and lowest return; an index-linked GIC has slightly higher risk and reward. Seg funds and the Manulife GIF share the next slot, and above these are pure equity mutual funds.

## Drawbacks to guaranteed vehicles

The marketing psychology behind these guaranteed vehicles is understandable. When retirees have their life savings at stake and can't afford to live on low-yielding, fixed-income products, a product that provides the possible gains of the stock market with a hedge against possible catastrophic loss seems a compelling one. For a young person investing for 20 or 30 years, the MER analysis in Chapter 3 would argue against paying the 1% or so that such hedges impose on the underlying MERs of the funds; on the other hand, if someone is convinced a bear market is a significant near-term threat, they may make a sort of market-timing decision that they'll pay the premium for a few years until they believe the threat of the storm has dissipated.

The appeal of these seg wrappers to older, conservative investors is that much greater for couples, since seg funds also provide a similar return of capital guarantee to a spouse upon the death of the fund owner.

But GIF and seg-fund guarantees aren't entirely loss-proof propositions. With the GIF, Manulife guarantees return of principal after 10 years, but not before. For example, if you invested $100,000 in GIF funds at their January launch, the market value might have risen to $110,000 by December. You could, if you wanted, reset the guarantee level to $110,000. Then, if stock markets crashed some time during the following 10 years and took the market value of the portfolio down to just $50,000, you could still get the $110,000 back. Five years from now, if markets took the GIF up to $125,000 in value, you could reset the level to a $125,000 guarantee, but the clock would also be reset.

York University professor Moshe Milevsky says the three- or five-year guarantee of index-linked GICs is more valuable than the 10-year guarantee for seg funds and GIFs because markets are unlikely to be lower in 10 years.

Apart from these market considerations, another feature of seg funds and the GIFs is creditor proofing, which is especially attractive to the self-employed. This is not bullet-proof, however, since seg funds purchased after an estate-threatening legal suit is commenced may not protect the creditor.

## Segregated funds

Given these tempting possible benefits, it's surprising the life insurance industry's original seg funds, which have been around for decades, haven't had a higher profile than their glamorous—but unguaranteed—mutual fund cousins.

Normally, you'd expect to pay a price for insurance, and this is the case with the new generation of seg-fund/mutual-fund hybrids. This comes in the form of what amounts to a higher annual management expense ratio. In the case of Manulife, this amounts to an additional annual fee of 0.3% or 0.4% for non-equity funds and 1% for equity funds. At C.I., the extra fee ranges from 0.4% to 0.8%. At BPI, it is 0.25% to 0.4% on equity funds, 0.15% to 0.35% on balanced funds, 0.15% to 0.2% on income funds, and 0.05% on its T-bill fund.

There's little benefit to paying a premium for a seg version of a money market or bond fund, which is why C.I. opted to include only equity and balanced funds in its seg wrapper. BPI includes some fixed-income funds, not because it thinks any fixed-income product will be under water for 10 years (possible only if there were huge and ongoing jumps in interest rates), but because of the creditor-proofing benefits.

The guarantee level on C.I.'s seg funds, which are mostly equity portfolios, can be reset monthly. "Our view is that the guarantee is pretty useless for fixed-income products," Holland says. "The guarantee becomes important when there is risk associated with the investment, as is the case with equity funds."

Investors must decide how much return they're willing to forgo. "Some people will knock off their tops in exchange for the bottom-side protection," says Jim Rogers, chairman of Vancouver-based The Rogers Group Financial Advisors Ltd.

## Cooking your own guarantees

There are ways to get around paying a premium for the market guarantee. As with index-linked GICs, savvy consumers can bypass the MER mark-up and "cook their own" guarantees by setting aside perhaps 60% of their initial capital to buy a 10-year strip bond, then invest directly in the markets, perhaps through options, with the remaining risk capital. However, points out Milevsky, index-linked GICs are based on a widely used stock index with easy-to-replicate payouts. Manulife GIF returns are based on underlying mutual funds, so "it is somewhat more difficult to replicate the pay-off using options/strips."

Also, you will not be able to "cook" up the life insurance protection or the creditor-proofing features. Milevsky suggests that young people avoid seg funds, but concedes that they become more attractive with age as the probability of death rises.

If it's these latter features that still appeal, the better deal may lie with the original, dull old seg funds, whose MERs are comparable to regular mutual funds. For example, Great West Life of Winnipeg has long sold the funds of third-party companies such as Guardian and AGF in seg fund versions. Many other insurance companies have been offering conservatively managed seg funds for almost 20 years.

Keep in mind too that you usually can't buy a seg fund in advanced old age, because of the rising mortality rate and the higher cost of guaranteeing the death benefit. The maximum age varies from 80 to 90.

## Chapter Eight

# Investment Funds Other Than Mutual Funds

While mutual funds may be the only type of investment fund that exists in the mind of the typical mass-market consumer, there are many alternatives that resemble mutual funds but have minor differences and are often available at a lower cost.

The segregated funds of the life insurance industry, described in the previous chapter, are just one example of the many other investment funds available that aren't technically "mutual" funds.

In the high-net-worth arena, pooled funds are almost identical to mutual funds and are frequently managed by the same people. The difference is that they are sold without a prospectus, usually require a $150,000 minimum investment, and typically have MERs about half the price of mutual fund MERs. For more about pooled funds, see Chapter 13.

Closed-end mutual funds and their siblings—royalty, realty, and income trusts—are the closest cousins of mutual funds. From a standing start five years ago, they have soared in popularity to hold $13 billion of Canadian investors' money in about 100 different fund/trust units.

They have become a mainstay of Canadian investing, but many investors have never considered them because they are not available through banks or most financial planners. These alternative products give investors an attractive way to have a professional, independent investment manager look after part of their savings. Their structure and portfolios look similar to mutual funds, and the individuals managing them are often the same people in charge of conventional mutual funds, but these structures are more efficient and cheaper to run, putting more return into investors' pockets.

Other products give investors the ability to invest in ways simply not possible through a standard mutual fund.

## Closed-end funds

Closed-end funds are conceptually similar to mutual funds, but with a few major differences. Canadian investors can choose between more than 150 U.S. closed-end mutual funds and about 20 Canadian closed-end funds. The household-name money managers, such as Altamira, Scudder, and Templeton, all manage closed-end funds in addition to regular open-end mutual funds.

When investors put money into a conventional open-end fund, they are buying new shares issued by the fund company. Open-end funds can always be purchased or redeemed on demand by the investor. The principal difference with closed-end funds is that they do not issue any more shares, theoretically closing the fund to new investors.

This does not, however, mean that new people cannot invest in the shares already issued by the fund. Closed-end fund shares trade on major stock exchanges just like any stock. As with stocks, the availability of units of a closed-end fund for a potential buyer depends on the willingness of an owner of the units to sell. Closed-end funds can be bought or sold on any business day, are RRSP and RRIF eligible, must meet standard disclosure requirements, hold annual meetings, and provide audited statements.

Some of the compelling advantages of closed-end funds are due almost entirely to their closed nature. Because no new shares will be issued, no cash reserves are held in the fund, either as a result of new money flowing in or as a reserve to meet redemption requests. This protects closed-end-fund investors from forced selling in the portfolio at a market low after a market decline and the inevitable redemption requests of some investors. It also means that there is never the risk that a closed-end fund will attract too much money and become an unwieldy Goliath.

Closed-end funds, unlike open-end funds, can be fully invested all the time. Also, because there will be no new shares issued, there are no large marketing budgets, television advertisements, and so on built into the fee structures. Closed-end funds also do not need to curry favor with advisers and do not pay trailer fees or sponsor "educational" seminars or golf tournaments. This translates into lower annual charges deducted off the top of the fund each year through the MER. Nonetheless, an additional cost is associated with a closed-end fund. While there are no load or sales charges associated with buying or selling units, a normal stock commission, typically about 2% through a full-service firm, is charged to buy or sell shares, just like trading any other stock.

Closed-end funds also offer an opportunity to pick up bargains. Unlike selecting a stock, investors considering a closed-end fund do not need to know finance or accounting to look for hidden value. It is printed every week in the papers in the form of discount/premium. Since a fixed number of shares exist, the price paid for a share depends on supply and demand in the market, rather than the net asset value per share (NAVPS) of the fund. In a conventional mutual fund, investors buy new shares from the fund company, paying precisely the NAVPS, or book value per share, on the day they invest. This means investors can potentially buy closed-end fund shares at substantial discounts to actual book value—like buying a dollar bill for 75 cents. They can also sell at a "premium"—a higher cost—than the underlying value of the stocks held in the fund.

The discount opportunity constitutes a double-edged sword. A discount effectively provides for a multiplier effect; not only can investors buy more shares, but hopefully the shares also go from a discount to a premium at the same time as the underlying value appreciates. Therefore, if a closed-end fund is selling at a discount, the investor is able to pick up a "bargain"—a fund selling at a 15% discount of its actual value gives you a chance to win twice: once on the subsequent capital gains, and a second time if the climate of that particular investment changes so other investors are suddenly willing to pay a premium for that closed-end fund.

The opposite can also happen, which is why closed-end funds are among the more volatile investments. There is always the risk that while the underlying portfolio—the book value or NAVPS—may appreciate nicely, the actual share price in the market may move in the opposite direction. This is because the discount or premium not only reflects the underlying portfolio but also a market consensus on the likely short-term future of the fund.

There is also a liquidity issue with closed-end funds. If a fund trades 5,000 shares per day and you wish to buy 10,000 shares, your buying interest will drive the price up that day. Similarly, a strong selling interest can drive closed-end-fund shares to unreasonably low levels. These factors mean that there is often little correlation between a closed-end fund and its comparable benchmark. Because of this, investors—particularly those with a short-term horizon—may want to consider investing in an index vehicle such as WEBS (see Chapter 9) rather than a country-specific closed-end fund. Generally, discounts should widen in a poor market with increasing pessimism, and narrow or go to a premium in a bull market.

The discount to NAVPS is one of the greatest causes of concern for closed-end fund investors. In recent years, many closed-end funds have consistently traded at substantial discounts of 20% or more. While buying at a discount, having significant portfolio performance, and possibly selling at a premium in the future sounds attractive, no one likes to see a consistent and significant discount on the value of their assets. In recent years, funds have introduced several discount closing features. Funds may buy back shares in the open market, often below a specific price, effectively putting a floor under the market price. Many newer funds also have a fixed wind-up date, perhaps 10 years after the original issue, ensuring that investors will eventually get the full book value. Some funds with seemingly uncloseable discounts have converted from a closed-end to an open-end structure to ensure that investors will get the full value from the fund. Closed-end funds also typically go to discount soon after their initial public offering. Closed-end fund discounts are quoted weekly in the better financial newspapers.

Closed-end funds also benefit from a shareholder activism unheard of in open-end funds, because closed-end-fund investors tend to be more sophisticated and invest in larger amounts. Closed-end-fund investors tend to see themselves as owners of a fund, rather then merely the consumers of a fund product put out by a management company. This shareholder activism, which shows up predominantly in U.S.-listed closed-end funds, typically takes the form of refusing to pass proposals at shareholder meetings, nominating shareholders to the board, and similar activities.

When Scudder Kemper merged last year, fund shareholders had to vote to approve the change of the appointed manager from Scudder to the new company, Scudder Kemper. Among the shareholders in the open-end funds, the approval was a virtual rubber stamp, but the closed-end fund was, as Morningstar noted, "practically a dead heat." Final approval was won only when Scudder Kemper made concessions to the closed-end fund shareholders.

Another factor that distorts the visible return is the way annual distributions are handled. Like conventional mutual funds, closed-end funds must flow through and distribute all capital gains and income to individual unitholders each year. This distribution reduces the NAVPS for both types of funds, although open-end fund investors normally have this distribution reinvested in new shares. Closed-end fund shares often can't have distributions reinvested, meaning that investors will receive cash while seeing the share value drop in proportion. Looking at share-price performance without knowing the dividend record is therefore pointless.

Because of minimal education requirements to sell mutual funds and the fact that traditionally most open-end fund investors are less sophisticated, government regulators have put significant handcuffs on how regular funds may invest. Closed-end funds and other trust units have fewer restrictions on how they may invest and can potentially use more aggressive strategies than their open-end relatives.

Surveys in the United States and the United Kingdom, where closed-end funds (or unit trusts, as they are also called) are much more popular, show, on average, consistently better returns than the more popular open-ended versions. Interestingly, many investors, novice and otherwise, are already familiar with what may be considered the most famous closed-end fund of all—Warren Buffett's Berkshire Hathaway, though it is not legally a closed-end fund. The definitive source of information on U.S. closed-end funds is Morningstar, while there is not yet an equivalent comprehensive source for Canadian closed-end fund information.

The table on page 152 compares four similar funds from the

same company, with the same manager and similar objectives. Other than different internal (hidden) MERs, investors will see some slight differences in portfolio holdings, mostly due to different dates the shares were acquired, and different reporting dates.

## Open and Closed Fund Comparison

| Fund | Templeton Emerging Markets | Templeton Emerging Appr –TSE | Templeton Emerging Markets –NYSE | Templeton Emerging Appr –NYSE |
|---|---|---|---|---|
| Type | Open-End | Closed-End | Closed-End | Closed-End |
| $ Size | C$1.1 Billion | C$55.5 Million | US$264 Million | US$71 Million |
| Mgmt Fee | 2.5% | 2% | 1.25% | 1.25% |
| MER | 3.24% | 2.67% | 1.67% | 1.83% |
| Manager | Mark Mobius | Mark Mobius | Mark Mobius | Mark Mobius |

## Segregated funds

The life insurance industry's segregated funds, or seg funds, were discussed at length in Chapter 7, along with similar "guaranteed" products such as the Manulife GIF and the banks' index-linked GICs. They are similar to mutual funds but subject to the life insurance industry's regulations. There are certain guarantees of principal (ranging from 75% to 100%) paid if markets are under water for at least 10 years or to a beneficiary on the death of the insured. There may be more creditor-proofing potential with seg funds than with regular mutual funds. Segregated funds are not to be confused with segregated management, which is the top end of the wealth products pyramid described in Part 3.

## Labor sponsored venture capital funds

Labor sponsored venture capital funds are investment funds that invest chiefly in early-stage Canadian companies, which may include some start-up situations. Their heyday was 1995–1996, when combined federal and provincial tax credits provided an instant 40% tax credit for investing in this relatively risky asset class. They're called labor-sponsored because in order to qualify for the tax credits, the venture capital pool had to be sponsored by groups representing Canadian labor and which therefore had an interest in creating new Canadian jobs. At one point, investors could get tax credits on $5,000 worth of such funds each year; in addition to the tax credits, they also generated the regular RRSP contribution deductions. In 1996, the maximum investment was reduced to $3,500 and the combined tax credits reduced to 15% federally and 15% in several provinces, for a 30% combined tax credit. The $5,000 was reinstated late in 1998.

When first launched, investors had to hold the labor fund for at least five years before redeeming, or else they'd have to repay the tax credits. In 1996, the maximum hold period was raised to eight years, arguably the time it takes for long-term venture capitals to pay off.

As an asset class, labor funds are closest to Canadian small-cap funds. In the U.S., historically, venture capital has yielded 15% a year net of fees. They are, in fact, micro-cap funds and somewhat riskier. However, this is mitigated by a requirement for the funds to hold at least 20% in cash at all times in order to meet possible redemptions. Also, because many of the underlying companies are not yet publicly traded, these funds may not appear to be as volatile as regular equity funds, particularly in a bear market.

One drawback is relatively high MERs: typically about 5%, or more than twice the MERs of regular mutual funds. This is in part due to the requirements for more hands-on, time-intensive research associated with pre-public companies. All LSIFs are sold on a declining redemption basis, ranging from 5 to 8 years.

One possible advantage of labor funds, which was pending legislation as this book went to press, is the ability to maximize foreign content.

Because the investments are considered small business properties, investors who buy labor funds for their RRSPs may be able to increase their foreign content from 20% to a maximum 40%. To compute how much, triple your total labor fund assets and add to your existing foreign content. For example, if you had a

$100,000 RRSP and had $3,500 worth of labor funds in it, you'd triple the $3,500 for $10,500 additional foreign content. You'd have a total $30,500 foreign content on this $100,000 RRSP, compared to the normal $20,000.

## REITs, RTUs, and ITUs

If you had enough money, would you consider buying an oil and gas well with a proven, long, and consistent production life and many tax advantages associated with it? What about buying a local strip mall, one whose major tenants are a food store, a drug store, a bank, and a liquor store, and that always seems to be fully leased regardless of the economy? In trying to satiate Canadians' hunger for higher yield, brokerages are converting many such "cash-cow" businesses into various types of investment trust units.

These trusts can be divided into three major groups: real estate investment trusts (REITs), resource-based royalty trust units (RTUs), and a wide variety of other income and investment trust units (ITUs). Through these various units, which trade on stock exchanges like a stock or closed fund, individual investors can own a piece of, and collect income from, a variety of businesses.

The key attraction is the consistent, tax-advantaged income they provide. With a five-year GIC paying less than 5%, and bonds only 0.5% better, the lowest, and perhaps most conservative, REIT is paying 6.6%, which, after a preferential tax treatment, is similar to an 8% GIC. The average REIT pays out about 8%, with the highest currently yielding 10.3%. RTUs range in a paid yield of 9% to 17%. Though a few ITUs do not pay a consistent income, most range between 7% and 12%.

The effective real return is often more than a comparable pure interest-bearing investment, because of the more favorable tax treatment accorded these trusts. All the tax advantages of real estate investing, the capital cost allowance, resource depletion, and other business expenses pass through to the individual trustholder. This means that in many cases investors get an 80% or more tax deferral, paying tax on only one-fifth of income actually received.

The amount deferred is considered for tax purposes to have reduced the cost base or adjusted cost base (ACB) of the units.

When the units are eventually disposed of, the deferred income is taxed as a capital gain, rather than as income, further enhancing the advantage. The relatively minor administrative burden of tracking the ACB is a cost associated with collecting the significant tax savings. To avoid the administration of tracking the ACB changes each year, some investors have placed their trusts inside an RRSP or RRIF, which also removes all the tax advantages. Investors should remember that trust units are not fixed-income investments like GICs or bonds, but are high-yielding equities, which can sometimes decline in value. As Canadian stocks went south in 1998, so did most Canadian REITs. They pay quarterly or monthly distributions.

Other than the management costs of the individual trusts, which are deducted before distributions are made, the other cost of investing in a trust unit is the standard stock-commission charge to buy or sell shares. There are never mutual fund-like loads of any sort. Often, investors buy their units when newly issued, and therefore do not even pay a purchase commission.

There are 26 Canadian resource-based RTUs with a value of about $6 billion. In each case, investors own an interest, through the trust units, in an underlying asset, typically a producing oil and gas field or similar property, that has been bundled and sold to investors who hope to earn the cash flow. In assessing the resource-based trust units, one must realize that part of the cash flow paid out is a return of capital as the underlying assets are depleted. It is possible that some of these units will eventually reach zero in value. Royalty trusts carry a special risk based on the accuracy of the resource life projections and commodity prices. The cash available to pay out to investors will fluctuate directly with changes in the price of oil.

There are 16 natural-gas-and-power-distribution ITUs and five independent-facilities ITUs, which invest in properties such as seaports, pipelines, and electric generating stations. Another 18 specialized income trust units are also available on the TSE. These ITUs are often like closed-end funds with a specific mandate.

In evaluating an RTU or ITU, many things need to be considered. Stability of income is key, which may depend on the expected reserve life of the resource, or the life span of the asset. For example, an oil and gas field with a 20-year life has more value than a field with a 10-year life. In assessing the underlying assets, the investor should consider the capital expenditures likely to be required to maintain the asset over its life span. It is also important to assess the sensitivity of cash flow to changes in the commodity price, to inflation, to interest rates, and to other factors that may affect it.

The relative tax structure and flow-through advantage of the trust also need to be considered. As mentioned below in connection with REITs, whether management is internal or external to a trust is crucial. With resource-based RTUs, reclamation costs for the eventual decommissioning of the property must also be considered, much like a sinking fund or building reserve fund that sets aside cash for known future expenses.

It is not appropriate to compare the cash-on-cash yield, or cash received compared to the amount of cash invested, between GICs and bonds, or RTUs, ITUs, and REITs. Not only is the return taxed in a different manner, but it often includes a return of capital, and includes compensation for increased risk and complication with the trust units. Some ITUs can cause confusion over the yield earned. There are often two different numbers: an internal yield, or the yield the portfolio earns; and an external or cash-paid yield, which is the amount that actually goes to investors.

## REITs

Another form of specialized closed-end, stock market-traded trust is the Real Estate Investment Trust (REIT). While most investors pay at least lip service to the idea of asset-class diversification, REIT investing has provided a new way to invest in this oldest of asset classes. While structured to generate excellent income, REITs also benefit from any long-term appreciation of the underlying real estate. Of course, the value of the same real estate may also decline.

From zero just a few years ago, there are now 15 REITs listed on the TSE, with a total value of $3 billion. In the United States, where they have existed for 30 years, more than US$60 billion is invested in some 200 REITs. The first REITs in Canada were conversions of open-ended real estate mutual funds that had been forced to suspend redemptions in the early 1990s when redemptions exceeded cash reserves. Because they did not have the cash to pay redemptions, they faced the unpleasant situation of selling properties at what many thought was the bottom of the real estate cycle. With a REIT, which is essentially a closed-end real estate mutual fund, there is a finite number of shares, meaning there should never be pressure to raise cash at an inopportune time.

Real estate may still be a dirty word for many investors, a hangover from the last boom-and-bust cycle, but REITs are quite different from real estate stocks or owning real estate directly. REITs are specifically intended to produce consistent, high levels of income, with growth potential a minor secondary objective. As part of this conservative focus, it is rare to find a REIT with more than a 45% debt-to-equity ratio, unlike real estate companies and developers, where 90% is common. Not only are the properties owned by the REIT selected specifically for their consistent cash flow, with lower leverage, there is less cash required for interest payments and more available to be paid out to investors. The more conservative balance sheet also means that—unlike with Olympia and York, Campeau Corp., Bramalea, and other troubled real estate companies from the early 1990s—should things get ugly, the risk of not being able to make the mortgage payments on the properties is greatly reduced.

In trying to decide which REIT is most attractive, it is essential to go beyond simply choosing the one with the highest yield. Like all companies, there are more conservative and more aggressive REITs. The more geographically diversified a REIT, the more it and its investors are protected from an economic downturn in a particular part of the country. Similarly, diversifying the mortgage and lease maturity schedule of the REIT is a key determinant of risk. Should much of its debt mature in a single year, there is the risk that interest rates will be particularly unattractive and cash flow available for investors will be curtailed. Also, should many tenants have leases that mature over a short period, there is a risk of significant vacancies. However, having, for example, 10% of leases mature each year means it is unlikely there will ever be a year in which 30% of tenants move out and need to be replaced.

One consistent feature of the best REITs is a high occupancy rate, typically over 90%. Another factor to consider is whether the properties are managed by an internal or external team. If the manager is external and has other business activities and interests, there is a potential for significant conflicts of interest. If they identify a particularly attractive property, do they buy it for your REIT, which may not be closely supervised by investors, or for the insurance companies' real estate portfolio that they also manage, or for themselves?

In the more sophisticated U.S. market, internal management is the standard, while in Canada about half the REITs use outside managers. Investors should also scrutinize the "yield-enhancement strategy" many managers talk about. The more aggressive the plans to "add value," whether through raw land development, revitalization of old properties, or by a niche focus, the greater the downside should they make mistakes. A hotel-only REIT, for example, will live or die based on hotel occupancy rates, which typically plummet during recessions. When this happens and they are awash in red ink, they may be forced to cut income pay-outs just to survive.

One of the most attractive features of a REIT is its closed-end nature, which gives it the liquidity of any stock. You can call your broker today and sell the REIT. This tremendous liquidity on what is fundamentally an illiquid investment comes at a price, however. Anything that affects general sentiment can drive down REIT prices. A decline in the real estate market, bad press about the manager, or problems with key properties can lead people to dump shares in the market. Whenever the number of sellers exceeds the number of buyers, the shares will go down, regardless of actual value or income paid.

Another risk is the potential unlimited liability of owners of REITs. Because the unit is a trust, liability can, in theory, be assigned to individual investors. If, for example, a building collapsed and a class-action law suit was lost, all the REIT's assets could be taken and individual unitholders pursued for the balance. Ensuring that your REIT has massive liability insurance is therefore essential before investing in one.

As anyone who has been involved in a landlord-tenant "situation" can attest to, there are hidden costs in investing directly in real estate. When you consider the many advantages of REITs, the simple access to a diversified portfolio of professionally managed properties, with all the tax benefits of owning real estate and none of the hassles, the recent popularity of REITs is understandable.

Mutual funds have not missed this new competition from the trust units and have introduced new "high-yield" or "income-trust" funds that invest in these types of trust units. While the costs associated with running various trusts are reasonable and, with so many different units available, always under competitive pressure, the justification for paying a mutual fund manager additional fees to oversee an already-managed portfolio is unclear.

Selecting any trust unit takes at least as much work as choosing a mutual fund, and the rise of mutual funds that invest in other managed products (trust units) is cause for concern. The problem is the same as the banks' junior Wrap programs or the mutual-fund/seg-fund hybrids described in Chapter 7: fees on top of fees. If investors should not pay 1% a year to a manager of a portfolio of mutual funds that charge another 2.5% themselves, why should they pay someone to oversee an already-managed product? Conversely, those investors without enough money to buy a minimum board lot of 100 shares of trust units directly (worth perhaps $2000), or those unwilling to use an adviser or do the work themselves, have no other option than to use a manager to manage trust units through "high-yield" mutual funds.

REITs and most RTUs and ITUs are primarily income investments. Therefore their share or unit price on the stock market varies from day to day, like all stocks in the interest-sensitive group. If interest rates drop, as in recent years, not only will they pay an attractive amount of income, but in the pursuit of yield, the share price will be bid up. The risk is that when interest rates rise, though the income paid may not change, the share price will likely fall.

The other major risk with trust units is the operational business risks. Bad management decisions might mean buying the wrong properties for a REIT. Can an investor with a REIT full of shopping-mall properties be assured that Internet shopping won't decimate all malls in 10 years? Royalty trusts have risk based on the accuracy of the resource life projections and commodity prices. The cash available to pay out to investors will fluctuate directly with changes in the price of oil. It's possible that new hydrogen technology like that being developed by Ballard Power in partnership with Mercedes and Ford will change the demand for oil and gas in the future, dropping the price to uneconomic levels. For example, if oil were to trade regularly at $10 per barrel, down from the current price of $15, most of the royalty income trusts would not be able to produce at a profit, and may have zero profit to distribute to investors.

Because of the additional issues in closed-end funds, royalty, realty, and income investment trust units, they must be bought from a fully licensed adviser with a TSE-member firm, rather than lower-licensed mutual fund salespeople and financial planners.

## Offshore funds

Offshore investment funds have long been perceived as a preserve of the super-rich, typically based in tax-free or low-tax centers that allow high levels of investor confidentiality.

There are several reasons why a wealthy investor might explore these funds. First, they typically have lower costs. Their annual management fees are about one percentage point less than that of the average Canadian open-end mutual fund. Second, historically, offshore funds have enjoyed fewer limitations from regulation, so fund managers can take more liberties in the search for higher returns. However, the offshore environment is changing to one of more regulations and restrictions, while the tax aspect is shifting from tax avoidance to tax efficiency. There are many offshore funds to choose from—more than 5,500 worldwide, according to Robert Milroy's *The Micropal Guide to Offshore Investment Funds* (International Offshore Publications Ltd. and Micropal Ltd., Guernsey, 1996, 1997, 1998). Like mutual funds, offshore funds hold equities, bonds, money market investments, and other assets, or a combination thereof. About 45% are equity funds, which benefit the most from tax-haven status since most tax-friendly jurisdictions have no capital gains tax.

Depending on the tax advice you receive, there may be more

scope to minimize taxes. Going offshore provides wealth protection whether from punitive taxes or, if the funds are wrapped up in an offshore trust, from creditors and excessive charges due to legal damages.

An offshore fund is a common fund managed by a professional investment manager on behalf of investors and is based in one of the world's tax havens or low-tax areas. These havens have high levels of confidentiality. Centers such as the Cayman Islands and Bermuda do not tax the profits or income of funds that are incorporated or domiciled there. A fund's domicile is where it is registered as a company and may not be the base of its administration or investment-management operations. Offshore financial centers aren't necessarily islands. In fact, more than half of all offshore funds are domiciled in land-locked Luxembourg.

While some offshore funds date from the 1930s, they began to multiply in the 1970s, when British fund companies set up subsidiaries in the Channel Islands of Guernsey and Jersey, the Isle of Man, Hong Kong, and Bermuda. These funds were initially designed for expatriate, non-tax-paying investors and foreign subsidiaries of British firms. They later became a refuge for people or companies wanting to safeguard assets held in the Middle East and Latin America.

The Income Tax Act requires that all Canadians report all foreign income. It's clear, though, that the confidentiality practices of the offshore tax havens are not there to help tax-hungry governments locate such assets. Some jurisdictions have made it a criminal offence to reveal information about investors. Often, only such outside bodies as criminal investigators will be allowed access to such information.

Most tax-friendly jurisdictions have no capital gains taxes, although the country an investor lives in will likely tax income as it is repatriated from the offshore portfolio. For that reason, many investors may prefer offshore equity funds to income funds.

Offshore funds can be purchased freely by Canadian and U.S. individuals if they are bought outside the country and in the minimum amounts that offshore funds have established—typically between $5,000 and $50,000. Inside Canada or the United States, few retail issues of offshore funds are sold directly because of regulations designed to protect unsophisticated investors; Canadian investors would have to meet the sophisticated-investor guidelines ($150,000 in Ontario, less in some other provinces) to buy them.

Most offshore funds can be held within an RRSP or RRIF, although most count as foreign content. To put one in an RRSP, you would have to buy directly, without a broker's assistance. It could then be transferred into a self-administered RRSP. The RRSP trust company would then re-register the fund units in the name of your RRSP.

The Canadian government does not make it easy for its citizens to buy offshore funds. Under the yearly income accrual interpretation of the Income Tax Act's section 94(1), any gains have to be accrued for income purposes yearly, whether or not any income has been received. This may not be a burden if the investor can substantiate the claim that the investment was made for long-term capital gains instead of creating income.

Interest earned within a bond or money market fund, however, is often taxed by the investor's country of residence. Investors should therefore allow their earnings to accumulate offshore by investing in funds that have accumulating units or allow dividends to be reinvested into more units of the fund.

Offshore funds can be either closed-end or open-end. Offshore fund sales fees are comparable to regular funds, although many charge a 5% front-end load. Most offshore funds also have switching fees, some have back-end redemption schemes, and some base fees on performance.

One complication is a dual pricing system under which there is a spread between the offer price (the price at which an investor buys units) and the bid price (the price at which one sells). That spread is one more reason for holding funds over the long haul and not trading too frequently.

There are single-country funds for at least 42 separate countries. Only six Canadian equity funds, defined as those investing more than 70% in Canadian securities, are included in the Micropal guide.

One of these funds, RBC Global Investments Canadian, is handled by Royal Bank of Canada out of Guernsey and sold to expatriate Canadians. The Canadian Imperial Bank of Commerce also runs offshore funds out of Guernsey.

## Managed futures

While any mention of derivatives or futures can scare some investors back into the bank, it is sometimes appropriate to consider a different asset class, known as managed futures.

Managed futures are active investments in baskets of futures contracts or options on futures, generally with a focus on commodities or sophisticated financial products. Futures are contractual promises to deliver or buy a commodity or financial security at a future date.

Some managed futures can be used to reduce risk in a portfolio while earning returns comparable to the stock market. Futures, for example, have historically been negatively correlated to the capital markets, meaning that when equity markets go down, futures typically go up and vice versa.

Other managed futures can increase the risk: the risk is greater if the manager is long in the market in the futures and the investors are also long in their own portfolios.

For years, institutional investors such as pension funds have not only diversified among stocks and bonds, but also into managed futures. One recent estimate put the amount of money already in managed futures at more than $20 billion, with about $1 billion of that coming from Canadian retail (non-institutional) investors.

Because managed-futures products are counter-cyclical to stocks and bonds, a 5% or 10% position in managed futures may help sophisticated investors to diversify a large portfolio, just as gold or real estate can act as a hedge against traditional asset classes.

As with stock portfolio management, different management styles in futures trading earn similar returns, but at different times. There are also many different types of futures contracts other than just commodities. Futures are traded on many commodities as well as on interest rates, stock markets, and currencies. Hundreds of different futures contracts trade in more than 50 categories every day in North America alone.

Because of the need for multiple managers in a variety of markets in many types of futures trading, and a typical minimum investment of $10 million per manager, a managed-futures program often makes sense for even the largest investors. In order to meet this need, many investors come together in a pool, which is then turned over to a team of at least a dozen different futures managers or commodity trading advisers (CTAs).

A new vehicle—the managed-futures certificate of deposit—functions much like a futures mutual fund and also carries a guarantee. The Bank of Montreal (BMO) has a popular managed-futures certificate of deposit, available to clients of Nesbitt Burns Inc. and other major brokerage firms. BMO has hired 10 firms to run its managed-futures portfolio, which resembles similar offerings in the United States from Merrill Lynch & Co. and PaineWebber Inc. Bank of Montreal's trading advisers have access to more than 50 international markets.

The net-asset value of the BMO certificate is set weekly and has a redemption period at least once a year. Because the growth is considered simple income and is highly taxed, the certificate is best held in an RRSP. Though the futures held are typically from around the world, the certificate of deposit is considered Canadian content for the purposes of RRSPs. Investors who wish to redeem early also face an early redemption fee of 3% the first two years. If they hold on until maturity, they have their principal guaranteed by the bank, although it is guaranteed like a corporate bond and is not insured by the Canada Deposit Insurance Corporation.

Smaller investors have limited options through mutual funds. There used to be two managed-futures mutual funds available to Canadian retail investors. However, Atlas Managed Futures was shut down due to lack of investor interest, leaving the field to AGF's 20/20 Managed Futures Value Fund, managed by John Di Tomasso. The fund suffered from the 1997–1998 slump in commodity prices. The Atlas fund featured multiple managers accessing a variety of financial futures products, such as interest-rate and currency futures.

The AGF fund, which requires a $2,000 minimum investment, is primarily a play on tangible commodities such as wheat, lumber, petroleum, cattle, or hogs, or soft commodities such as coffee, cocoa, soybeans, and sugar. The Victoria, British Columbia-based Di Tomasso Group also manages another futures fund, the Equilibrium Fund, that is sold only to institutional clients and foreign investors, so as not to compete with the AGF fund.

There is, however, an offshore version for non-U.S. investors: Di Tomasso Turbo Fund Ltd., administered by Olympia Capital International Inc. of Bermuda. It has a US$250,000 minimum investment. A Canadian version of the Turbo Fund includes options on the Standard & Poor's 500 composite index, enabling the fund to go long on commodities and short on U.S. stocks. Canadian Turbo has a $500,000 minimum investment.

Managed futures, as with hedge funds described below, create problems for investors with other investments. This is because the managers will normally disclose what they are allowed to do, but not what they are actually doing. There is no way of knowing whether the portfolios are long or short, so investors cannot tell what level of risk their overall portfolios are under.

## Hedge funds

One phenomenon of the 1990s bull market was the emergence of more than 3,000 hedge funds, 87% of which are based in the United States. There are two basic types of hedge fund: those that hedge, or protect, against the danger of negative events, such as a stock crash; and high-performance funds that use a manager's expertise in a particular area to beat the general market.

As with other forms of investing, there is a risk involved. With hedge funds, the risk derives from the techniques they use, such as short-selling, and the investments they target, such as futures contracts.

Hedge funds are less constrained by government and industry regulation than mutual funds and are more free to use leverage, derivatives, and other exotic financial instruments. Smaller hedge funds often have the flexibility to outmaneuver larger competitors.

Many hedge funds also allow personal contact between the

manager and the investors. And a manager can control liquidity, making the fund less susceptible to the redemption pressures faced by popular mutual funds.

Typically, a hedge fund is launched when a hot money manager with an acknowledged edge in a specialty area decides to set up a limited partnership or an offshore investment corporation. The motivation is lucrative performance fees—typically 20% of the market gains generated—plus an annual management fee of 1% of assets.

Apart from high returns, hedge funds often tout their lack of correlation to major stock indexes. In theory, they can provide wide diversification and, as the name implies, hedge against danger.

While some Canadian investors can buy offshore hedge funds, only a handful are managed in Canada. The biggest category— 37% of all hedge funds, according to Hedge Fund Research Inc. of Chicago—are macro funds, which invest in futures and derivatives. There are also funds that focus on growth and value stocks, emerging markets, fixed-income, and other areas that have counterparts in the traditional mutual fund market.

There are niche-oriented funds, such as those that make bets on distressed stocks or debt, and merger-arbitrage funds that play corporate takeovers by buying stock of a company to be acquired and then shorting it. There are convertible-arbitrage funds that buy convertible bonds and sell short the underlying equities, as well as market-timing funds, short-seller funds, sector-shifting opportunistic funds, and multi-strategy funds that shift strategies to wherever money can be made.

Ironically, most hedge funds are not true hedge vehicles in the sense of hedging against market downsides. Many pay lip service to this, but are heavily committed to the upside fueled by rising equity markets.

When a major stock-market correction occurs, it will become apparent how many high-performing hedge funds were truly protecting the downside. Such funds' main strategy is short-selling, which allows managers to profit by selling a stock first, then buying it back on a decline—if it declines.

The true short-selling hedge funds have been the worst performers throughout the 1990s, producing just 3.7% a year compounded compared to the 13% to 14% produced by the S&P 500 composite index or market-neutral hedge funds. This picture, of course, could change dramatically if the 1998 developing bear market deepens.

Eric Kirzner, associate professor of finance at the University of Toronto's management faculty, says a true hedge fund is one that isolates the talent of a particular manager. For example, the best mining-stock picker in the world might start a hedge fund, going long on the best mining stocks and short on the general market. If the market crashed, his or her stocks might still do well—a result Kirzner considers characteristic of a true hedge fund.

The other class of hedge funds, which don't truly hedge, are better termed "performance" or "spec" funds, Kirzner says, such as BPI Canadian Opportunities or Friedberg Currency.

One alternative for Canadians is HR Strategies Inc. of Montreal, a limited partnership that offers a fund-of-funds approach to five different hedge fund managers. This is also a growing trend in the United States. Funds made up of other hedge funds offer more diversification and access to some funds that might not otherwise be available. They have outperformed the S&P 500, but have not done as well as the specialty funds.

Hedge funds remain products in search of a market. Young, aggressive investors seeking high returns might prefer the performance funds, while older, conservative investors worried about capital protection would want the true hedge funds.

The average track record for hedge funds is less than four years. So investors are betting first on a high-risk strategy, and second that a manager who looks like a genius in a bull market will also be a genius in a bear market. That's a big bet.

In the United States, wealthy investors searching for the next hot asset class have looked to hedge funds and venture capital for higher returns.

But other investors have given up entirely on the notion of finding a human manager who can beat the markets. A rising percentage of savvy investors are doing exactly the opposite— turning to passively manage "indexing" products. These merely replicate the returns of the S&P 500 or TSE 300 but do so at a lower price. The next chapter looks at this in detail.

## Chapter Nine

# Passive Investing:
# If They Can't Beat the
# Indexes, Why Pay Them?

So you don't have the time to pick stocks yourself and you now know that mutual funds are not the panacea you once thought they were. What next? Index or passive investing has been popular in the United States for several years and may be the next wave in consumer investing in Canada. With the power of the Canadian banks behind new index funds launched last year, passive investing could become as popular as the banks' managed no-load funds became in the early 1990s.

Index investing, or simply indexing, is the practice of passively investing in a stock market index or, more precisely, in an instrument that attempts to mirror major market indexes. In 1994, index products attracted only 3% of new investments by consumers. This rose to 11% in 1996 and was higher still in 1997–98. Index investing is growing at 18 times the rate of the mutual fund industry, according to Global Strategy Financial Inc.

This trend has been strengthened by the inability of most active managers to beat the indexes, particularly after fees. Perhaps the best measure of the new popularity of indexing is the new initiatives by the major banks. Canada's Big Five (possibly soon to become the "Humungous Three") banks seem to see index investing as the latest and greatest way to make money from the small investor. In terms of numbers of index funds, the leaders are CIBC Securities Inc. and TD GreenLine, both of which have a line of index funds with MERs well below 1%. If the parent banks merge, the new entity would become the closest Canadian equivalent to Vanguard in the United States, as far as low-cost indexing goes.

Indexes were initially developed to provide a measure of the

market for purposes of monitoring and comparing institutional pension portfolios. Financial innovators then decided to offer individual investors the ability to buy the index. In Canada, the Toronto Stock Exchange (TSE) introduced TSE 35 Index Participation Units (TIPS 35) in 1990.

## What are the indexes?

Stock exchanges and other institutions create indexes in a variety of ways, depending on the goals they are trying to reach. Some are arbitrarily selected by committees, while others are set by market size and weightings based on market capitalization. The indexes are primarily used as benchmarks. Within each are many sub-indexes.

Canada has several major indexes, of which the TSE 300 is the most widely known and followed. The TSE 300 is a market-weighted portfolio of the 300 largest public companies traded on the Toronto Stock Exchange. The TSE also has many sub-indexes. These include the TSE 35, the 35 largest companies; the TSE 100, the 100 largest companies; and the TSE 200, which tracks 200 smaller companies from the TSE 300. The TSE is also segmented into four major sector indexes, 14 industry sub-indexes, and dozens of industry sub-sub indexes.

For example, the TSE Gold Index is 5.2% of the TSE 300, and is composed of the many gold companies in the TSE 300. This industry sub-index is market weighted, so the largest companies, such as Barrick Gold and Placer Dome, each comprise a significant part of the sub-index. The other major indexes in Canada are the Scotia McLeod Bond indexes and the Nesbitt Burns Small Cap index. As the table on the next page summarizes, large companies play a large role in the indices, and overlap each other.

## Canadian Index Comparison

| TSE 35 | | TSE 100 | | TSE 300 | |
|---|---|---|---|---|---|
| Bell Canada | 10.29% | Bell Canada | 7.64% | Bell Canada | 6.27% |
| Northern Telecom | 7.36 | Royal Bank | 5.19 | Royal Bank | 4.26 |
| Royal Bank | 5.41 | Northern Telecom | 4.43 | Northern Telecom | 3.64 |
| CIBC | 5.37 | CIBC | 4.14 | CIBC | 3.40 |
| Canadian Pacific | 5.32 | Bank of Montreal | 4.02 | Bank of Montreal | 3.30 |
| TD Bank | 4.97 | TD Bank | 3.82 | TD Bank | 3.14 |
| Bank of Montreal | 4.61 | Scotia Bank | 3.79 | Scotia Bank | 3.11 |
| Seagram | 3.87 | Canadian Pacific | 2.82 | Canadian Pacific | 2.31 |
| Thomson | 3.64 | Seagram | 2.70 | Seagram | 2.22 |
| Scotia Bank | 3.32 | Barrick Gold | 2.36 | Barrick Gold | 1.94 |
| Top 10 as % | 43.97% | Top 10 as % | 33.35% | Top 10 as % | 27.38 |

The principal indexes representing the U.S. stock markets are the Standard and Poor's 500 (S&P 500) composite index, a market-weighted measure of the 500 largest U.S. companies; the Dow Jones Industrial Average (DJIA) of 30 blue-chip companies, based on price weighting; and the Russell 2000, an index of 2,000 small to medium-size companies. The broadest index of all, the Wilshire 5000, represents about 6,500 public companies.

Outside the United States, many of the major indexes are from Morgan Stanley Capital International (MSCI). For example, the MSCI-EAFE (Europe, Australasia, and Far East) index is frequently used to track investments outside North America. Each country also has at least one internal index considered to be representative of that country's stock market. For example, *The Financial Times* of London has an index that tracks the top 100 British companies in the FTSE 100. In Germany, investors watch the Dax. Japan is often measured by the Nikkei, which tracks 225 Japanese companies. Investors looking for an index or sub-index need only open *The National Post* to find more than 50 listed every day. In fact, in the spring of 1998, *The Financial Post* launched FPX, three investable indexes that give investors benchmarks to evaluate the performance of income, balanced, and growth portfolios.

It is important to understand the differences among indexes and to remember that weighted indexes are substantially influenced by the largest companies comprising each index.

## How to index

The goal of all indexing is to invest in a portfolio or investment vehicle that can be expected to earn returns similar to a market index, with similar or lower amounts of risk. Investors who choose indexing have several distinct choices. Institutions create and sell index units, which trade on the stock exchange like a regular stock. Fund companies and banks offer index funds. In recent years, dozens of indexed-linked securities have been created, again mostly by the banks. Some even have guarantees of initial principal, as discussed in Chapter 7. Some people try to index themselves, buying a portfolio of shares directly and holding them for the long term. Because of commission costs, the difficulty of achieving diversification, and the complication of rebalancing, this approach has lost ground to the other methods.

## Index participation units

Index units are a legal trust, administered by an institution with a tight mandate to invest the entire amount of the trust in the shares of the individual companies comprising a particular index. Index units are bought like any stock and can be held in RRSPs, and sold short, and even have traded options. Units can be bought on margin or held as security for a loan. Index units pay a regular dividend, which is the aggregate of the dividends of the underlying companies, and is eligible (for Canadian index units) for the Canadian dividend tax credit. Some index units have automatic reinvestments of dividends. Units can be bought and held for the long term or actively traded as part of a larger portfolio. Index units are normally among the most liquid securities in the markets, with tens of millions of dollars' worth traded every day.

Because index units are open-end trusts, they will issue or redeem shares as appropriate to ensure an orderly market should demand exceed supply. Market price may temporarily deviate from the index level. It is this feature which ensures that index trusts will never trade at significant discounts or premiums to their index—which usually happens with closed-end investment trusts. Within each index trust's mandate is a rebalancing formula, which allows the weighting in the component companies to be changed, sometimes yearly. This passive, formula-driven occasional rebalancing of a broad portfolio of leading companies is a key attraction of index investing.

The open-ended feature and periodic rebalancing mean that returns on an index unit should mirror the underlying index. This is not without cost, however. Other than a normal brokerage commission to buy the units, there is a hidden cost, much like a mutual fund MER. These charges cover the cost of running the trust, custody, trust services, and reporting. Unlike a fund MER, the costs are almost entirely administrative, rather than for management services. Similarly, there are no television advertisements built into the budgets nor any adviser compensation, trailer fees, or load schedules. This annual cost is one of the major causes of tracking error (the deviation of the units' return compared to the underlying index).

### Example of index unit—TIPS 35

Among the earliest index units were the TSE Index Participation Shares, or TIPS, which proportionally invest in the companies that comprise the TSE 35. The TSE passively manages the trust, investing, for example, 10.3% in shares of Bell Canada or 5.4% in shares of the Royal Bank. The TSE manages the trust, buying and selling shares in the underlying stocks and issuing and redeeming TIPS units as required. The MER charged to the units is about 0.05%. TIPS have proven to have an extremely close correlation with the TSE 35. At this point, the only other index unit in Canada is the TIPS 100 (formerly HIPS and still traded on the exchange as HIP/TSE), which similarly invests in a weighted portfolio that mirrors the TSE 100. TIPS can be included in RRSPs and RRIFs, and dividends from the underlying stocks are paid quarterly. They are also eligible for the dividend tax credit if held outside tax-sheltered plans.

## U.S. index units

Three domestic and 17 international index units are available on U.S. stock exchanges. Diamonds, which stands for the Dow Jones Industrial Average Model New Depository Shares, invests in the 30 stocks that make up the Dow. A more diversified index unit, available since 1993, is the Standard and Poor's Depository Receipts, known as Spiders (SPDRs), which invests in the S&P 500. It trades on the American Stock Exchange as SPY. Also available is the mid-cap Spider, which represents the 400 companies in the S&P 400. These companies are under US$1 billion in market cap and are not included in the S&P 500. World Equity Benchmark Shares (WEBS), traded since March 1996, represents 17 different country-specific indexes from Morgan Stanley. WEBS do not follow the commonly known domestic indexes. For example, WEBS-Canada is not trying to mimic the TSE 300, but rather the MSCI-Canada index, which has 80 stocks. Until early 1997, investors could also buy shares in country baskets, on the New York Stock Exchange, which matched *The Financial Times* and S&P indexes in various countries. These have stopped trading, and investors now only have the WEBS option. Unlike domestic index products, WEBS have an MER of about 1% and provide a 95% correlation to their indexes.

## Index funds

Index mutual funds have become the latest rage in the United States, attracting about 20% of all new fund investments, up dramatically in recent years. The major Canadian banks and some insurance companies have launched a variety of index funds to meet the hoped-for demand in Canada. At their best, index funds could be much like TIPS, with low tracking error and tiny fees.

Unfortunately, to differentiate themselves, and perhaps as an excuse to justify higher fees and allegedly add value, most index mutual funds are less like an index and more like a mutual fund. They could be more aptly named "managed index funds." In some cases, someone is appointed to tinker with the actual investments within the fund; in others, the rules for the fund specify only a quasi-index mandate. For example, one of Royal Mutual Funds' new strategic index funds can only invest in 25 of the companies in the TSE 35 (and TIPS). Similarly, another bank's index fund is only 75% invested in the index, with 25% assigned to active management. Some banks also use proprietary in-house indexes as their target, rather than the more widely known, published indexes.

The most contentious issue with Canadian index funds is their costs. Unlike the United States, where index fund MERs are substantially lower, Canadian index fund MERs range from a low of 0.75% to a massive 2.57% on Great-West Life's Equity Index Fund (a seg fund with the insurance guarantee). When you consider that only about 1% of fund MERs on Canadian funds go to the money manager (the balance going to advisers, marketing, and administration), index funds in Canada are not cheap by any measure. The average index mutual fund MER is above 1.25% annually, not substantially cheaper than the 2.1% average for active funds, and in line with total costs of low-MER managed funds such as Trimark Canadian's 1.52%.

The Great-West Life Equity Index Fund is worth further scrutiny. Not only does it have a higher than average fee, but it also has its hands tied, investing only in the largest 250 companies from the TSE 300. Little surprise, then, that it has substantially underperformed the TSE 300 in every period (by 0.25% over moving four-year periods, according to GWL). It has earned less than the average actively managed fund over the last 10 years, with 9.3%, compared to 10.7% for the average fund and 11.8% for the TSE. While investing in an index may be attractive, index funds are often not the index. As with so many things in life, it is a buyer beware situation. While the returns of an index unit should virtually mirror the index, index mutual funds with clouded mandates and significant fees likely will not.

## Why index?

Investing through an index unit seemingly offers many attractions to investors. At the top of the list is recent market returns. These have been substantial in the last few years, handily beating most active managers without seemingly taking on any risk. Recent returns are, however, only one of several reasons to consider indexing.

One of the greatest advantages that indexed products offer compared to managed products is comparatively lower fees. When investing in an index (or more likely index units) or a low-cost U.S. index fund, the ongoing and management costs can be dramatically cheaper. With no superstar management team, and often little or no marketing, index investing should be substantially cheaper. As discussed in Chapter 3, MERs on actively managed mutual funds routinely take one-fifth of all returns just for management. Typical U.S. index funds, which are not available to Canadians, have annual MERs of less than 0.4% and, in some cases, 0.2%. For Canadians, the cost argument is true for index units but is less compelling for index mutual funds.

Less talked about is the additional tax cost of high-turnover, actively managed mutual funds. Because many mutual funds trade frequently, there is little year-to-year deferral of capital gains. In an index investment, there are fewer changes in the underlying portfolio. For example, the TSE 300 has a turnover ratio of about 18%. The TD GreenLine Canadian Index Fund has a turnover ratio of more than 20%. This means there is a higher level of deferral of capital gains in index funds than in most actively managed funds.

The simplicity of index investing is the most compelling reason to consider it. When investors buy index products, they are as close as possible to having a buy-and-ignore strategy. Without ever having to read a paper, talk to an adviser, attend an annual meeting, or surf the Internet, index investors should be able to sleep well at night, particularly if they also have bonds or bond index products to balance their equity index exposure. Regardless of how much or how little work they do, or how smart or educated they are, the index investment will grow, and occasionally fall, in line with the general market trend. When there is a significant change among the companies and the index, the index administrator will change the weightings and the holdings of the underlying portfolio. Investors learning about index investing are often surprised how few options there are. The lack of choice is because there is little need for it. If an investor wants the lowest possible management costs on a weighted portfolio of the 35 largest public companies in Canada, there is only one choice compelling—TIPS 35.

The security of an index investment is also an attractive feature. As with any reasonable portfolio, diversification represents the single biggest source of safety. The passive management of the index, where sinking companies are removed because of a decline in size, and growing companies similarly added, adds an additional layer of safety. Ten of the 35 companies represented in TIPS today were not there in 1990. There is also added security knowing that the room for human error by an active manager cannot happen. Although career-ending catastrophic errors from active managers are few and far between, they simply can't happen in an index.

All active money management looks to capitalize on market inefficiency, which many believe is lessening. This makes it harder for managers to find bargain values in hidden gems. The advantages to indexing, particularly in that most transparent and efficient market—the United States—are compelling. There are, however, reasons to think twice about indexing, particularly in less efficient markets, depending on your tolerance for risk. It seems clear that active managers can consistently outperform indexes in small-cap investing and in less efficient foreign markets.

All is not sunshine and roses with index investing in North America, either. In recent years, as is common late in every cycle, greed overcomes fear, and people, often those who are less experienced and knowledgeable, pursue an unrealistic goal for consistent top performance. Having moderate returns becomes not only unacceptable, but tantamount to failure, when seen through their rose-colored perspective. In fact, the very word "moderate" in some circles has become synonymous with "mediocre." With this mind-set there is a risk that people who in the past chased hot mutual funds, hot stocks, hot real estate, and other "no-brainer" sure things, now view indexing as the easy road to riches.

## Why not index?

Conditions in recent years have worked against active managers. The enormous drop in interest rates has transformed the interest-sensitive stocks, which include banks, pipelines, and utilities, into market darlings. These large, conservative businesses make up what many would consider to be an unreasonably large weighting in most indexes. For example, the financial services sector comprises more than 20% of the TIPS 100. When the rest of the interest-sensitive group is considered, this sector accounts for 42.5% of the index. It is the phenomenal return of this one sector that has driven the index to outperformance. The other sectors (industrial, resource, and consumer) may only have broken even. Luckily for index investors in the last few years, the index was overweight with interest-sensitive, rather than resource, stocks.

The change in the nature of investing and the rise of mutual funds have also contributed to the momentum of passive approaches. While the economy has grown strongly, centered in small and medium-sized businesses, the market has had a strong large-cap bias, driven in part by the flow of funds from retail investors. This may have been accentuated by the index effect, particularly in the United States.

During any raging bull market, it is difficult for active managers to outperform because of an inevitable lag from holding cash in the funds. As investors give the funds more money, the funds are not automatically invested, as an index would be. Any fund with a more conservative bent that is trying to reduce risk has dual objectives and may not even be trying to beat the market: the manager may be more concerned about protecting capital in a market down-draft.

Comparing the returns of a conservative, actively managed fund to an index may be like comparing apples to oranges. In a flat- or rising-interest-rate environment, active managers may once again outperform. When leadership shifts back to small-cap stocks or away from the interest-sensitive large cap group in Canada, the trend of index outperformance may well be reversed.

Trimark chairman Robert Krembil still believes that good managers can beat the index. "It's better to own a collection of good businesses. . . . I look at the index, and there are so many things I wouldn't want to own. In the long run [10 years], we can beat the index."

## Index effect and cash-flow momentum

The very popularity of indexing can itself push the markets, and hence the indexes, higher in a classic virtuous cycle. This is particularly the case in the United States. With repeated ballooning in index heavyweights, the indexes have strong returns, attracting more money into the now even larger and more expensive index components.

### Cash flow momentum may reverse index effect

When sentiment changes against indexing, perhaps because of a typical 25% bear market, the legions of recent converts to indexing, many of whom have no adviser to protect them from themselves, may reverse this cash flow and crush the index returns. This is not unlike the situation 25 years ago in which investors were enamored with the so-called "Nifty 50." These were 50 large U.S. companies (such as IBM and Polaroid) that investors believed could never go down and that were driven to astronomical valuations. In the bear market of the mid-'70s, they dramatically led the market south, sustaining larger proportional losses than the broader market. Many of the Nifty 50 stocks took almost a decade to regain their lofty prices, and some still have not rebounded.

With low cash reserves, index funds would have to sell their component stocks to raise money for those investors who, without an adviser's perspective, might start selling after a market correction. This selling to raise cash would drive the market in reverse, creating a vicious cycle exactly the opposite of the virtuous cycle of the late 1990s. Should a concerted pressure exist to get out of the large-cap index heavyweights, the scenario would resemble the proverbial fire in a crowded movie theater. The first to reach the exits may be fine, but those only a few meters behind are crushed in the stampede.

**Tax advantage lessened with inevitable selling in correction**
With the potential for such a reverse index effect, and significant selling, the tax deferments of recent years would also come home to roost. Hefty stock sales would entail significant realization of capital gains for every investor, whether or not they actually sold. These capital gains taxes, perhaps 20% of the market value of index portfolios, would require additional sales to pay and could further exacerbate the reverse index effect.

Investors must be aware that some index products, particularly for foreign indexes, use derivatives rather than equity investments. This means the gains produced are highly taxed as income rather than the lower taxed dividends and capital gains.

For all their positive attributes, indexes are not necessarily equivalent to the general economy or even the stock market. The 30 stocks in the Dow Jones are arbitrarily picked and do not reflect broader industry weightings. The TSE 300 is heavy in interest-sensitive stocks and resources and has reasonable exposure to telecommunications, but is light on consumer products, automobiles, pharmaceuticals, and computer giants. TIPS represent only the companies in the index, not the broader economy. Some of the 14 major industry groups in the Canadian market are not even represented in TIPS 35.

Because of the 20% foreign-content limit in RRSPs and RRIFs, an all-Canadian index approach lacks true diversification, both of industries and geographies. One-third of all Canadian index products are necessarily in the higher-risk and deep cyclical sector.

An index may also be slower to dump securities that have soured. If a company is going bankrupt, it is normally not removed from an index until five days after the bankruptcy notice, whereas an active manager can get the fund out and save something.

## Lack of control

Index investors are at the mercy of the index and, to a lesser degree, those who run the product. Most indexers and the indexes themselves were victims of the biggest stock fraud in history. Because of its large market capitalization, Bre-X Minerals Ltd. was added to the TSE 100 in 1997, immediately attracting hundreds of millions of dollars of new investment money from the index products.

Investors who also want a moral component to their investing simply cannot use the index product or strategy because they will inevitably be putting their money, through the index, into tobacco stocks, liquor stocks, and the like. The Ethical Group of Funds encountered criticism in 1997 when it invested part of its Ethical Growth Fund in TIPS. Unitholders objected that TIPS contained firms that are normally screened out by the Ethical Growth Fund managers. The company later announced it would make no further investments in index products.

## Costs in everything

While low cost is a major advantage of index products, they are by no means free. Index units (like TIPS) are dramatically cheaper than index funds (like the bank no-load index funds). Some index funds cost even more than actively managed funds, particularly those from life insurance companies. Index products are not some sort of commission-free charity. Commissions have to be paid to buy and sell the underlying stocks, just as anywhere else. If index products are available, it's because they were created by someone who thinks they can make money by doing it.

TIPS are normally bought and sold through the market, meaning someone else sells the units you are buying. They can be redeemed for cash from the TSE itself, albeit not at face value. They will be redeemed at a discount-to-book value, based on the number of shares redeemed. For example, if you redeemed 200 TIPS, you would receive 96% of the value. If you redeemed 20,000 units, you would get the maximum 99.5% amount.

## No service or advice

If you have mostly index products in your portfolio, expect zero advice or support from your investment adviser. The asset-mix planning, financial and estate planning, hand-holding, and emotional insulation an adviser often provides at no cost in traditional stock or fund portfolios cannot be provided in a mostly index portfolio. If investors end up doing this work themselves, that is in itself an extra cost. In the worst case, the do-it-yourselfer will make a major mistake that will cost far more than the fees saved through passive investing.

## Risk

Despite their image, index products are not risk-free. If active managers sense a coming market downturn, they may build cash by selling off overvalued securities. That doesn't happen in an index product because valuation does not come into play. The index product is 100% invested in the market. On the downside, actively managed index products may be even worse than pure passive index products.

There is also some currency risk involved in non-Canadian index products such as WEBS and Spiders. There is no human available to hedge currencies, as there may be in actively managed global mutual funds.

In the compulsive drive to earn the largest possible return every month or year, less experienced investors seem to have forgotten the oldest investment rule of all: "If it seems too good to be true, run like hell."

### Case Study—Johnny Indexer (JI)

JI is a 45-year-old investor, with $98,000 in his RRSP, and no time for or interest in investments. He heard about indexing after his financial planner made a slip of the tongue. He was surprised to find out that the star fund managers he was paying big annual fees to were not beating their "benchmark" indexes. When he realized they could not prevent him from losing money either, he started looking for an alternative. He was disappointed when his financial planner, who he later found was only licensed to sell mutual funds, could not offer any helpful advice. He ended up discussing it with an acquaintance who was an investment adviser at a major stock brokerage firm and to whom he soon transferred his RRSP.

Luckily, JI had paid front loads for his mutual funds and the adviser was able to remove his money without incurring any other costs. JI told the adviser he wanted to put 100% of his savings into the stock market for the long run, and was not concerned about periodic drops of 20 or 30% for two or three years. "I probably wouldn't even notice: I never read my statements, and it's RRSP money anyway." He also told his adviser he wanted to use an index product, and though he would be happy to hear from the adviser afterwards, did not expect to invest any more than the annual RRSP contributions. After what JI thought was an unnecessarily lengthy discussion on the risk of putting everything into stocks, and a discussion on where to locate his foreign content, the adviser made the following recommendation.

For foreign content, he bought 100 S&P 500 index units (Spiders) on the American Stock Exchange, and for the rest of the RRSP he bought 1700 TSE 100 units on the Toronto Stock Exchange. The Spiders cost US$110 per share, which after a commission of US$130 came to a total of US$11,130. After the currency exchange, the total cost was $15,693 Canadian, or 16% of his foreign allotment. The 1700 TIPS 100 units were bought on the TSE at $46.85 per unit, which after an $890 commission cost $80,535.89. The remaining $1,772 was invested in the brokerage's no-load money market mutual fund, pending additional RRSP contributions. The total cost of $1,072 in commissions equaled 1.1% of the investment of $95,158 in two of North America's most diversified indexes. If JI had been prepared to do all the work himself, and did not want the reassurance of an adviser making recommendations, he could have executed the same orders through a major discount brokerage for less than half that commission. In either case, he would not have any additional costs to pay, and will never see his RRSP growth throttled through high MERs on mutual funds. If he holds these units for 20 years, and adds new contributions in the same way every year, his RRSP will grow at the blended rate of the two underlying indexes, and likely will beat most actively managed accounts.

## Why you seldom hear about indexing

Regardless of whether they should be indexing, most investors have not and likely will not ever consider passive investing, because true indexing does not have any salesperson who will help you up the learning curve. Advice and indexing are mutually exclusive. Because of the time and energy an adviser must exert to gain the trust and confidence of a new client, advisers naturally limit themselves to products or services that compensate them.

The undeniable truth is that if someone is spending time and money trying to sell you on indexing, they expect compensation. If their compensation is not a flat fee from you, then it must involve a hidden add-on, meaning it is likely not an index at all. For this reason the MERs on indexed funds in Canada are much higher than the costs for index trust units (TIPs, Spiders, and so on) or U.S. index funds.

If investors retained investment advice the way they retain lawyers, accountants, plumbers, or auto mechanics—namely, paying by the hour—more people would probably be partially invested in an index.

## Chapter Ten

# Direct Investing, Hybrid Strategies, and Hazards of Picking Individual Stocks

If there is "Life After Mutual Funds," it follows that there was always "life before mutual funds." While mutual funds waxed and waned in the 1920s and the 1960s, before the singular mania of the 1990s, the traditional alternative has always been to do what the funds now do on investors' behalf: invest directly in the stock and bond markets.

We mentioned earlier the paradoxical phenomenon whereby many intelligent mutual fund investors are now devoting as much time and energy to mutual fund analysis as old-time stock investors used to devote to actual stocks. That's fine if it's a hobby and you enjoy it, but consider that you are already paying a mutual fund manager to analyze stocks on your behalf. Consequently, much of your energy will be counterproductive and result in second-guessing your fund manager.

If you are the type of person who likes to analyze mutual funds—and many computer-literate baby boomers are—you likely possess the very skills needed to invest in the markets directly. The same energy you spend surfing fund-analysis sites could instead be expended on analyzing stocks or bonds, and you could pocket the management fees yourself.

Hundreds of books exist that address the art and science of picking individual stocks. The brokerage alternative is not a radical suggestion and will not even seem novel to veteran investors. However, for newer, younger investors weaned on mutual funds, it's worth a reminder that this old-time alternative to funds continues to exist. As Barron's noted in its "Beyond Mutual Funds" supplement, many U.S. fund investors are rediscovering stock ownership.

Stock-picking is not the dominant theme of this book, but one can hardly avoid the subject altogether. The April 1998 issue of *Money* magazine devoted a cover story entitled "Stocks or Funds: What's Right for You?" What's interesting about that piece was its implicit assumption that stocks or equity mutual funds are the only asset class worth considering. The article concluded, "Stocks give you a shot at explosive gains, while funds offer a smoother ride."

One could build a portfolio of quality, dividend-paying large-cap stocks and hold them, like Warren Buffett, for years and decades. Except for the initial commissions, you would not pay annual management fees (except the small fee for self-directed RRSPs), and you would also receive regular dividends, either in cash or reinvested in more of the stock in question. Similarly, you could assemble a "ladder" of strip bonds or Government of Canada long and short bonds, paying only the initial commission to acquire them. The resulting mix would be equivalent to a balanced mutual fund, but with only a negligible annual management fee. Such a direct approach to the markets can be executed through either traditional full-service stockbrokers or the discount brokers that have developed in Canada in the wake of the 1984 establishment of TD GreenLine's discount brokerage operation.

With a full-service broker, you would not be completely on your own, and, of course, you would pay the broker commissions to buy and sell stocks. If you're highly cost-conscious, enjoy doing your own research, and are competent enough to make your own decisions—three big ifs—you can cut brokerage commissions to the bone by using one of the 11 discount brokers in Canada. In addition to GreenLine, which has the lion's share of the discount market, most of the other big banks offer discount brokerage arms. There are also newer independents such as Groome Capital of Montreal and Priority Brokerage of Toronto, and Internet discounters such as E Trade Canada.

A typical full-service trade involves a minimum commission of $70 to $80, which means you should wait until you can make a $5,000 trade to keep the commission to a reasonable 2% or 3%. Discount brokers such as Royal Bank Action Direct (RBAD) charge as little as $29 for an electronic trade mediated by a personal computer or the Internet, and $45 for a human-mediated telephone order. At RBAD, two-thirds of discount trades are still mediated by a human.

Full-service and discount brokers have great flexibility: you can invest in mutual funds as well as many other securities mentioned in other sections of this book: for example, the fund alternatives described in Chapter 8 or the passive indexing products discussed in Chapter 9.

## Hybrid strategies

In the real world, the affluent clients of investment advisers do not usually commit to a 100% funds or 100% non-funds strategy. Most adopt various "hybrid" strategies, incorporating several products. You could use mutual funds where it's likely the managers can add value and justify the fees—such as small-cap stock funds, "EAFE" (Europe, Australia, and Far East), or non-North American global equity funds, or specialty funds covering technology or precious metals. Then you would invest directly in, say, large-cap Canadian stocks or U.S. large-caps—where a manager is less likely to add value and beat the indexes—and in strip bonds or a bond index fund.

Typically, when an all-fund portfolio held at a discount broker passes $25,000 in assets, the investor branches out into stocks, says Michael Bastian, president and CEO of Royal Bank Action Direct. He notes that one in five investors who have held funds for a year or two also start buying stocks. They may hold previously purchased funds and direct new purchases to stocks.

One advantage of such a hybrid funds/stocks approach is that you could cut the effective total MER. For example, say 50% of your portfolio is in 2% MER funds and 50% is in directly held securities you plan to hold for 20 or 30 years. Disregarding the one-time brokerage fee on the stocks, the "effective" MER of the portfolio would be 1%—exactly the annual fee most wealthy people pay in the products and services described in Part 3. You'd still have professional stock-picking help on the tricky aggressive parts of your portfolio, but the stable large-cap/fixed-income component would bypass the professionals and save some fees.

## Mimicking fund portfolios

By combining stocks with funds, you can also get ideas for direct stock purchases from the mutual fund reports that the companies send you regularly. This strategy is known as "mimicking" the fund portfolios. Of course, you have no guarantee you will be purchasing such stocks at the same price as the fund, but if you were considering a particular stock anyway, the fact that your favorite fund manager has acquired it may give you a little more comfort in your selection abilities.

The fund unitholder report will tell you what stocks your large-cap Canadian equity fund is in, to take the most likely example, and frequently the fund's cost on the stock. Using this information, you can calculate what price the stock was trading at and compare it with the current price. If your personal investment style matches that of the fund manager, there's nothing preventing you from buying directly a few of the large-cap stocks in that fund. If you are in two or three fund families, you may notice that particular stocks are owned by funds in all three families. That would indicate a fairly safe bet for you to buy, even if you're not entirely confident of your own stock-picking abilities.

There is, of course, an inherent danger that a situation has changed radically between the time the fund purchased a stock and when it was publicized in the unitholder reports. That's more likely to be a problem in the small-cap or medium-cap arena, as occurred with Bre-X Minerals Ltd., which showed up even in conservative Canadian balanced funds. But in the large-cap area, any significant changes are likely to have been reported already in the financial press. If you have concerns, you could list the stocks you're interested in, flag them when you notice them in a few favorite funds you track, and then watch the newspaper stock pages, focusing on the "new lows" section. When your target stock hits a low, that may be a buying opportunity. That's exactly what some fund managers do: the first thing they read in the newspaper every day is the "new lows" listings.

If you enjoy comparing mutual funds, or going through their list of stock-holdings, you will probably also enjoy tracking individual stocks. Instead of poring through mutual fund statements of stock holdings, you'll be going through the annual reports of actual stocks you own. The companies don't send you their reports when you own them indirectly through funds, but they do when you own their stocks directly.

As discussed earlier, one of the main reasons for the popularity of mutual funds has been its ability to free investors from the supposed drudgery of tracking individual stocks, poring through annual reports, assessing quarterly earnings, and so on. Edward Trapunski, author of *The Secrets of Investing in Technology Stocks* (Wiley, Toronto, 1998), has noted that it takes three hours a day or 21 hours a week for an investor to stay abreast of stocks just in the high-tech industry. For investors who don't want to make that commitment of time and energy, high-tech mutual funds can make a lot of sense. You may not need a fund manager to pick IBM, Microsoft, Intel, or Northern Telecom for you, but once you enter the realm of small- and mid-cap tech stocks, you're in potentially dangerous territory.

As with tech stocks, the dangers are greater in choosing small- and mid-cap stocks. But there's little downside in choosing large-cap dividend-paying stocks of established companies such as the big Canadian banks, BCE Inc., Barrick Gold Corp., Inco Ltd., Alcan, and other such stocks. In fact, any investor who cautiously bought bank stocks in recent years has outperformed most aggressive equity fund managers.

Say, for example, that you've chosen to buy a fund company's Canadian small-cap fund and global equity fund. Those are two places where the fund company is likely to add some value.

On the other hand, it's arguable that you don't need to pay 2% a year for a large-cap Canadian fund that purchases essentially the TSE 35 or TSE 100. Because most large Canadian equity funds own the big banks, BCE Inc., Canadian Pacific, and similar securities, and provided you can afford to buy stocks in $5,000 chunks at a time, you can get the best of both worlds by buying such stocks directly and using funds in the more dangerous asset classes. After all, you're more likely to suffer big losses from buying junior gold stocks or money-losing Internet stocks.

We note that many investment advisers who started with just

a mutual fund license are working to be registered as brokers, which would allow their clients to adopt such hybrid portfolios of both funds.

## Strips and TIPS

Another low-cost hybrid approach suitable for RRSPs has been dubbed the "strips and TIPS" strategy, and doesn't use traditional mutual funds at all. When Mercer's Hamilton first raised the MER issue on mutual funds, he suggested that some investors would be better served with a low-cost TIPS-and-strips strategy using a self-directed RRSP and a discount broker. TIPS, or Toronto Index Participation Shares (TIP/TSE), are described in Chapter 9. Unlike index-linked GICs (see Chapter 7), TIPS pass along dividend income. And unlike mutual funds, there is no annual investment management fee. A further refinement would be to maximize your 20% permitted foreign content in an RRSP or RRIF by buying some of the passive foreign products described in Chapter 9, such as Spiders for U.S. stock exposure or WEBS (World Equity Benchmark Shares) for global stock exposure.

Strips are strip coupon bonds, where a government bond is separated into its principal ("residual") and coupon (interest-paying) components. On the bond side, there is little product available to mimic the Scotia Capital Markets universe bond index. Investment advisers suggest instead building "ladders" of bonds maturing at various times. We looked at how to create a "ladder" of strips in Chapter 6.

Some brokers like strips to hedge against deflation and real return bonds to hedge against inflation. The federal government introduced real return bonds in 1991, and these bonds guarantee a fixed rate of return above inflation. The first real return bonds provided a 4.25% coupon over 30 years, plus a monthly percentage rise in the value of the Canadian consumer price index. These bonds are also stripped, and the strips can be purchased with maturities ranging from six months to 30 years. Given the current round of interest-rate hikes, it may be safer to keep to the short end of strip bond maturities or stay in cash until yields rise.

You will have to monitor the overall asset allocation resulting from your mix of TIPS and strips. The mix may be the normal balanced fund proportion of 60% stocks to 40% fixed income, but this may vary.

You also won't pay as much in fees as you would in a balanced fund, but the two are not directly comparable. In a balanced fund, you have active management of equities and the bond managers actively manage interest rate risk.

If "strips and TIPS" is so effective, why haven't you heard more about it? "Part of the reason Canadians are pretty ignorant about this is that nobody has a vested interest in telling you to open a self-directed account and use strips and TIPS because there's no money in it for anyone," Hamilton says. "The price you pay for low fees is you have to know how to do it yourself."

Of course, you get what you pay for. Fund fees include professional management. If you do not want to pay, be prepared to do it yourself. And not all investment advisers support a strips and TIPS philosophy. In fact, RBC Dominion Securities investment adviser Nathan Mechanic, who some credit for the phrase "strips and TIPS," does not believe that indexing is a valid strategy in a topped-out stock market that is moving sideways or downwards as North America appeared to be in 1998.

## Hazards of direct investing

The move from funds to stocks, whether partial or wholehearted, does entail greater risks. A mutual fund has double protection: professional stock selection and diversification. Typically, a fund will not have invested more than 5% in any one stock, whereas do-it-yourself stock pickers can concentrate 100% of a portfolio in a single stock, or even more with leverage. While the full-service brokerage offers human advice, discount brokerage customers are left to their own devices, and with it the potential for disastrous mistakes such as Bre-X. Even discount brokers, however, are required to monitor trades and ensure that any trade is not outside the investment profile the customer established when setting up the account. For this reason, a discount trade may be refused until the customer revises his or her profile to fit the new trading mode.

Even the best brokers, those with 20 years or more of experience, impeccable ethics, great communication skills, top-flight designations such as Chartered Financial Analyst (CFA), and a life-long commitment to doing the best they can for clients, treat most investors poorly. This is not a comment about personal character but rather about the underlying economics of the brokerage industry. The typical broker oversees about $40 million of investments for about 500 clients, with an average investment of $78,000 per client. This simple business reality means that when something happens with a stock, only so many people can be reached quickly. If you were the broker, would you call the client with 1,000 shares or 100 shares first? As well, as the following chart shows, the ideal stock portfolio should have perhaps 20 to 30 stocks, but few investors have enough money to diversify this much.

## Security Specific Risk (Above Market Risk) for Canadian Equities

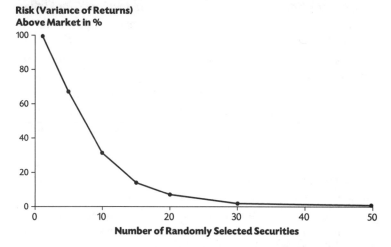

**Risk (Variance of Returns) Above Market in %**

**Number of Randomly Selected Securities**

*Source: Lawrence Kryzanowski, Concordia University*

Most brokerages provide advisers with software that allows them to instantaneously list, in order of size, who owns how much of a particular stock. By the time they reach the regular clients, it may be too late to do anything. The next time the market has a particularly bumpy day, try to contact your broker for a discussion on the merits of a particular company. Also ask yourself who is minding the shop when she is taking you out to lunch the following week, or when her voice mail tells you she's on vacation.

While we mention these brokerage options, they are more appropriate for sophisticated investors who probably have no need for this book. Investors who gravitated to mutual funds because they valued professional management, diversification, and the many other advantages of funds should be considering other Managed-Money alternatives to funds, not direct participation in the stock and bond markets. This is the purpose of Part 3 of this book.

In the 1991 bestseller, *Serious Money* (unrelated to *The National Post*'s column), author, speaker, and investment adviser Nick Murray declared the "death of do-it-yourself investing." Do-it-yourselfers were shaken by the 1987 market crash, an event that drove many into the arms of mutual fund managers. Should a late 1990s or year 2000 millennium bug-inspired market setback materialize, the current discount broker/online trading/internet wave of do-it-yourselfers could become equally disenchanted with their own efforts to call markets.

Murray was on the leading edge of mutual fund marketing (the subtitle to *Serious Money* was *The Art of Marketing Mutual Funds*). His premise was that the world had become too complex, with events unfolding too suddenly, for individual investors to function comfortably. The mass-market Managed-Money product of choice at the time was, of course, mutual funds, although his book also explored many alternatives. Murray also predicted that individual investors would be unable to handle the proliferation of choices in the mutual fund arena any better than they handled individual stocks: hence his belief in the need for personal advice delivered by an *Excellent Investment Adviser* (the title of his self-published 1996 follow-up to *Serious Money*).

Such advisers are normally compensated through commissions on "load" mutual funds. Investors who try to do it themselves with directly sold "no-load" funds often end up buying aggressive growth funds at market tops, liquidating during events such as the 1987 market crash, and forcing portfolio managers to sell more stock at depressed prices, after which, the no-load do-it-yourselfers lick their wounds in a bond fund. In short, Murray argues, no-load investors always inflict maximum damage on their portfolios by buying high and selling low. His premise was that investment advisers aren't needed so much for their technical expertise and asset-allocation knowledge as for their simple ability to understand the normal human emotions of greed and fear that wreak such havoc on the average do-it-yourself portfolio.

We agree that average investors need help or professional advice. In order to succeed, the individual and hybrid investment strategies outlined in Part 2 depend on having a good adviser and being knowledgeable. That's a tall order for most people. But rather than gambling on such hit-and-miss strategies, there is, we think, an easier way. The approach is called "Managed Money," a subset of which is mutual funds. It turns out the mutual fund investor has been on the right track all along. But further along that track lie some more cost-effective and customized solutions.

The products introduced in Part 3 can be similar to mutual funds: pooled funds and mutual fund "Wrap" programs. Or, at the high end, there are "segregated" accounts that resemble the do-it-yourself stock approach described in this chapter. The difference is that with "seg" or "separately managed" accounts, a professional manager is again making bets on your behalf. Unlike funds, however, he or she customizes it to your unique requirements, and does so at a lower cost.

# Part Three

# Eat Well and Sleep Well with Managed Money

*Chapter Eleven*

# Becoming a High-Net-Worth Client

## How to eat well and sleep well with your investments

Investing directly in the stock markets reflects a desire for growth: to "eat well" in some distant-future retirement. But as the last chapter showed, investing directly in individual securities does not always bring with it the ability to also "sleep well."

If you are or have been a mutual fund investor, you've had the right idea. You quite rightly regard the huge number of variables involved in modern industrial economies as too complex for casual investors, whose interests lie elsewhere. In fact, it's pretty tough even for professional investors to match the markets, which is why we looked in Part 2 at such passive alternatives as indexing.

The capital markets are complex and often dangerous places. Until mid-1998, they didn't seem dangerous, they simply seemed very profitable. In fact, the markets have been heading up since 1982 and the last four years have been a joy for anyone investing in stocks and bonds. However, the "nervous Nellies" holding GICs have not been as fortunate.

As a result of declining interest rates and low yields on GICs, many savers have become true investors only recently. After all, it all seems so easy: buy a few blue-chip stocks and watch them increase in value. But, of course, things are not that easy. If they were, we would all be millionaires.

In light of this, it is useful to consider the following analogy. If you decide to try white-water rafting on your vacation, you would probably consider the risks of doing it yourself. While the river can appear to be peaceful and calm, there are risks and dangers under the surface. Investing is the same. During a bull market, investing looks easy, but the bear always lurks beneath the surface.

If you were going white-water rafting, you would hire a guide. By choosing the Managed-Money option, you are hiring a guide to the capital markets. It may seem like a waste of money in a bull market but money managers earn their keep during times of uncertainty, and especially during full-fledged bear markets. Perhaps this time *is* different and we will never see another protracted bear market, but do you want to bet your long-term financial security on "this time it's different"?

Many people think they have hired a guide when they work with a broker or financial planner. As long as markets are going up and they have profits, they don't examine the relationship too closely. Only when they hit choppy waters do they begin to ask the fundamental questions that they should have asked at the outset.

Before deciding which guide to hire, investors should first decide whether they want a guide at all, and, if so, what kind. The investment equivalent of not having a guide is doing your own research and executing your trades with a discount broker. Or it could mean following the "Rip Van Winkle" two-fund strategy outlined in Chapter 6, the "Strips and TIPS" passive strategy of Chapter 9, or studying annual reports and choosing your own stocks, as discussed in Chapter 10.

As part of this decision-making process investors must consider both value and cost. The value is in the advice and guidance you receive. The cost is what you pay for it. A recently completed preliminary research study by Winans International Investment Management, reported in *The Wall Street Journal* on August 14, 1998, revealed some surprising information about this value equation.

This study looked at the direct costs of various ways of investing in U.S. equities over three, five, and ten year periods. These costs included mutual fund loads where applicable, direct investing commissions, mutual fund MERs or direct management fees. The cumulative costs assumed a lump-sum investment, no market growth and an ending portfolio value for each time period. The costs were taken from published schedules and average fund turnover ratios, calculated by Morningstar, were used. Turnover ratios for direct investments in stocks was assumed to be 25%.

For investors with a portfolio value of $200,000 the conclusions were enlightening. Investors purchasing no-load funds would incur costs over a five year period of 6.9% of their total investment. The same investment in front-end load and back-end load funds would incur costs of 11.3% and 15.5% respectively. Investors going direct to an Investment Advisory firm (the U.S. equivalent of our Investment Counselling firms) and paying a management fee of 1.2% would incur costs of 8.1%. The least costly method was to directly invest in stocks without any advice or assistance at 4.7%.

For high-net-worth investors, the choice of guide will have an impact on the costs of having your money managed and these cost differentials will have an impact on your returns over time. It is interesting to note that the 1.2% management fee used in this study is higher than the typical 1% fee charged by most investment counselling firms for pooled fund investments.

Most investors have decided that while the do-it-yourself approach may be fine for building a deck or refinishing furniture, their long-term financial well-being is worth the price of added expertise. For such investors it is important that they understand what expertise they want and how they expect to use it.

Following are three pairs of statements that will help investors determine the kind of expertise they are looking for:

1. I like to discuss each holding or idea before making any decision.
2. I generally do whatever my adviser recommends.

3. I can generally assess when the advice is good and don't worry about overtrading of my account.
4. I am concerned about too much activity and other conflicts of interest.

5. I like to speak with my adviser frequently about my holdings and the current action in the market.

6. I prefer to have a quarterly review of my entire portfolio and its performance relative to my goals and objectives.

If you agreed with statements 1, 3, and 5, you should be dealing with the advisory side of the industry. As outlined in Part 2, these are the brokers and planners who can distribute a wide range of investment products and options to clients.

If you agreed with statements 2, 4, and 6, you should be focusing on the management side of the industry, either through managed products available from distributors or by dealing directly with the investment manager.

The time to assess whether you want an adviser or a manager is when times are good. In a bull market, everyone can eat well. Stocks are going up and wealth increases. It's like enjoying a five-course gourmet banquet that someone else is paying for. Times are great. In uncertain, volatile markets, however, it can be a gut-wrenching roller-coaster ride, as most investors have discovered in 1998. Times are uncertain and there may be some sleepless nights caused by newspaper headlines and television reports about churning markets.

Investors may not have been "nervous Nellies" during the good times but uncertainty tends to change that. For many people it makes sense to hire experts to guide their portfolios through the difficult stretches. When investors decide to have investment experts manage their money, they are hiring their own guide.

The most important part of the Managed-Money process is determining an investor's objectives and developing an asset mix appropriate for both an investor's return expectations and risk tolerances. Risk tolerance relates to more than just volatility, although most of the risk measures available focus on this one aspect. To most investors, risk means the potential to lose money. As investors move through their personal life cycles and approach the time when they will need to live off their investment income, the ability to tolerate losses decreases. For example, a 30-year-old investor still has a long time horizon to recoup a loss in any given year before she needs to use her capital. A 70-year-old has much less time, however, so he has a lower tolerance for losses.

With Managed Money, clients have an investment expert who integrates their long-term objectives, risk tolerance, the current and expected state of the money markets, and the time horizon to develop a unique investment strategy and policy for each investor.

Developing this investment strategy is the most important decision an investor has to make. The seminal study on this issue is known as the Brinson Study. *Determinants of Portfolio Performance* by G.P. Brinson, L.R. Hood, and G.L. Beebower was published in the July/August 1986 edition of the *Financial Analysts Journal.* This study of pension fund and institutional portfolios showed that approximately 90% of an investor's return is determined by the asset mix; that is, the relative proportion of stocks, bonds, and cash.

Numerous other studies have supported this theme. While some have determined that security selection and market timing can also be important, none has questioned the fundamental principle that getting the right asset mix is the most important decision an investor must make.

If most of an investor's success or failure is determined by asset mix, then it makes sense to have the best-trained and most highly qualified experts making those decisions. This underscores the benefits of Managed Money.

For investors with jobs, families, and normal everyday interests, the benefits of Managed Money are enormous. Unless you enjoy studying financial markets daily and are confident that you know as much as the best professionals, it makes sense to consider Managed Money as an integral part of investment planning.

For most people, Managed Money is an evolution of the investment approach they are using. Most investors now own mutual funds because they like the diversification that the funds offer, combined with the management expertise of top-flight investment professionals. Mutual funds *are* Managed Money, targeted at the mass market. The new managed products and services that are available simply add this professional expertise to the asset-mix decision.

There are a number of related issues, many of them demographic: increasingly, older investors have to consider taxation, estate planning, income splitting, and the myriad complexities that accompany wealth creation. Chapter 15 looks at these issues in more detail.

## Understanding the Managed-Money industry

The investment industry can be a confusing world for new and even experienced consumers of financial services. Unfortunately, the industry has done little to reduce this confusion. There is a legal concept called "informed consent." When it comes to our investments, however, many consumers and financial services providers seem to operate on the principle of "misinformed consent."

To begin to understand who the players are in the investment industry and what a consumer can expect from each, it's necessary to understand the structure of the industry. Similar to other industries, there are two major parts to the investment industry: manufacturing and distribution. On the manufacturing side are the investment managers—the money managers who invest your savings for, hopefully, healthy returns. They are registered as investment counsel and portfolio managers with either a provincial securities commission or with the Investment Dealers Association. Most of these individuals hold their registration through provincial securities commissions. These are the firms and individuals registered (i.e., permitted) to provide continuous management of investment portfolios. These firms and individuals manage investment portfolios such as mutual funds, pooled funds, pension funds, and individual—or "private client"—portfolios. In the mutual fund industry, examples of these firms include Altamira Investment Services Inc., Trimark Investment Management, Royal Bank Investment Management, Phillips Hager Investment Management, and J. Zechner & Associates. The actual day-to-day management of the mutual funds takes place at these firms.

The other side of the industry is distribution, or sales. This end of the business—the mutual fund dealers—delivers the manufactured investment products to consumers. The average consumer tends to have more experience with this part of the industry. Some investment management firms, such as Altamira and Phillips, Hager & North, distribute their own products directly to consumers. Others, such as Royal Bank Investment Management and other bank-owned investment firms, distribute through their parent companies. Still others, such as Trimark, Mackenzie Financial Corp., and C.I. Mutual Funds, distribute through external sales networks. These are the brokerage firms and mutual fund dealers, including Wood Gundy, Nesbitt Burns Inc., Merrill Lynch Canada (formerly Midland Walwyn), and Fortune Financial.

Consumers can think of an analogy to the household appliance business. They can buy a microwave oven or television from the company-owned store or from an independent retailer. In the investment industry, a fund available from the company-owned store is not usually available from the independent retailer. A case in point: just try buying the low-fee Phillips, Hager & North or Bissett Investment Management funds from an independent mutual fund dealer. These funds charge low management fees because they have eliminated the cost of the distribution network for clients who wish to go directly to the manufacturer. It's the same difference as wholesale versus retail.

## The money managers

The managers are those firms registered to manage investment portfolios on a continuous and discretionary basis. (The term "discretionary" is explained in the next chapter.) The portfolio managers who make the day-to-day decisions on what to buy and sell must meet rigorous standards of education and experience, as outlined in the following table.

Most of these firms are registered as investment counsel. Their expertise is in investments. They are not financial planners, and investors should not expect them to have expertise in insurance, financial planning, or retirement planning.

The distinction between some financial advisers and planners and investment counselors may be starting to blur as financial planning firms upgrade their expertise by hiring individuals with the CFA designation or equivalent experience. Such financial planning firms may, as a result, become registered as investment counselors.

The most common professional designation for investment professionals is the Chartered Financial Analyst (CFA), which is an internationally recognized designation. The CFA is a three-year program and the body of knowledge covers investment research and portfolio management. Less common is the Certified Investment Manager (CIM), which is awarded by the Canadian Securities Institute. The CIM is a two-year program that covers financial planning in the first year and investment management in the second year. The FCSI designation, or Fellow of the Canadian Securities Institute, is granted to individuals who, in addition to the normal brokerage education and licensing exams, hold the CIM designation, have a minimum of five years' experience, and meet ethical and continuing-education requirements.

If a supplier tells you it is a money manager, the prospective customer should ask what its registration is. If it is not registered as an investment counsel/portfolio manager, it is not a manager. If the supplier is managing client assets without the registration, it is ignoring securities laws and consumers should be extremely wary of having any dealings with such individuals and firms.

## The distributors (sales channels)

Distributors come in a variety of shapes and sizes. They range from the banks to independent mutual fund dealers, such as the Financial Concepts Group and Regal Capital, to large proprietary fund dealers, such as Investors Group Inc., to insurance companies and brokerage firms.

Those firms licensed as mutual fund dealers can only distribute (sell) mutual funds. Others may be licensed to sell insurance products, while others are licensed to sell a full range of securities that may include mutual funds, stocks, bonds, closed-end funds, and trust units.

A critical distinction to make here is that distributors are advisers, not managers. Advisers can offer advice and make recommendations, but investors make the actual decisions. When dealing with an adviser, investors are acting as their own manager.

The distributors that act as advisers come with an alphabet

## Investment Service Providers

| Firm Type | Regulatory Supervision | Qualifications for Registration |
|---|---|---|
| **Investment Counsel** | Provincial Securities Commission | Portfolio Manager/Investment Counsel: Level I Chartered Financial Analyst (CFA) program, Certified Investment Manager (CIM), plus five years experience in research or portfolio management |
| **Broker/ Investment Dealer/ Securities Dealer:** Advisory and Discretionary | Investment Dealers Association | *Advisory*—Financial Adviser: The Canadian Securities Course and the Conduct and Practices Handbook exam. *Discretionary*—Portfolio Manager/ Investment Counsel: Level 1 CFA, CIM plus five years experience in research or portfolio management. |
| **Mutual Fund Dealer** | Provincial Securities Commission<br><br>Moving to self-regulatory status under the IDA | Investment Adviser/Investment Planner/Financial Planner: One of the Canadian Securities Course, Canadian Investment Funds Course, Investment Funds in Canada Course or Principles of Mutual Fund Investment. |

| Revenue Sources | Advantages | Disadvantages |
|---|---|---|
| Fees for continuous management of investment portfolio | Continuous management of investment portfolio. Freedom from bias toward transactions. Lower execution costs. No conflict between principal trading or underwriting and portfolio management. Highest minimum qualifying standards for professional staff. | Generally not available to clients with smaller amounts of capital. Clients served from larger financial centers. Difficult to identify service providers due to limited advertising and promotion. |
| *Advisory—* Commissions for execution of transactions. Trailer or service fees from product sales. *Discretionary—* Fees for the management of portfolios and commissions for the execution of trades. | *Advisory—*Can provide advice and execution to clients of all sizes. Wide selection of product availability. Available in communities of all sizes. *Discretionary—*Continuous management of the portfolio Due to the commission revenue, often able to handle accounts of smaller size. | Potential bias toward high-commission products due to transaction compensation. Combination of sales commissions and built-in product fees can be expensive. *Advisory—*Lower level of minimum qualification and training. Wide variety in investment experience, training and expertise. |
| Revenue from commissions for product sales, known as load fees, and trailer or service fees paid by fund companies | Ability to process transactions of relatively small dollar amounts and can usually offer regular installment purchase plans. Wide selection of product availability. Available in communities of all sizes. | Potential bias toward high-commission products due to transaction compensation. Combination of sales commissions and built-in product fees can be expensive. Lowest level of minimum qualification and training. Wide variety in investment experience, training and expertise. |

soup of different qualifications, but there are three basic categories of registration: broker, mutual fund rep, and life insurance agent.

A broker (or financial adviser) who wishes to sell securities must be designated a Registered Representative, which requires passing the Canadian Securities Course (CSC), sponsorship by a provincially registered dealer, and a requirement to have been supervised for a specified period of time. Advisers must have completed the CSC and licensing exam. For several years new advisers have also had to complete the Professional Financial Planning (PFP) program within 30 months of becoming licensed. The PFP is different from the Personal Financial Planner program offered to bankers, and was previously known as CIM Part 1. A subcategory, investment representative, which is typically attained by discount brokers and full-service administrative and support staff, is more junior. Investment representatives can take orders but cannot offer advice. They need the CSC and three months' experience but don't need to take the PFP course.

Mutual fund reps must pass the Canadian Investment Funds Course, offered by the Investment Funds Institute of Canada, or the equivalent course on mutual funds offered by the Institute of Canadian Bankers. By itself, a mutual fund license does not allow the individual rep to sell other securities, such as stocks.

Finally, life insurance agents need a life insurance license—or life license—regulated by the provinces. This must be renewed annually and requires 30 hours of additional education annually in most provinces. There are two levels: Levels 1 and 2, and the latter must be taken within two years of attaining Level 1. A voluntary extra credential is the Chartered Life Underwriter (CLU) designation, offered by the Canadian Association of Insurance and Financial Advisors. To sell stocks or funds, the life agent would need to get the relevant qualifications and end up dual-licensed.

Within these categories of registration, many professionals have taken additional training to provide more expertise to clients. The most common type of additional training is in financial planning.

Financial planners are, or should be, generalists. They should have a broad knowledge of retirement planning, insurance, estate planning, capital accumulation strategies, investments, tax, and legal issues. They are not an expert in any one of these areas. Think of them as a financial general practitioner, not a specialist; a family doctor, rather than a neurosurgeon. Financial planners should bring in the experts once they have identified the investor's requirement for expert advice, whether tax, insurance, estate planning, or investment.

Most investors have simple needs when starting out. They need to save and invest in RRSPs for retirement, need some life insurance and disability insurance, and a will. A good financial planner will develop a plan that considers these needs and long-term goals. As this plan is implemented, needs will change. This is the nature of personal life cycles. As responsibilities increase with marriage and children, more insurance is needed. As a financial plan works and wealth is accumulated, more complicated tax advice may be needed. As wealth increases, there is also a greater need for investment expertise.

Often, the more success a good financial plan has over the long term, the more a consumer's needs shift from financial planning to investment planning and management.

There are fee-for-service financial planners, but they are a minority in the investment industry. Most financial planners are paid when they implement the plan, whether that involves buying insurance or investment products. Consumers must understand that a plan may be biased toward the products that the planner can sell. This is only realistic since financial planners have their own personal financial commitments just like anyone else.

With the exception of Quebec, anyone across Canada can call him- or herself a financial planner—and many do. After all, "financial planner" sounds much more professional than "mutual fund salesperson" or "stockbroker." However, such a broad and all-encompassing term leaves consumers floundering about what expertise and qualifications a financial planner has. This is not because there are no standards but rather because there are too many competing standards. In fact, there is an alphabet soup of designations. Current financial planning designations include CFP, CIM, RFP, CHFC, CLU, PFP, and SFC. It is tough enough for those within the industry to remember all these acronyms, let alone for consumers to understand what they mean. The following table

## Financial Planning

| Designation | Conferred by |
| --- | --- |
| **CFP**<br>Certified Financial Planner | Financial Planning Standards Council of Canada (FPSCC) |
| **RFP**<br>Registered Financial Planner | Canadian Association of Financial Planners (CAFP) |
| **CHFC**<br>Chartered Financial Consultant | Canadian Association of Insurance and Financial Advisors (CAIFA) |
| **CLU**<br>Chartered Life Underwriter | Canadian Association of Insurance and Financial Advisors (CAIFA) |
| **PFP**<br>Personal Financial Planner | Institute of Canadian Bankers (CB)* |
| **SFC**<br>Specialist in Financial Counseling | Institute of Canadian Bankers (CB)* |

## Investment Planning

| Designation | Conferred by |
| --- | --- |
| **CIM**<br>Certified Investment Manager | Canadian Securities Institute (CSI)** |
| **CFA**<br>Chartered Financial Analyst | Association for Investment Management and Research (AIMR) |

\* Designation owned by the Canadian Bankers Association
\*\* Designation owned by the Investment Dealers Association of Canada

outlines what the various letters mean. The designation that has broad international recognition is the CFP, or Certified Financial Planner. For two years, various groups had been working together under the joint banner of the Financial Planning Standards Council of Canada to bring some sense and consistency to the standards applied to all those engaged in financial planning. One designation with uniform qualifications would make life easier for consumers, who would then know what to expect of someone who claims to be a financial planner.

In the spring of 1998, the Canadian Securities Institute and the Institute of Canadian Bankers both withdrew from the Standards Council. Whatever set of letters are used to describe qualifications, consumers should hope that all the players can join forces and set standards to which all the players will adhere.

Investors must understand who will be implementing their financial plan—a distributor or a manager. Increasingly, investors are choosing managers to implement their plans. The distribution side of the industry has responded by developing a whole new type of product that can be labeled "managed product."

Many investors run into trouble when they attempt to implement their long-term plan. There is a tendency to buy, or be sold, the flavor of the month, usually based on the previous year's hottest fund or asset class.

Investment products are typically structured on an asset-class basis. Bonds are one asset class, cash another. But even within the equity, or stock, asset class, Canadian equity may be designated as a separate asset class, as well as American, international, and others. Distributors would typically recommend that a client use a variety of asset classes to implement the investment plan.

The problem for investors is they are dependent on the distributor to create and advise on an investment plan that is based on asset classes. Most investors don't care which asset class they use as long as their objectives are met. They are objective-driven investors, not asset-class-driven investors.

Mackenzie was the first Canadian investment firm to bring an investment focus to implementation based on investors' objectives. Its STAR asset-allocation service was developed by Gordon Garmaise based on a precursor used at the TD Bank. STAR packages up several Mackenzie funds in configurations ranging from "aggressive growth" to "conservative income." STAR has stimulated similar approaches in other financial services firms, which use a variety of managed account programs based on investors' objectives.

These programs have placed both parts of the investment management process in the hands of investment professionals rather than in the hands of distributors. The two parts of the process are the asset allocation or asset mix—that is, the mixture of different asset classes such as bonds, cash, and equities—and the individual security selection within those asset classes.

## Marketing strategies versus investment strategies

Consumers of investment products and services are inundated with information and advertising every RRSP season. The poor consumer has a hard time differentiating valuable investment information from mere marketing hype.

Much marketing information is based on good information but has been developed beyond its applicability in the real world of investing. One of the most glaring examples is the use of "star" fund managers. The earliest and best-known star for modern investors was Peter Lynch, former manager of the Fidelity Magellan Fund. There is no question that Peter Lynch was the portfolio manager who "pulled the trigger" on the trades in the fund, but to think that he was solely responsible for the excellent performance of the fund under his tenure is ridiculous. Such a premise may sell a lot of books, but it is not how money is managed. In his book *One Up On Wall Street*, Lynch acknowledged that a dozen analysts were working for him, researching possible holdings and following the stocks the fund owned. Lynch would not have been able to keep up with the volume of information on all of the fund's holdings without help, so it really was a team that contributed to the management of the fund.

The star manager approach is much easier for the investment companies to market. Focusing on an individual and bringing that person's personality and image to life for investors helps to sell funds. One-person bands are rarely an effective way to manage money. By comparison, the team approach seems bland and potentially bureaucratic, yet in reality many of those teams are dominated by one or two individuals.

The Templeton organization is one that has always managed to combine both the star and the team. The star, of course, is Sir John Templeton, who, while ostensibly retired, remains the focus of the Templeton Growth Fund annual meeting held every spring at Toronto's Roy Thomson Hall. The team is the scores of portfolio managers and analysts around the world who are responsible for researching industries and geographic regions. The investment process is structured so that all investment professionals support and depend on each other. Although this approach may not make for snappy advertising copy, it has made for successful investing over the years.

Another investment strategy frequently used as a marketing strategy is the benefit of diversification. No one disputes that diversification can reduce the risks of investing. By combining different investments that behave in different ways, the inevitable volatility of investing in financial markets can be lessened. Diversification is one of the best investment strategies that individuals can implement in their portfolios. However, diversification can also be misused when applied as a marketing strategy. When the concept of diversification induces an individual to own 25 different mutual funds, it has definitely been abused. As a marketing strategy, it helps to sell the latest, newest, hottest fund, but it is unlikely to enhance the investment experience.

When trying to assess whether what is being promoted is an investment strategy or a marketing strategy, consumers must ask some tough questions. They must look beyond the glib statements to see if they make sense and if there is depth behind the idea.

## The investment process

One of the buzzwords in mutual fund circles is "the investment process." Brokers, the media, and the public are all trying to analyze whether a particular manager uses a "top-down" or "bottom-up" approach to picking stocks, or whether the basic investment philosophy can be categorized as "growth" or "value." Most consumers are left wondering what this jargon actually means, but they simply nod in the right places, just as the general populace agreed that the nude emperor in the child's story was actually wearing clothes. These concepts are not that complicated, however, and there is no right or wrong approach. Each investor must decide which is the best approach for his or her individual situation.

A top-down approach means that managers start with the big picture in economic and business cycle. From this analysis they develop an outlook for interest rates, economic growth, commodity prices, and other factors that affect stock and bond prices. This outlook determines what types of assets to own, such as stocks or bonds, and how to structure holdings within each asset class. A manager who is a "theme investor" takes a top-down approach in the development of these themes, which can vary widely. One manager may take the view that commodity supplies are shrinking and he should buy resource stocks. Another judges that demographic trends are so overwhelming that a portfolio should have a heavy weighting of wealth management companies or health care companies.

Bottom-up managers declare that such big-picture events can't be forecast, and they instead concentrate on finding good individual companies. They will get to know a company's management and study the balance sheet and the income statement to identify great companies they want to own.

The reality is that all portfolio managers must pay attention to both the top-down and bottom-up aspects of securities. A fund manager can identify an industry with an excellent outlook from a top-down perspective but he or she must still examine the individual companies within that sector. One key element that must be considered in assessing a company's prospects is the outlook for its products, and how the larger economic outlook affects those prospects. The issue is where to start their process because they need to look at both aspects.

The most important part of the investment process is to be driven by the investor's needs. The client's objectives must be identified so they can be properly matched with an appropriate investment process.

Until recently, only the wealthiest individuals could have an investment professional directly involved in providing advice, guidance, and management in this key decision-making aspect. These were the individuals wealthy enough to deal directly with an investment counselor.

The introduction of new products and services in recent years have made this service available to individuals with more modest investment capital. Some of these services, such as Mackenzie's STAR and Bank of Montreal's Matchmaker asset-allocation service, are available to clients with modest portfolios of just a few thousand dollars. Others, such as CIBC's Personal Portfolio pooled funds and the "Wrap" accounts of the brokerage firms, are geared to more affluent investors (with $50,000 and up).

These services come in two main types: those that set a long-term asset mix and rebalance that asset mix periodically, and those that adjust the asset mix on an active basis to incorporate a forward-looking outlook for the capital markets.

Whether static or active, the asset mix is determined by the investment managers rather than the distributors or the investor. All the investment research literature has shown that the asset mix is the most important single decision in the investment process.

## A framework for investing

While most advisers and planners talk the language of planning and wear a few designations, far too often it is merely a one-time exercise of making some assumptions and doing some projections, or at worse, merely lip service. It is the age-old idea of "How will you get where you are going, or know when you arrive, if you do not have a map?" A financial plan should be a living document that establishes in writing exactly what is needed in terms of insurance, estate planning, tax planning, and asset-mix recommendations. It should also include a formula for an occasional, perhaps annual, review.

If the last page of a financial plan is a list of products to buy, you have really just been handed a subtle sales package. A financial plan should not include investment recommendations other than perhaps an asset mix, a rate of return objective, and a draft investment policy statement, as discussed in detail in Chapter 12.

Unfortunately, those people most in need of sound financial planning typically have the least to invest and are ignored by most product-pushing planners. Conversely, the people whom planners like to serve are those who have achieved financial independence and may not need much planning. People at this level typically need investment services. They also tend to already have a good accountant and a lawyer who have ensured that the basics are covered. Financial planning is often said to be 90% common sense, 5% tax planning, and 5% estate planning. To get the last 10%, a planner—regardless of designation—is unable to help. Other professionals are needed for these services.

Financial planning differs fundamentally from investment planning. Good investment planning depends on a sound financial plan, particularly in the area of tax. Investment planning must be done by an investment professional whose day-to-day business is recommending specific investments and investment strategies. A good accountant, for example, may help you with your financial planning, but typically she is not licensed or well versed in the myriad of investment options available. Investment planning involves establishing a strategy within a financial plan, short-listing the types of investments to consider, and then choosing particular services (if a managed approach is taken) or investments. The most basic investment plan should include quality controls and risk parameters, for example, "no bonds rated less than A" or "never more than 10% in any particular investment." It should also include a process for at least semi-annual or quarterly reviews.

## Setting objectives

As discussed earlier, determining investment objectives is the most important aspect of the investment process. It requires taking a step back from the advice, advertising, media commentary, and general discussion about investing and the markets. This is difficult for people to do because most of the financial services industry is based on selling some kind of product or service.

Most of the advertising and marketing material promises to help investors achieve their objectives if they buy a particular product or service being promoted. This is approaching matters in a backward way since until investors have identified their objectives, they can't determine which product or service is most likely to achieve them.

Everyone has a bias. Mutual fund dealers are confident that their products are the best for achieving someone's objectives; insurance agents are convinced segregated funds are the best; investment counselors can't understand why anyone would go anywhere else, and brokers will tell you they offer the widest array of products and services. None of these people is necessarily wrong; they are just coming at the process from their own perspective and biases. Readers must form their own beliefs and reach their own conclusions. This can only be done after they have determined their objectives.

When setting objectives, an investor needs to answer one main question—"What is this money for?" Whether you are just starting out or have accumulated significant investment assets, this question still needs to be posed. The answers will be as varied as the individuals providing them. The answers will vary depending on where the individual is in the life cycle of investing, and could include any of the following:

- To provide the down payment for a house or condominium
- To provide capital for starting a business
- To provide for children's education
- To provide a cushion to provide flexibility in career choices
- To travel and enjoy life
- To provide for retirement
- To provide financial security for a surviving spouse
- To help children with their expenses
- To give grandchildren a good start in life
- To support worthwhile charitable and philanthropic causes

The answers will also vary depending on an individual's stage of life. For example, any of the above objectives could apply to the same individual at different points in his or her life. Some of the objectives will require an emphasis on savings and the subsequent investment of those savings, and some will require a pure investment focus.

Once you have determined the answer to this question, you can look at the components of building an investment strategy. Typically if someone asks "What are your investment objectives?"

the answer is to make money or to provide income. By dealing with the "why," we have a better chance of achieving our objectives. In building an investment strategy to meet objectives, there are six key factors to consider:

- time horizon
- liquidity
- return requirements
- risk tolerance
- regulatory constraints
- special considerations

An example is a 30-year-old professional woman living in an apartment in Toronto. She has set up systematic withdrawal plans to save money for a house and would like to buy within three years. Since Toronto is the land of high real estate prices, there are two possible approaches. The first is an aggressive savings plan, which leaves little for dining out or other forms of expensive entertainment or vacations. The second is an aggressive investment strategy that entails a higher degree of risk but could pay off handsomely in added return and get her into a house sooner. The advantage of the first strategy is that she can be assured that the objective will be met with little risk, assuming the savings are invested in low-risk money-market, GICs, or other relatively short-term investments.

The second strategy may or may not work, depending on how short term the time horizon is. Before deciding which strategy to follow, the investor must decide if she can live with the risk of not meeting the objective. This example highlights the importance of time horizon in matching investment strategies to objectives. The shorter the time horizon, the less volatility can be accepted. RRSP investments generally have long time horizons and therefore can tolerate more volatility and be invested more aggressively for growth.

Liquidity is related to time horizon. If you need to access some of your investment capital, whether to buy a house, start a business, or as a reserve in case of unexpected emergency or job loss, this money must be kept liquid. The amount of capital to be kept liquid depends on individual circumstances but many experts suggest a six-month reserve. This amount could equate to 5% to 20% of the portfolio.

Liquid investments can be turned into cash in a short time frame without suffering losses or penalties. Therefore equities, long-term bonds, or any rear-load mutual fund do not qualify. Disasters rarely strike at convenient times and having no liquid investments would only make a disaster worse.

Once you have assessed your time horizon and liquidity needs, you can think about the return you want and level of risk you are willing to take to get it. Return is never free: risk will always be associated with it. The secret to successful investing is to accurately assess the risks you are taking.

There is no such thing as high return with no risk. But even taking a lot of risk doesn't necessarily guarantee high return. Rewards are commensurate with returns. There will be periods when it seems like some mutual funds or stock sectors or types of investments are generating great returns. They may have been on a roll for a long time. The market will often give investors the return side of the equation for long enough that they become convinced there isn't much risk. About the time everyone jumps on board, the market provides a painful lesson about the risk side of the equation. Investors always chasing after last year's hot investment can attest to this truth.

Regulatory requirements for most investors will be the foreign-content limits on RRSPs. Limiting foreign content may not be the optimum strategy from a pure investment perspective, but Canadians have no choice and cannot ignore this restriction if they wish to have the benefits of tax-sheltered investing.

Special considerations will vary with each individual. Some investors have none while others may want to invest only in ethical companies. If someone works for a particular company and wishes to participate in an employee share purchase or stock option program, they may want to avoid other companies in the same industry on the principle that they already have enough exposure. Special considerations are unique to each investor.

Once a preliminary set of objectives has been developed, investors can begin to look at the options available for meeting them. They now have a framework for evaluating which alternatives best meet those objectives.

## Chapter Twelve

# The Concept of Discretionary Management

All the products or services described in Part 3 can be categorized as Managed Money. They cater to investors who are looking for someone to manage their money on their behalf, and are willing to pay 1% to 3% a year for the privilege. This is called discretionary management, wherein investors empower a money manager to buy or sell securities or funds on their behalf. The decision to implement a big asset-allocation shift or a sale of a particular investment is at the discretion of that manager.

The discretionary approach is in direct contrast to what investors normally experience with a stockbroker, and which we described in Chapter 10. With a full-service broker, there is collaboration between the investors' own investment choices and those of the broker. Perhaps the broker pitches something from the brokerage's buy-list and the investor probes the suggestion and asks to see the green sheets and analyst research. Sometimes it's the other way around: the investor has come across an idea or received a tip from a third party and "bounces it off" the broker for evaluation. Together, the client and broker decide whether to hold a particular security—but the client has not given the broker full discretionary power over the account. This approach may work, particularly if the investor is sophisticated and has strong ideas about what makes good companies and good stocks, and has found a competent broker. But it is not discretionary management.

While a full-service broker may or may not save investors from their mistakes, it's also possible for a stockbroker to provide the type of bad advice we described in a mutual fund sales context in Chapter 4. When you read about high-profile cases of abuse of affluent elderly people by brokers, it's often because the broker was either given, or acted as if she were given, full discretionary authority over an investment account. The occasional cases of stockbroker abuse generally involve overly passive investors who have allowed the broker to take control and churn the account to earn higher commissions. There is a phrase called "virtual discretion," in which clients essentially do whatever the broker suggests. However, clients should keep in mind that these brokers do not have the legal authority to manage on a discretionary basis.

Mutual fund investors go through a similar process. If you have mostly load funds, a broker or financial planner should provide a certain amount of advice. Both of you work together to make decisions.

No-load fund investors, however, are like discount-brokerage customers—they make decisions on their own. In a way, though, do-it-yourself no-load investors are hybrid creatures. The managers of the funds they hold decide which securities to buy and sell in their portfolios. But when no-load investors make their own decision to acquire or redeem the fund—or make high-level decisions that alter the overall asset mix of their fund portfolio—then, to an extent, they are overruling the decisions of the fund managers.

If you study the markets and are accustomed to initiating transactions with a broker or financial planner, it may seem somewhat disconcerting to enter a discretionary relationship with an investment manager. But you may also appreciate the peace of mind that comes with engaging a professional, as in any field. After all, you wouldn't want to fill your own teeth or perform heart by-pass surgery on yourself.

## What is discretionary management?

Discretionary management is when you, the investor/client, authorize your investment manager to handle the day-to-day operation of your investment account. This means buying and selling securities as well as collecting dividends and income on your behalf. Your manager literally has the "discretion" to act for you.

Upon first hearing about discretionary management, many individuals think they would have to give up all control of their investments and that their investment manager can do whatever he or she wanted. If you are dealing with a qualified, competent professional, however, this is not the case at all.

As outlined in Chapter 11, individuals who can manage portfolios on a discretionary basis must meet the highest standards of education and investment experience. Their role is to determine, with the client, an appropriate strategy for managing the investment portfolio and to report to the client on a regular basis. In essence, the investor is hiring a professional to do a specific job and should view it the same way they would hiring any other type of employee. You assess their ability to do the job, provide a job description, let them do the job, and periodically review how well they are doing it.

As a client of discretionary investment management, you are not relinquishing all control. Rather, you are hiring an expert to handle the day-to-day details of your investments. Anyone who owns mutual funds has already done this. In a mutual fund, the fund manager makes the day-to-day decisions on actual security selection.

Some investors who own mutual funds wonder whether the managers of discretionary portfolios are as good as the fund managers. They make the dubious assumption that since mutual funds cost more in management fees, they must therefore offer better returns or better managers. Often they have been told this by a mutual fund dealer, broker, or financial adviser, who wants to keep them in the high-fee product and to retain them as a client. It's not true. Many investment counseling firms that manage pension and mutual fund portfolios also manage brokerage-sponsored Wrap accounts, as well as portfolios of both funds and segregated accounts for individuals. There are also many firms that manage discretionary portfolios for individuals that do not manage pension or mutual fund portfolios. This should not be viewed as a negative. As with mutual fund managers, a wide range of discretionary managers are available to clients. Some are great, some are awful, and most fall in the middle range of competent professionals who do a reasonably good job. Each investment firm will have its own focus, based on how it wants to develop its business.

## Discretionary portfolio of funds (mutual or pooled funds)

Discretionary investment management can be obtained in two forms. The first is with pooled funds or mutual funds. With this option, the manager will manage a portfolio of funds and make the day-to-day decisions regarding what proportion should be invested in various types of equity funds or fixed-income funds.

If you are a client of discretionary portfolio-of-funds investment management, the manager has clear guidelines on how big the shifts between different funds will be. These guidelines or constraints may be imposed by either the client or the manager as part of the investment process.

Many clients don't want to see wild shifts occurring in asset mix from one quarter to the next. The "sleep-well" objective will not be met if they see one statement with a mix of 30% U.S. equity, 20% Canadian equity, 10% international equity, and 40% bonds, and the next statement shows 50% international equity, 20% U.S. equity, 10% Canadian equity, and 20% bonds. Not only would such large portfolio shifts be considered very aggressive—essentially market timing—but they would also be tax inefficient.

Typically, managers don't make these kinds of significant asset-mix shifts on a quarter-by-quarter basis. Rather, they prefer making shifts over a longer time frame. Each manager will have his or her own process and it is not uncommon to see an investment process that restricts changes in asset-mix weighting in any single quarter to a maximum of 5% to 10% of the total portfolio. This is an excellent risk-reduction technique since it is widely accepted that no single individual can pick the absolute market top or bottom every time. Since most clients of Managed Money include preservation of capital as one of their objectives, this type of investment process is usually a good fit for most.

It also has the added benefit of being more tax efficient. Every time asset-mix shifts are made in a portfolio of funds, units of one or more funds are sold and units of one or more other funds are purchased. This creates a tax event. The unrealized gains held in the pool being sold are then realized and a capital gain tax liability is created.

Although this tax inefficiency won't affect investments in RRSPs since they are non-taxable portfolios, it will have a large negative impact on investments held outside an RRSP.

## Discretionary segregated management ("separately managed")

The second way to get discretionary portfolio management is through segregated management. When we use this term, we are not referring to the insurance company segregated funds covered in Chapter 7. Rather, segregated management means that each client's assets are segregated, or separated, from the assets of other clients. That is, instead of holding units in a pooled fund or mutual fund, the investor owns individual stocks and bonds— just like an investor who buys stocks directly from a stockbroker.

With a separately managed account, the manager has more flexibility about how to make asset-mix changes. Changes can be made in two ways. The manager can decide to reduce equities and increase bonds, and sell sufficient equities to make the bond purchases at one time. Or when an equity is being sold for other reasons, they can reinvest the proceeds into bonds rather than other equities. Sometimes a manager uses both approaches.

This method can be more tax-efficient because the manager could choose to sell only a small number of stocks with large capital gains built in or they could choose to sell those that have not appreciated greatly. As with portfolios of funds, managers of segregated accounts make asset-mix shifts gradually rather than aggressively every quarter.

An added benefit is that the inefficiencies of the pooled structure discussed in Chapter 5 are eliminated.

## The investment policy statement

Regardless of whether investors choose the discretionary portfolio-of-funds approach or the discretionary segregated-account approach, it is critical that they give the manager a job description. In the world of discretionary management, this job description is called an investment policy statement. This statement should describe, in simple English, the parameters and constraints under which the manager can operate the account.

Evidently, when investors decide to enter into discretionary relationships with investment managers, they are placing a high degree of trust in those managers. However, they should never place that trust blindly or without proper governance procedures. A client who turns over a portfolio to a manager with the instructions, "Oh, do whatever you think best," is asking for problems and will probably get them. Similarly, a manager who accepts an account on this basis is also asking for problems.

When homeowners decide to renovate a kitchen, they don't simply call a contractor and say, "Do whatever you think best." Instead, they work with the contractor to identify their needs and design a kitchen accordingly. With a kitchen renovation, the needs may include cupboard and pantry space, and built-in appliances such as a dishwasher and microwave oven. It may also include an eating area for young children or access to backyard space. The kitchen should reflect the family's needs and wants. Once agreed upon, the contractor builds the new kitchen; there's a reasonable expectation that the resulting kitchen will be the one agreed to and specified in the contract.

The investment policy statement is the investment equivalent of the kitchen design and contract. You and your investment manager will identify your needs and develop a long-term investment strategy to meet those needs. The investment manager will then take care of the day-to-day implementation of that strategy and report back at regular intervals.

A comprehensive investment policy statement addresses four key areas of concern. All four areas must be addressed and the entire document should be written in English, not investment jargon. The purpose of the document is to establish a clear understanding between client and manager, not to show how smart the managers are or how many big words they know. The following four sections must be included:

- *Background and Overview*
  This is a brief description of who the client is and answers the question "What is this money for?"

- *Investment Objectives*
  This section should address the investment time horizon, liquidity needs, income needs, and any regulatory or special constraints (more on this in Chapter 13).

- *Asset Mix and Security Selection*
  The long-term benchmark asset mix should be clearly identified as well as the manager's ability to vary it. Any constraints on security selection, such as minimum credit quality ratings for fixed-income securities, should be outlined.

- *Reporting and Evaluation*
  This is the section that some managers would prefer to leave out. Clients should always insist on including it. It should specify how investment performance will be evaluated and the frequency of written reports and personal meetings.

The most commonly overlooked part of the investment policy statement is the section on reporting and evaluation. And not just individual clients find that this section has not been addressed—often, large institutional portfolios also overlook it. It is as important as the other sections because this is where your manager tells you not only how your portfolio has performed, but also, and more importantly, whether your manager has done what you hired him or her to do.

In terms of reporting, a manager should provide a full portfolio valuation at least quarterly. This will include a full portfolio statement showing the asset mix of the portfolio both at cost and at current market value. The percentage of the portfolio represented by each asset class should be indicated. The next section of the valuation should provide a complete list of holdings in the portfolio, with the cost basis or book value, the current market value, and the percentage of the total portfolio represented by each holding. The third section of the valuation should provide details on the portfolio transactions, the buys and sells, including the execution costs. There should also be a summary of the actual return from the portfolio for the current quarter and various annualized time periods.

As part of this quarterly reporting, the investment manager should discuss what happened in the capital markets during the previous quarter and the impact of these events on the portfolio. He or she should summarize what is expected to happen in the coming quarter and explain how the portfolio has been structured to take advantage of expected opportunities or avoid anticipated risks.

The final section compares the portfolio's performance against the agreed-upon benchmark—a reference point showing relative performance. For example, the TSE 300 might be the benchmark against which a Canadian equity manager might be evaluated. Although getting managers to report against a benchmark can sometimes seem like pulling teeth, as a client you should insist on it. All investment counselors are accustomed to reporting against a benchmark for their institutional clients. Most professional and high-quality firms will automatically report against a benchmark for individual clients.

## Choosing a benchmark

Building a benchmark may seem like a complicated and confusing task, but there's no need for investors to fret about it. Benchmarking is no more complicated than comparing a mutual fund to the underlying stock indexes. The benchmark you select should be directly related to your needs and objectives and to the management that will be provided.

If an investor has hired a manager with a clear mandate to be conservative and to keep most assets in fixed-income investments, the benchmark should be related to the fixed-income markets. If the investor wants aggressive growth from the small-cap sector, however, the benchmark should be related to small-cap equities. These are relative benchmarks—performance relative to the performance of established benchmark indexes.

Some clients always think in terms of target rates of return and absolute benchmarks. They may say to their manager that they want an 8% or 12% return from their investments. Other clients approach it by setting a target rate of return that equals inflation plus X%, where X might vary from 1 to 4. For clients who are dependent on their portfolios to provide regular income, there should be some reference to the annual income requirements that must be met, in addition to the total-return expectations.

There are pros and cons to each method. Most clients would be best served by using a combination of benchmarks and specifying the time frame over which a manager will be evaluated.

The advantage of relative performance benchmarks constructed from index returns is that they are neutral. Neutral benchmarks are an excellent means of separating personal and professional considerations. An investment manager may be a nice person and wonderfully attentive, but he or she has been hired to do a reasonably competent job and must be evaluated by his or her performance.

The disadvantage of neutral benchmarks constructed from the indexes is there may be periods when the managers' underperformance may be justified based on the client's stated objectives. A good example in the Canadian equity markets occurred in 1993 and 1994. In 1993, Canadian small-cap stocks, especially the junior resource and gold stocks, did well; in 1994, the large caps did well. If the client objective was to hold conservative equities (providing stable dividend income), a portfolio should have underperformed the TSE 300 in 1993 but performed well in 1994. The reverse is true for investors who hired managers to run small-cap portfolios; they would have performed well in 1993 and poorly in 1994.

Over longer time frames of three to five years, relative benchmarks work well for most clients. The benchmark return is what a competent investment manager can be reasonably expected to produce. By comparing returns to the relevant benchmarks, investors can see whether their managers added value to or detracted value from the benchmarks.

Absolute benchmark returns can also work over longer time horizons. Since most investors understand that to obtain higher returns they must take higher risks, an absolute target helps clients quantify how much risk they want to assume; this can be based on the long-term historic returns of the capital markets. The benchmark return over the long term might be 8% to 10% annualized over a four-year period for a conservative account or 12% to 15% over a four-year period for a growth-oriented account.

Sample investment policy statements are included below. The first is for a discretionary portfolio-of-funds account and the second is for a separately managed account.

## Investment Policy Statement (Portfolio of Funds)

### Background and Overview

Stuart Roth is 58 years old and has taken early retirement from his position as an engineer. His wife, Sandra, has not worked outside the home. They have decided to retain an investment manager to handle their investment portfolios. Their assets are divided between RRSP and joint accounts.

The Roths own their own home and cottage and have no liabilities. Their children are grown and established in their own careers. With retirement, the Roths expect to spend more time at the cottage and anticipate moving to a smaller city home within the next five years. Stuart will receive a pension from his company but they will require income from the portfolio to supplement this pension income.

Although Stuart and Sandra have been good savers over the years, they only began investing in the last four years. As both are in good health and have no history of health problems in their families, they realize that the time horizon for their investment portfolio is more than 20 years.

### Investment Objectives and Asset Allocation

The Roths' primary objectives are to protect the capital they have, provide a modest income, and some growth. At this point in their investment lives, they are concerned with volatility and any impact it may have on their ability to draw income from the portfolio.

Some of their assets are held in an RRSP, which will be maintained to take advantage of the tax-free growth available and the long-term time horizon of the overall portfolio. The assets in the RRSP total $450,000. The assets in the jointly held account total $300,000.

The following asset-allocation ranges have been determined and the "normal" asset allocation will form the benchmark portfolio. The cash component of the portfolio will be held within each pool and will not be managed as a separate asset class. Canadian equity funds held in the joint portfolio should have a bias toward holdings that provide dividend income.

### RRSP Portfolio

|  | Minimum | Normal | Maximum |
| --- | --- | --- | --- |
| Fixed Income | 25% | 40% | 55% |
| Equity | | | |
|   Canadian | 45% | 60% | 75% |
| Benchmark Portfolio | | 100% | |

### Jointly Held Portfolio

|  | Minimum | Normal | Maximum |
| --- | --- | --- | --- |
| Fixed Income | 45% | 60% | 75% |
| Equity | | | |
|   Canadian | 0% | 5% | 10% |
|   U.S. | 10% | 20% | 15% |
|   International | 5% | 15% | 25% |
| Total Equity | 25% | 40% | 55% |
| Benchmark Portfolio | | 100% | |

### *Evaluation and Reporting*

Stuart and Sandra expect to meet with their portfolio manager quarterly to review the investments and overall performance. The manager will be expected to meet the benchmark total return, net of all fees and expenses, on a three- to five-year rolling basis. The manager will also be expected to generate a cash yield in the jointly held portfolio of a minimum of 3% to meet the income requirement.

In addition to regular meetings, the manager will provide a written quarterly valuation of the investment portfolio, including the investment performance of the portfolio against the benchmark portfolio. The benchmark return will be constructed from the following indexes:

Cash—90-Day Canadian T-Bills
Fixed Income—Scotia McLeod Bond Universe Index
Canadian Equity—TSE 100 Index
U.S. Equity—S&P 500 Index
International Equity—Morgan Stanley EAFE Index

This policy statement will be reviewed annually and revised as appropriate.

Accepted by:

_____          _____
Stuart Roth                          Mary Jones, Supersmart Investment


_____
Sandra Roth


_____          _____
Date                                 Date

## Investment Policy Statement (Separately Managed)

### Background and Overview

Jim and Susan Wilkes retained Supersmart Investment Counsel as their investment counselors in July 1998. They understand that the firm is registered as an investment counselor with the Ontario Securities Commission and that Mary Jones will be their portfolio manager.

Jim is age 46, Susan is 44, and they have a five-year-old daughter. Jim has just sold 40% of his company and will continue to be actively involved in the business on a full-time basis. Susan expects to return to work as a graphic designer on a freelance basis once their daughter is attending school full time.

The assets are the proceeds of the sale of Jim's business, valued at approximately $1,000,000. They do not require income flow from the portfolio over the next 10 years; therefore the portfolio should be managed for long-term total return with an emphasis on capital appreciation.

### Investment Objectives and Asset Allocation

Jim and Susan understand that investment markets can be volatile and are comfortable with short-term volatility. They are prepared to accept a higher degree of volatility and risk with part of the portfolio in order to achieve greater growth. Although they are prepared to be somewhat aggressive in the investments when warranted, they are not interested in speculation. They are balanced investors with an equity orientation and require both asset-class and geographic diversification.

They do not wish to hold investments in the tobacco industry, nor in any companies whose primary business is armaments.

The following asset-allocation ranges have been determined and the "normal" will form the benchmark portfolio.

|  | Minimum | Normal | Maximum |
|---|---|---|---|
| Cash | 2% | 5% | 35% |
| Fixed Income | 20% | 35% | 70% |
| Total Fixed Income |  | 40% |  |
| Equity |  |  |  |
| Canadian | 10% | 25% | 55% |
| U.S. | 10% | 25% | 55% |
| International | 5% | 10% | 25% |
| Total Equity |  | 60% |  |
| Benchmark Portfolio |  | 100% |  |

### Evaluation and Reporting

Jim and Susan expect to meet with their portfolio manager quarterly to review the investments and the overall performance of the portfolio. The manager has wide latitude within each asset class to shift the portfolio and will therefore be expected to outperform the benchmark portfolio, net of all fees and charges, on a rolling three- to five-year basis.

In addition to regular meetings, the manager will provide a written quarterly valuation of the investment portfolio, including the investment performance of the portfolio against the benchmark portfolio. The benchmark return will be constructed from the following indexes:

Cash—90-Day Canadian T-bills
Fixed Income—Scotia McLeod Bond Universe Index
Canadian Equity—TSE 300 Index
U.S. Equity—S&P 500 Index
International Equity—Morgan Stanley EAFE Index

This policy statement will be reviewed annually and revised as appropriate.

Accepted by:

_____          _____
Jim Wilkes                       Mary Jones, Supersmart Investment

_____
Susan Wilkes

_____          _____
Date                             Date

## Chapter Thirteen

# Graduating to Serious Money: The Products and Services

Just how much money is "serious money"? The answer depends on where you stand and what product is being sold. For the average person, any money they have invested is "serious," whether it is $5,000 or $5 million. To financial services firms, it depends on which product or service you are considering. Minimum account sizes range from $25,000 or $50,000 to $1 million or more, with plenty of overlap.

Minimum account sizes provide a good indication of the options a client has. Combining that with the structure of the industry outlined in Chapter 11 will help investors to sort out where they should be looking for discretionary management of their portfolios.

This chapter deals primarily with those programs and services that are fully discretionary in nature. That is, the manager makes asset-mix decisions on an ongoing basis as required by the client's objectives and capital markets. This does not include automatic rebalancing services such as Mackenzie's STAR program. While rebalancing programs may be a good solution for many, they do not involve discretionary management of a portfolio of funds. Rebalancing services set a static asset mix and the mixture of funds is adjusted each quarter back to the original mix. They do not involve any judgments based on current market events, or the outlook for capital markets, or change in investor circumstances. In the following diagram, these programs are shown as the entry level for investors wanting a higher level of service and expert input. They are services and products designed for the mass market and provide some degree of customization.

Discretionary management of investment portfolios used to be available only to the very wealthy—those with more than $1 million of investable assets. Recent developments in the marketplace have brought a plethora of managed products and services to investors with as little as $50,000 to $100,000.

Product and service availability for discretionary investment management can be grouped into four categories, based on asset size, and these categories overlap. They can be thought of as a pyramid, with mutual funds at the bottom, asset allocation services and mutual fund Wrap accounts next, and fully segregated management at the top. This represents the size of the marketplace that would be appropriate for any of the categories with the smallest number of investors able to access segregated management.

## The Managed Money Hierarchy

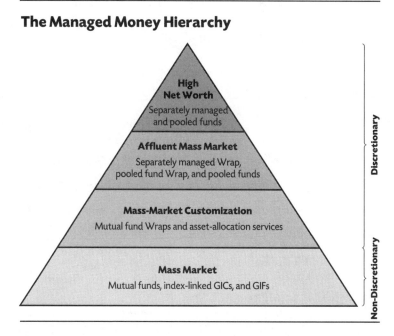

## *Mass market*

These products are non-discretionary in nature and were addressed in Parts 1 and 2 of this book.

## Mass market customization

The products and programs available to this segment of the market are targeted at investors with less than $250,000 of household investable assets. However, investors with as little as $5,000 can access some of these services and gain additional assistance with their asset-mix decisions. These services will have a fee on top of the fees charged in the mutual funds selected. The issue of high cost addressed in Chapter 3 is even more relevant for these programs.

With these types of rebalancing programs, the investor never strays far from the long-term asset mix. The downside of this type of automatic service is that there is no forward-looking investment planning within the program. That is, there is no way for the programs to take advantage of or anticipate changing environments such as the recent collapse of the Asian markets. For example, if the long-term asset mix calls for an allocation to Asia, the rebalancing will automatically include Asia. To accommodate a dramatically changed outlook for these markets, investors must change their long-term asset mix on their own without guidance from these products.

These types of programs are offered by brokerage firms, banks, and increasingly by financial planning firms and mutual fund dealers. The dominance by the banks in this market category reflects their overall client base. Every investor and potential investor deals with a bank for at least some of their financial needs. They also have a massive distribution network through their branches.

Some of these programs, such as Mackenzie's STAR, give good value for the additional fee. Others, such as Royal Trust's PAM, Scotia Leaders, and CIBC Choices, seem expensive when a 1% management fee is added to the mutual fund fees of 1.5% to 2%. As the portfolio size moves over $100,000, more choices are available that provide better value.

While $100,000 may seem like a large portfolio, it is not when defined as investable household assets. For example, a family with two RRSPs and other savings can find themselves well over this amount without thinking they have serious money. Someone who receives an inheritance can easily move over this threshold with a single bound.

## Affluent mass market

The affluent mass market is where most professionals will find themselves. For example, a two-career couple with RRSPs and savings will have a much wider range of services to choose from. Most investors over the age of 50 and many retired people will easily be over the threshold for these services. This group represents about 20% of Canadian households. This is the market segment that most financial services firms have targeted in their marketing programs as "high net worth."

Many members of this group have been investing for years with a broker or planner as their adviser. Many are looking for more from their investment experts. They want more help and better advice. In fact, many of them want management. There are three types of services or programs that investors can access who have assets in the range of $100,000 to $1 million.

The first is pooled funds directly from the investment counselor. The second is pooled fund Wrap accounts. And the third is segregated Wrap accounts. Wrap accounts or Wrap programs combine all aspects and costs of discretionary investment management into a single fee: they literally "wrap in" all the costs of investment management.

There are no exact distinctions regarding the asset level for which one product is no longer appropriate; rather, there is much overlap, so prospective clients must understand the distinctions among the various products.

### Pooled funds

Pooled funds can be characterized as funds for the well-to-do. They are similar to mutual funds in that assets of many investors are combined (i.e., pooled) and invested in one portfolio. But they are available only to investors who can meet much higher minimum investment sizes. In Ontario, the minimum investment is $150,000. This is because pooled funds are sold under the "sophisticated investor" rules and sold by offering memorandum rather than prospectus.

Pooled funds were first developed so small pension and institutional funds could gain access to portfolio management directly from investment counseling firms. From the investor's perspective, the key is that fees are charged directly to each client and the fee schedule is tapered so the rate of the fee declines as the size of the investment grows.

During the 1980s, many investment counseling firms began making their pooled funds available to individual clients, as long as they could meet the high minimum investment requirements. Some investment counseling firms, notably Sceptre Investment Counsel and TAL Private Management, set up pooled funds specifically for individual clients. These funds were designed for investors with significant assets outside their RRSPs who wanted professional, cost-effective investment management and wanted to receive service directly from the investment firm rather than from a distributor. These pooled funds took advantage of the investment and administration efficiencies available to the managers from the pooled structure. At the same time, they avoided the high cost of paying trailer fees, since the funds were available only to clients of the counseling firm.

Many firms offer more than one pooled fund so it is relatively easy for clients with $500,000 to obtain discretionary management of a portfolio of pooled funds. Clients are able to have professional management of both the asset mix and the security selection of their funds.

Typical management fees for pooled funds begin at 1% of assets. Even with custodial and brokerage costs added, the total fee is typically 1.25% to 1.35%, a big difference from the 2%-plus costs charged to mutual funds. As Chapter 3 makes clear, reducing your annual costs of obtaining investment management is the surest, lowest-risk way to enhance wealth building in the long term.

Because they pay no commissions or trailer fees, pooled funds have been the best-kept secret of investing for clients with assets of up to $1 million. While the increasing availability of pooled funds directly from investment counseling firms certainly adds to the value equation for investors, they are not perfect solutions for everyone. They have high minimum investments—typically $150,000 per fund—and present all the same tax inefficiencies of regular mutual funds. Investors are still buying into a pool of securities that may contain large embedded realized and unrealized capital gains. Other problems with pooled structures discussed in Chapter 5 also apply, albeit to a lesser degree, to pooled funds.

The banks, trust companies, and investment counseling firms have taken up the cause of pooled funds and are big supporters of them as an efficient way to manage portfolios. They are extremely efficient for managers and therefore more profitable, but they are not always as efficient for clients.

CIBC Trust offers a pooled fund program called Personal Portfolio Services to investors with as little as $100,000 or as much as $1 million. At the low end of this range, it is competitive with mutual fund fees; at the high end, it has better pricing than the Wrap accounts. The program is based on five model portfolios defined by the investor's objectives, ranging from conservative income to aggressive growth.

Other financial institutions that offer cost-effective discretionary investment management services targeted to this market segment include Canada Trust and TD Trust. In some cases, the fees are significantly lower than Wrap accounts. Typically, the investment management is offered by the institutions' own managers, thereby eliminating the need for a consultant to provide manager selection services. Clients should carefully consider whether the promised higher returns and lower risk of the multi-manager Wrap programs are worth the guaranteed extra costs.

## Pooled fund Wrap accounts

Pooled fund Wrap accounts are those programs that offer co-mingled (pooled) investment vehicles using proprietary funds, typically with a fee schedule tapered downward as asset size increases. Of lesser importance is whether the fund is offered by prospectus or offering memorandum.

Their characteristics include manager search and selection, multiple managers in multiple asset classes, and ongoing monitoring of those managers for a single all-inclusive fee.

The largest and most well-known of these programs is RBC Dominion Securities' Sovereign Program, originally introduced by a predecessor firm, Richardson Greenshields. Brokerage firms took the idea of professional management for clients who have outgrown mutual funds and packaged it using proprietary funds for their clients. When a fund is proprietary, it is available only from that particular sponsoring firm.

Firms have three good reasons for promoting these products. The first is that they are highly profitable. These programs are typically priced at a beginning fee level of 2.5% to 2.75%, about the same level as the pricier mutual funds. Therefore the problems of high fees described in Chapter 3 apply here as well. While these programs provide consulting services as part of the program and no sales commissions are involved, the annual fees make up for that to the benefit of the sponsoring company and the detriment of long-term investors.

The second reason firms love these proprietary products is they cannot be transferred to another brokerage firm if a customer or adviser changes brokerage firms. Investors would have to convert their investments to cash and realize all capital gains if they wanted to follow the broker to a new firm. While many clients have an excellent relationship with their brokers, few are willing to pay unnecessary taxes simply to continue the relationship. This is why senior, experienced brokers are less willing than junior brokers to promote this kind of product.

A third reason brokerage firms like pooled fund Wraps is because they reduce their risks of being sued for inappropriate investments. It would have been difficult to find any Bre-X in Wrap accounts. There is less risk of individual investment advisers giving bad advice to clients, or of juniors or rookies using clients as a learning experience, when their investments are in a Wrap program.

Evidently, these are good reasons for the firms to promote Wraps, but what are the investor's reasons for buying them? Up to $250,000, they are reasonably competitive with mutual funds, have no acquisition or redemption charges, and have the value-added benefit of consulting services that select the investment managers. They provide professional management of both the asset mix and the security selection and meet the client's objectives of more professional management than they can obtain from an adviser or planner. They are also convenient.

As with mutual funds, convenience comes at a price. For investors with up to $750,000, these products can be considered; but at the high end of that range, other alternatives should also be investigated. For some clients, the convenience of having a single advisory relationship through which they can obtain both managed services and traditional brokerage services may be worth the added costs.

For years, there has been talk of competition resulting in the reduction of fees for mutual fund investors. So far it hasn't happened, although it may be beginning in this market segment, with direct competition between the multi-manager (broker-sponsored) programs and single-manager portfolio of funds services.

While some firms and advisers market these programs to investors with large, multimillion-dollar investment portfolios, investors have shown they are smarter than that. The typical account size in a pooled fund Wrap is between $100,000 and $150,000.

**Segregated Wrap programs**
As investors move up the scale of assets under management, another choice emerges. With assets of $250,000 or more, investors can access segregated Wrap programs. Segregated accounts in this context means that the assets of each client are segregated, or separated, from the assets of other clients. It means that instead of owning units in a fund that owns Northern Telecom shares, the investor would own that company's stock directly. All the brokerage firms offer these programs. The first such program introduced in Canada was the Burns Fry Advance program. This program continues with Nesbitt Burns and has been joined by programs at all their major competitors.

The typical client asset size in these programs ranges from $400,000 to $600,000. This is the high end of the affluent mass market but not quite truly wealthy. Some clients will have larger assets, but investors with more than $1.5 million must seriously evaluate the value being received for the higher fees.

The advantage of segregated portfolios is that they allow for customization of both asset-mix management and individual security selection. That is, a client can tell the manager that he or she wants an ethical portfolio, for example, holding no tobacco stocks. Another advantage is the investor finds it easier to terminate the management relationship. If investors want to fire their manager in a pooled fund, however, they must sell the units and receive cash, creating a tax event. In a segregated portfolio, they can transfer the actual securities and make changes in the portfolio at a later date if desired.

Segregated management does not cost the client more but has a higher minimum point of entry. A larger asset base is necessary to achieve proper diversification. Many pooled funds can hold 60 to 100 securities. Some investors think the more diversification the better, yet research shows that once you go beyond 40 holdings, additional benefits from diversification are not achieved. Managers have large numbers of holdings because they are looking for somewhere to put the money without having too large a stake in any one company.

The costs are high to investors in these programs, with fees starting in the 2.5% to 3% range. The programs are structured on a multi-manager, specialty-asset class basis. This means you might have a choice of two Canadian equity managers, two U.S. equity managers, two international equity managers, and two or three fixed-income managers. Most programs also offer a choice of balanced managers. From this selection of managers, you will build an overall portfolio to meet your personal objectives.

Experience shows that most people who use Managed Money products or services are looking for capital preservation and growth. This means most investors will end up with a balanced portfolio. In a Wrap program, the financial adviser and brokerage firm pull together the separate parts and put them together into a balanced group. Many clients prefer to hire a balanced manager so they can match their overall objectives to the mandate being given to the manager.

The theory behind the multi-manager, specialty-asset class approach is that clients can hire the best manager for each asset class and improve returns. In theory, this works perfectly but real life is often different. The theory presumes that the client or consultant can always choose the best manager in each asset class. If one of those managers turns out to be a poor choice, it brings down the returns for the entire portfolio. If this happens, the investor has received no added value for the higher costs incurred.

Because these programs are relatively new, there is little experience to go by. One institutional multi-manager product has a 10-year performance history, but its balanced portfolios show consistent below-average performance over those 10 years.

With all the brokerage-sponsored Wrap accounts, clients are dealing with the distributor rather than the manager, which is another consideration for investors.

## High net worth

Once all your saving and investing have paid off and you require management for a large portfolio, typically in the range of $750,000 and up, a new service opens up: fully discretionary investment management provided directly by the investment management firm. Historically, this service has been provided "by invitation only" and is available only to the top 5% of households. As baby boomers expand their own wealth and begin to inherit their parents' estates, however, this elite service is expected to grow rapidly.

At this level of assets, investors can deal directly with the investment manager using either pooled funds or segregated management. Investment firms will have different minimum account sizes for segregated management, which can be as low as $500,000 or as high as $4 million. A wide range of choice is available, including bank-owned investment counseling and trust company subsidiaries as well as both large and small independent investment counseling firms.

Dealing direct with the investment manager is the high net worth equivalent of the mutual fund Rip Van Winkle approach discussed in Chapter 6. Your investment manager can tailor your investment portfolio to your needs and you can develop a relationship with the manager.

This service is more cost effective than Wrap accounts and clients with this level of assets can obtain whatever consulting services they require on their own, at additional cost. Many investors with seven-figure portfolios are quite content and have been well served historically by building a long-term relationship with a single manager. Many do not consider hiring multiple managers until their assets exceed $5 million.

## Portfolio of funds

When a client selects the portfolio-of-funds discretionary management approach, the investment manager will oversee the overall asset mix using a variety of pooled funds managed by their firm. The asset mix will be managed according to the overall objectives of the client and the manager's outlook for the capital markets. This type of portfolio structure allows the investment manager to make shifts in the portfolio, for example, from Asia to Europe, without moving money from one manager to another.

Fees for these services are typically 1% on the first $2 million in assets and decline from there. Often, an expense is charged to the fund for custodial and administration services. This additional fee is generally 0.10% to 0.15%. Transaction costs charged to the fund for the purchase and sale of securities would not exceed 0.10% to 0.15% for a balanced portfolio. When costs for all aspects of the investment process are added up, it comes to a maximum cost of about 1.5%—significantly lower than Wrap account fees.

## Segregated management

Clients who want separately managed accounts and have assets of $1 million or more can access segregated accounts from the investment manager. In addition to the ability to customize the asset mix and security selection, clients of segregated management can also customize the timing of transactions. For many wealthy investors, this is an important consideration for integrating their investment planning with their tax planning.

Segregated management has always been considered the elite wealth management service. The fee schedule is similar to that of pooled funds from investment counselors, although some firms charge a premium of 0.25% for segregated accounts.

A wide variety of firms offer this service, from small independent firms to large, institutionally owned firms. Many of the largest and best-known pension management firms also have "private-client" divisions. Some of the same firms that are managers on Wrap account programs also serve individual clients directly. Two such examples are McLean Budden and Bissett Investment Management. Both firms participate in Wrap programs and offer portfolio-of-funds services and segregated management directly to individual clients. The minimum assets needed to deal directly with these firms vary from $500,000 to $1 million.

## Hybrid managers

One category of manager offers discretionary services not directly comparable to Wrap programs or investment counseling services: brokerage firms and securities dealers who manage accounts on a discretionary basis. Investors should be extremely cautious when dealing with such hybrid managers because there are a number of potential problems.

The first is cost of trade execution. All trades must be directed to a broker for execution and costs are associated with execution. With these hybrid firms, the trade execution is normally done at retail commission rates, which can be four to five times as high as the institutional rates obtained by investment counselors on behalf of clients. Institutional rates are about half the rates charged by discount brokers, typically around four to five cents per share.

Some firms, such as RBC Dominion Securities and Nesbitt Burns, have addressed this potential conflict by quoting a management fee that includes all transactions. This, however, does not mean they have eliminated problems. Since all the stock trades must be executed within the firm, clients cannot be sure they are receiving the best execution at the best price. These brokers who handle discretionary portfolios cannot shop the market for clients to ensure either the availability of particular securities or competitive pricing; they must take whatever their own firm's trading desk will offer. The portfolio managers in these firms have access only to their own firm's research, where an investment counselor has access to all of the research from all the brokerage firms in the market.

These hybrid managers usually charge the client the same management fee as investment counselors but provide more expensive trade execution and have no formal access to alternate research. These services represent a "buyer beware" situation for investors. Their customers pay the same or more, but they receive less value.

The one advantage is that because of the commission revenue, many of these hybrid firms can accept segregated portfolios for clients with assets of less than $500,000. Investors at this asset level who absolutely require segregated management would be better served by a Wrap program. The quality of the investment management is higher and the conflicts of interest have been removed.

## Flat-fee brokerage accounts

Most brokerage firms will also offer clients an advisory service, which may or may not use some managed products, such as mutual funds, that are non-discretionary. In these accounts, clients will have the option of paying an annual fee rather than transaction charges. Examples include Nesbitt's Freedom account or Dominion Securities' Advisor account. Most of these accounts cap the number of transactions.

While this is not Managed Money, there is the opportunity to include some managed products, while eliminating some of the conflicts described in Chapter 4.

## Evaluating investment performance

When looking for an investment manager for the first time, or when considering a change, most clients want to know about investment performance. Advisers and managers can assist clients in evaluating past performance in terms of client objectives. Since the investment counseling profession was first developed for pension fund management, these managers are used to providing performance data to prospective institutional clients and can also provide this information to individuals.

When evaluating performance data, clients should always remember that past performance is no guarantee of future performance—just like the mutual fund advertisements always declare. Historical performance data should only be used as an indication of a manager's past professional competence and should always be evaluated within the context of a client's individual objectives and the market environment over that time period.

Investment managers might present performance data to prospective clients in one of four ways. Often, if the firm manages mutual funds as well as private accounts, it will use the performance data from these funds to illustrate historical performance. These performance numbers will have a high degree of integrity and will be publicly available. Prospective clients should ensure that they understand the fund's objectives to make sure the style is appropriate. Most investment counselors will manage portfolios with similar objectives on a consistent basis, so these fund portfolios can be a good representation of a firm's capabilities.

Another method of evaluating a firm's investment performance is on a relative basis. Firms that manage pension accounts often have external performance measurement that they can show to prospective clients. Their portfolio would be ranked in a universe of other pension and institutional accounts, and prospective clients can see how, for example, a firm's balanced account performance compared with the balanced account management of other institutional managers. When evaluating this type of performance data, it is important to understand the constraints placed on both the portfolio and the universe. The main question a prospective investor is trying to answer is "Given the same constraints as other managers, how did you do?" Consequently, it is important to understand the constraints. Relative performance can also be measured against an index or a hypothetical portfolio return constructed from several indexes.

The third method is to provide actual performance from a sample account. This is the least acceptable method because this sample account may not be representative of the firm's other portfolios. In theory, this sample account would be one in which the objectives were similar to those of the prospective client. However, there is no guarantee the managers haven't just chosen their best account.

The fourth method is the best option, but it is not yet universally used. This method is to present the performance data of a composite of accounts in accordance with AIMR (Association of Investment Management & Research, based in Charlottesville, N.C.) standards. To comply with these standards, all of a firm's managed accounts would be included in a composite with accounts that had similar objectives. The resulting performance numbers are therefore truly representative of all portfolios managed by a firm. This method is likely to become more common both as prospective clients demand it and as investment managers upgrade their technology and systems to allow for the capturing of historical data and the calculation of time-weighted returns.

AIMR performance presentation standards require that all Wrap account performance be presented or shown net of all fees and expenses. In fact, few Wrap accounts in Canada actually do this.

One other method that is used occasionally to represent performance is the presentation of investment returns from a model account. Model accounts are never accepted within the institutional and pension business, and private investors should view them with skepticism. Model portfolios do not deal with real money so there will be potential questions as to whether the model investments could have actually been made for clients at the time and price used in the model. Some model portfolios either do not account for transaction costs or use commission rates that could not be achieved by actual clients. A final difficulty is there is no way of assessing whether actual accounts are managed in accordance with the model portfolio or whether there is a wide variance from the model.

*Chapter Fourteen*

# Consulting Services: Finding a Fee-based Adviser

Large institutional investors have always used investment and pension consultants to assist them in ensuring that proper and prudent management is applied to the portfolios under their care. Pension-plan sponsors and other institutional investors oversee billions of dollars for their plan members. Consultants are used to ensure that funds have both the proper asset mix and the proper managers.

These portfolios can range from $30 million to several hundred millions of dollars. Traditionally, pension consulting has been a fee-for-service business. Fees are charged based on the time and work involved, similar to the way in which accountants or lawyers are paid. Large funds often have higher consulting bills but that is because they often require more work, not because they are large.

There is always a risk with professionals who bill by the hour that they will recommend unnecessary work to build up the billable hours. Although most consultants are reputable professionals, prospective clients should be aware of this potential risk nonetheless.

Individuals have access to a wide range of consulting services. Some are available independently while others are built into packaged managed programs. To find services right for you, the first step is understanding the service and how it is delivered. Different clients will choose different services depending on their needs and preferences.

A consultant plays the role of matchmaker—introducing an investor to a number of prospective managers and helping them determine which is most effective for their needs. This is the manager search process. Before hiring a consultant, investors must ensure that they understand the consultant's approach.

## The consulting process

The consulting process should evaluate investment firms from a number of perspectives. The most important is to look at how the investment firm manages their own business. Is this a firm that has managed to grow their business steadily by providing consistent service to clients or have they grown in fits and starts, seeing a big influx of new clients after a year of good returns and then trailing off? Does the firm have a large staff turnover or is it stable? You want your consultant to know the investment firms well enough that they know which firms have the potential for trouble before it becomes public knowledge.

A consultant must also assess a firm's investment process. Consultants probe this issue and verify how the firm actually manages money, as opposed to what its marketing material says. This requires portfolio management experience. One investment firm defines its investment process as being fully invested at all times within their pooled funds. They had a large influx of cash into a fund that resulted in the fund being 80% in cash for months in a rising market. This hurt the returns of the existing unitholders. This does not happen frequently with reputable investment firms but the consultant must be on the lookout for them.

These are continuous processes. You can't look at a firm one day and decide it is good for the next five years. Rather, consultants must monitor investment firms and meet with them regularly. Simply looking at the raw investment returns doesn't give any insights into what is currently happening at the firm and what the future implications are for clients.

Consultants also look at historical performance. They assess whether investment returns are consistent with the investment process, or whether it confirms the insights gained from the previous analysis. If the performance has been lagging is it due to the manager's style or other problems at the firm? Simply maintaining a data base of investment returns for a thousand managers won't reveal which managers are good. Performance data bases are backward looking; much of the consulting process should be forward looking.

## Qualities and expertise of consultants

Anyone can hang out a shingle and call themselves an investment consultant. Many professionals advise clients on what manager to select or how to evaluate different managers. If you are not managing investment portfolios or selling securities, there are no requirements for registration so it is "buyer beware."

People with significant assets who are looking for an investment manager often ask a trusted adviser, such as their lawyer or accountant. Unfortunately, many of these professionals know little about the investment industry and the full range of options available. They may only be involved in investment manager searches once every few years and so they tend to lack a detailed current knowledge of what is available and who potential managers are.

When evaluating consultants, keep in mind that you are looking for assistance in selecting an investment manager, so the consultant should have demonstrated investment expertise. Some consultants have had direct experience and practical knowledge in portfolio management before becoming a consultant, while others will have a more academic knowledge, having taken many courses but with no practical experience. Still others have had extensive pension or institutional experience with non-taxable portfolios of more than $50 million but little or no experience with taxable portfolios of $500,000 and up.

## Acting as your own consultant

Some investors effectively act as their own consultant. Once they decide they want a discretionary investment manager, they collect names from friends and associates and then interview managers. This can be considered an "accidental list." That is, they will be interviewing firms they have found out about by accident rather than through expert knowledge. Often the connection is someone from the golf club or their accountant. The common thread is that the names of prospective managers have been obtained from individuals who are not experts. There are significant differences in how investment management firms operate and the resulting costs to the client. These differences are often difficult to detect except by those with expert knowledge.

For those who choose this route, there are two sources of information that will identify potential managers. The first is a series of regional *Private Client Investment Counselling* directories published by Rodgers Investment Consulting and available free of charge. Firms in the directory range from large, institutionally owned firms, to small, independently owned firms. The second source of names of prospective firms is the Investment Counsel Association of Canada membership directory. Membership in this association is dominated by Ontario-based firms, and all firms are independently owned. Due to membership restrictions (most bank subsidiaries are precluded), this organization is dominated by smaller firms.

## Consultants inside Wrap programs

One of the benefits of Wrap accounts, and the justification for their higher fees, is that ongoing consulting services are provided to the sponsoring firm. This ongoing consulting work involves selecting, monitoring, and replacing managers when required. Most of the consulting firms in these programs are well-established pension consultants with Canadian offices, although some U.S. firms have made inroads into this market.

Since the value of a consultant is in bringing superior knowledge to the manager-selection process, investors should make a realistic assessment of the consultant's capabilities. Questions should be asked about the consultant's process in evaluating managers, such as how often they meet with managers. Do they meet with the marketing people or the portfolio managers? One U.S. consulting firm involved with a Canadian Wrap program provided much amusement when it asked Canadian managers how many IRA and KEOGH accounts they managed. Since these are U.S. tax-exempt accounts and are not applicable to Canada, it raises the question of how much they know about the Canadian marketplace. Another consultant to a Wrap program had not met with the managers selected for more than two years.

Wrap clients receive two levels of consulting. The first is from the institutional consultant who selects the managers to participate in the program. The second level is from the investment adviser who deals with the client and assists them in determining objectives and servicing the account. Determining objectives is the most critical part of the process so the broker should have expert knowledge. Unfortunately, there is a wide range of expertise. These two levels of consulting is one reason why Wrap accounts are more expensive than going directly to the managers. Their fees—which are built into the management fees—are charged each and every year, not just when the manager is hired or replaced.

Fees within Wrap programs include the consulting services and are based on the portfolio size. Typically, the larger the portfolio, the lower the rate. Such a tapered fee schedule is provided because it doesn't take twice as much work to handle a $500,000 portfolio as it does to handle a $250,000 portfolio.

## Public accounting and fee-only financial planning firms

In recent years, accounting and fee-only financial planning firms have made a push into private wealth management and begun offering consulting and manager search services. Often their practices have evolved into investment consulting from a financial planning and tax perspective. Their investment planning can sometimes be secondary to their main line of business. Because their investment expertise and experience can vary widely, prospective clients should investigate the depth of investment, tax, and financial planning expertise within the practice.

Traditionally, consulting by professional services firms was done on an hourly or project basis. Once the professional had a sense of how much work was involved, he or she quoted a fee. Pension consulting firms still work this way.

In bringing these consulting services to individual clients, most of these firms have chosen to follow the Wrap account fee model of a percentage of assets, rather than for work actually done. This means complicated searches are subsidized by relatively simple searches. Some firms try to keep down costs by negotiating with managers to lower their fees for clients of that firm. While it sounds good, it is a negative because it is effectively the same as a fee-sharing agreement and the top-quality investment firms have not agreed to these arrangements. The firms that will agree tend to be those who need the business the most, but are unlikely to be the one a client wants to hire. These asset-based fees are charged every year, not just when a manager is hired, and are often at the same rate for selecting a manager as for the ongoing supervision of the manager.

Firms tend to focus on different areas. With some, this business has grown as an add-on to their financial planning and tax services. They may be primarily focused on using mutual funds for the investment management rather than pooled funds or segregated accounts.

## Independent planners and advisers

A number of independent firms have been established as this market has grown. These independents manage a portfolio of mutual funds using both load and no-load funds. They charge an asset-based fee that may be tapered. This is in addition to the fee charged in the mutual fund. Some will collect the trailer fee while others will reduce the amount of their own fee by the amount of the trailer fees. Because these are often small firms, prospective clients should carefully evaluate their investment and portfolio management expertise and experience.

When a consultant or adviser charges a management fee, no commissions, either front-end or rear-end, should be charged on the purchase of mutual funds. Clients should not pay twice. There are some cases of unscrupulous dealers charging a management fee even after having collected the commission from a rear-load fund sale and collecting trailer fee.

## Independent investment consultants

Some independent consultants are available to assist individual investors in choosing investment managers. Their business is focused only on manager selection and they do not provide tax or financial planning services. Some charge an asset-based fee, while others bill on an hourly basis so clients pay only for the actual service they receive. Some firms accept finder's fees, fee rebates, or commission rebates from investment managers and brokers. Prospective clients should carefully evaluate their experience, expertise, and knowledge. Investors often incorrectly assume that any experience in the financial services industry, such as banking or accounting, is relevant to investment management. This is not true. After all, would you want your eye doctor performing heart surgery?

Since these firms can be small, they can often customize the service they offer. They can assist in manager selection and provide an annual or biannual review. If the client prefers, he or she can monitor the manager quarterly and be, in effect, a "manager of managers."

## Manager structure

There is a debate within the industry about whether a client should have a single manager or multiple managers. Another is whether they should hire managers based on overall objectives or by specialty asset classes.

The Rip Van Winkle approach to manager selection outlined in Chapter 6 suggests that investors should hire one or two good balanced managers and let them manage the portfolio. There isn't a lot of consulting work to be done after the manager has been selected. Using a similar approach, a client with $5 or $10 million would hire two complementary firms and develop a long-term relationship with each investment manager.

The typical consultant structure is to recommend a multi-manager, specialty-asset class structure. The above client might end up with five or six managers or more. This is a complicated structure that requires the services of a consultant to keep it on track. The client's primary relationship will be with their consultant, not their investment managers. This becomes essentially the same as dealing with the distributor. All reporting and contact is filtered through the consultant and the consultant becomes responsible for making the all-important asset-mix decisions.

It will not necessarily enhance the client's investment experience but it will enhance the consultant's billings.

# Conclusion

*Chapter Fifteen*

# Taxes, Trusts, and Estate Planning for the Wealthy Boomer

While most of this book has focused on investment products and services, there are a number of related topics we can only address briefly and urge the reader to investigate further.

Wealth, for all its attractions, does not bring with it simplicity. In their youth, boomers may have liked the simple life. In their dotage, wealthy boomers will be carrying a lot of baggage. As the classic "sandwich" generation, they will have to worry not only about the generation that came before, but also the one following. Aging and sometimes infirm parents must be cared for; children must be raised and educated. Family businesses must consider succession planning.

There are concepts and skills needed that many boomers will not have encountered before, or even considered. Just as they will look to an excellent investment adviser or to Managed Money for guidance for their financial assets, boomers will need to seek expert help in a number of new domains.

They will need to engage the services of top-flight lawyers, accountants, insurance specialists, and tax professionals. A single point of contact may be a *real* financial planner who is qualified to talk to all of these specialists—not the pseudo-financial planner/fund flogger encountered in Chapter 4, but someone with at least a CFP (Certified Financial Planner) or equivalent credentials.

Boomers with such multiple responsibilities will have to re-address their insurance needs: not just traditional life insurance, but also critical illness insurance, disability insurance, and long-term care insurance for themselves, their spouses, or their aging parents. Entire books have been written on these topics.

As wealthy boomers progress further up the corporate ladder, they will have to examine the intricacies of employee stock-option plans, which will have an impact on their long-term investing choices and affect their overall asset mix. Many will have to learn about both the traditional Defined Benefit corporate pension plan and the more flexible Defined Contribution plan. They will need to work with the right kind of financial planner to consider the weight of the present value of their earned pension as part of their overall asset mix.

Those who do well as executives will learn there is a limit to the Canadian government's willingness to provide tax-assisted retirement saving. The whole area of supplemental or "top-up" pensions will gain a new meaning. Those less fortunate will have to learn how to "fire-proof" their career and develop back-up financial reserves to start their own business or find or develop alternative careers.

And despite their youthful lessons that "love is all you need," other boomers will go through painful divorces and child-custody cases. Family law will be a growth area.

Those boomers fortunate enough to reach the retirement finish line in good time will have to deal with early retirement planning and consider second careers.

## Trusts and estate planning

Sadly, the day will come when wealth must be transferred from one generation to the next. This is the domain of estate planning and beyond the scope of the present work; again, there are several excellent books on this topic.

Estate planning is an important component of any high-net-worth financial plan. On the one hand, boomers will have to deal with the financial and other implications of the death of their own parents. But they will also have to confront their own mortality and learn about wills and other legal necessities, to ensure that their wealth is passed on to a surviving spouse and their children.

A key tool in estate planning is the trust, a concept that may be new to boomers who are just on the cusp of wealth. A trust arises when a person transfers legal title on a property to another person (the trustee), with instructions as to how the property is to be used for designated beneficiaries. The earliest trusts date back to the Middle Ages, when they were used widely to provide for families during prolonged absences of knights during the Crusades. As the centuries passed, the trust concept developed in countries using the English common-law system.

Modern trusts come in many varieties—personal, private, family, corporate, and pension—and cover a myriad of tax and legal issues. A personal trust is, as Royal Trust points out in a brochure on the topic, "a powerful tax, estate, and financial planning tool." There are two main purposes for trusts: they let you control how money is used—while you are alive and after your death—and they can generate tax savings. Sometimes, trusts can also help to protect assets from creditors.

All types of assets can be placed in a trust, including financial assets such as bank accounts, stocks and bonds, mutual fund units, and limited partnerships, as well as private businesses, residential or commercial real estate, and other types of assets.

The role of the trustee is a fiduciary one (see also our discussion of the fiduciary concept in Chapter 4) and carries potential liability. If a trust is set up while you're alive, it's called an inter vivos trust, or a living trust. You can also set up a testamentary trust as part of your will, which will allow your wishes to be carried out after you die.

Trusts can be established and administered in Canada, or set up under the laws of an international jurisdiction and administered by a foreign trustee.

You can set up a trust to provide benefits for a child, while the parent retains control over it; to split income earned by various family members; to provide for disabled family members; or you can set up a charitable remainder trust to donate a cottage or artwork to charity, generating a tax credit now and allowing you to use the item while you're still alive.

Eventually, most trusts must be collapsed. There was a time when trusts were considered primarily for tax reasons, but the tax reforms of the past decade have eliminated many of these advantages. Thus, trusts should be considered primarily for non-tax reasons.

Many smaller investors may already have trusts and not realize it. For example, if you are putting money into a mutual fund for a child's college fund, it may be "in trust" for them. There's no written document but there is an intention to create a trust in that situation. The problem is that all contingencies may not be covered, such as what would happen to the assets upon the premature death of the child. In such cases, a more formal trust will have advantages.

Self-directed RRSPs are also a form of trust, in which you are your own beneficiary. RRSPs do not have formal trust agreements, they are not as flexible, and the fees are lower than the broader legal trusts described here.

The core document is called the trust agreement; it sets out in writing the terms of a living trust. This is where the settlor—the original owner or transferor of the property—clearly sets out what he or she wants done, and gives the trustees the power to carry out their duties. For testamentary trusts, the terms are contained in specific clauses within a will.

Because an irrevocable trust cannot be changed, it's essential that the trust agreement, or will, be properly drafted and accurately reflects the individual's wishes. The trust agreement should be drawn up by an estate and trust lawyer but any estate-planning expert can help frame the issues and wishes.

## *Dying broke: annuities and reverse mortgages*

The antithesis of estate planning is the seemingly selfish doctrine of dying broke, which, believe it or not, is the title and central thesis of authors Stephen Pollan and Mark Levine in their book, *Die Broke* (Harper Business, New York, 1997). They believe that inheritance is a bad thing for families, both for parents and children. Instead, they favor giving away your money while you're still alive and spending to the limit of your income (but not beyond), putting aside some savings, but not obsessing about it.

Rather than taking complete retirement at age 65 or some

other arbitrary age, they counsel gradually slowing down, replacing employment income with income from other sources only as it becomes physically or spiritually necessary to do so. In advanced old age, Pollan and Levine counsel converting some retirement savings to annuities, as a hedge against outliving their money. This can be an effective strategy, as long as purchasers understand that annuities are not an investment and that they die with you. An annuity is a lump-sum purchase today from an insurance company of a future stream of payments, which will continue as long as you live. The purchasers of the annuities are gambling that they will live longer than average; the insurance company, on the other hand, is betting you won't live as long as the average.

Elderly homeowners are similarly encouraged to eventually get a reverse mortgage. The idea is to leave no estate; the income stream from both annuities and reverse mortgages ends when you do, so children are out of luck.

Reverse mortgages are one of those kamikaze techniques that are controversial enough that they've been slow to develop in Canada. A reverse mortgage is one of the few financial arrangements that becomes more attractive as you age. While potentially a life-saver to cash-strapped seniors committed to their homes, the decision to obtain a reverse mortgage is a serious one. It has the potential to change the rest of your life—either for good or for ill, depending on the advice you get and the care you take in understanding what you are getting into.

A conventional mortgage allows you to borrow money you do not yet have. By contrast, a reverse mortgage lets homeowners access what is essentially their own money. With a traditional mortgage, the borrower makes regular repayments of principal and interest to the lender and the balance owing decreases. The equity in the home slowly rises until after, say, 15 or 20 years, the borrower owns the home free and clear. With a reverse mortgage, everything happens, appropriately enough, in reverse. The homeowner receives payments from the lender and the share of equity in the home gradually decreases. The mortgage terminates when the house is sold, the homeowner moves out, a pre-set term ends, or the homeowner dies.

At this point, the amount owing plus interest must be repaid. It is possible the debt may exceed the equity in the home, but normally the borrower only has to repay the part of the debt equal to the property's value: the lender absorbs any extra debt. The homeowners gamble that they will live long enough that they end up with more cash than the home would otherwise have generated.

With a reverse mortgage, you can receive either a monthly income stream or a lump sum, or get a line of credit. The loan term can be over a lifetime, or restricted to the period in which the borrower lives in the house, or some other predetermined period.

Reverse mortgages suffer from the image of being a desperate last resort for the elderly homeowner to avoid poverty. However, as the baby-boom generation approaches retirement, reverse mortgages may become more popular. Boomers have long embraced the notion of taking on debt to finance immediate consumption. One could argue that reverse mortgages are the perfect product for a "me generation" that does not mind depleting their children's inheritance.

There are, of course, potential pitfalls to this approach. No lender will provide a reverse mortgage for 100% of the value of a home. The lenders are essentially gambling on market values and your age, and therefore play it safe and typically lend less than 50% of a home's market value.

The older you are, the more the lender will give you. As with annuities, they are banking on the odds you won't live to an advanced old age and collect more in payments than the home is worth.

The decision to convert home equity should not be entered into quickly or taken too lightly. Be prepared to ask a lot of questions of the lenders who provide reverse mortgages before signing anything. There is usually no cooling-off period, unless you specify one in the mortgage contract.

## Innovative tax planning

Taxes are another topic addressed in specialized books. While this book has dealt at length with the high cost of mutual fund MERs, they're trivial compared to the amount of taxes Canadians pay over a lifetime. The difference is there's not a lot the average salaried employee can do to avoid taxes. Apart from the RRSP, the last frontier of tax minimization is self-employment and business ownership.

Taxes will loom ever larger as boomers build wealth. If they're not careful, taxes may even become the tail that threatens to wag the investment dog, rather than the other way around. In the early years, employees who contribute regularly to RRSPs are somewhat sheltered from taxes and the need to plan for them. They may not like the amount they're paying in taxes deducted at source, particularly if they're in the 52% tax bracket we assume in this book, but such employees are accustomed to living on after-tax dollars. The RRSP also builds up with relatively few tax consequences, other than the immediate tax refund generated by the annual contribution.

Investors just starting out tend to have most, if not all, of their investible financial assets in the RRSP. For decades, such investors are shielded from such considerations as capital gains taxes, the respective merits of dividend income versus interest income and other considerations. They do, of course, pay a price in returns, since the Canadian government insists that 80% of an RRSP or RRIF must be Canadian content. There are ways of getting around this—chiefly through derivative-based foreign mutual funds—but studies show that most Canadians are not maximizing even the 20% foreign content they are already permitted to use.

The Wealthy Boomer, on the other hand, will increasingly be building assets outside the RRSP, in so-called "open" or "taxable" investment plans. These portfolios are not constrained by foreign content limits, although they are subject to capital gains taxes, lesser taxes on dividends, and highly taxed interest income.

If you look at the investments in most taxable portfolios managed for high-net-worth individuals, they tend to be concentrated in North American equities, and primarily U.S. stocks. That's always where the wealth has been, and the most recent leg of the bull market has made that truth ever more clear. In fact, far from being risky, this strategy has helped investors avoid foreign crises such as the Latin America monetary crisis or the Asia flu.

Some iconoclastic analysts have questioned the wisdom of the RRSP, despite its motherhood status as an unquestioned plank of retirement planning. RRSPs only defer taxes—they do not prevent them—and many pensioners whose RRSPs have turned into RRIFs have come to the belated realization that the government owns half their RRIF. They are forced to liquidate a percentage of the RRIF each year, taking it as income and paying tax on it as they do.

When you consider the Old Age Security clawback there may even be a case for ending RRSP contributions at some point and building up more tax-advantaged income streams through an open or taxable investment plan. Joel Hoffman, a Markham chartered accountant and software developer with What If Software, has developed financial planning programs that can calculate the optimum point that will maximize after-tax income and government benefits. His paradigm-shifting concept entails ceasing RRSP contributions some time in your 50s and saving instead in dividend-paying stocks or other securities held outside an RRSP. Hoffman likens this to "pre-paying" the taxes that will ultimately be imposed on RRIF withdrawals, which can amount to well over 50% if OAS clawbacks are factored in. (Late in July 1998 the government killed the proposed Seniors Benefit, which would have debuted in 2001.) Again, we would urge readers to get professional assistance in such matters: we raise the point only as an example of thinking outside the box when it comes to such givens as taxes and RRSPs.

As the government continues to shut down popular tax shelters, such as computer software and mutual fund limited partnerships, the options for minimizing taxes are rapidly dwindling. Short of self-employment or taking the drastic step of leaving the country for some dubious offshore tax haven, there remains one viable, tax-effective area in Canada. Surprisingly, it is the seemingly staid field of life insurance.

Apart from their basic insurance functions, life products such as universal life may have a tax-advantaged investment value. There are some interesting possibilities for linking insurance, financial planning, investments, and tax planning. An example is the Insured Retirement Plan (IRP), marketed by Manulife and

Dominion Securities. On the other hand, universal life policies have mixed reviews. Some regard the high commissions and sales techniques as being every bit as questionable as the mutual fund practices outlined in Chapter 4.

This is an area where a well-qualified financial planner with knowledge of insurance, taxation, accounting, and investing is a must—or someone who has a good network of such experts.

## Offshore trusts and emigration

The super-affluent often look into offshore trusts as a way of lowering their tax burden. There is a view that as national borders vanish and Internet-based commerce evolves, that every wealthy person will become a "sovereign individual" who will set up shop in whatever tax jurisdiction offers the most favorable terms. This world view is described in *The Sovereign Individual: How to Survive and Thrive During the Collapse of the Welfare State* by James Davidson and Lord William Rees-Mogg (Simon & Schuster, New York, 1997). They see a future in which countries will have to compete for the honor of providing services to the affluent, just as businesses must cater to consumers. In similar fashion, individuals will privately contract out such traditional government-provided services as defense or health insurance.

Davidson and Rees-Mogg provide a sobering analysis of the lifetime losses imposed by predatory taxation. Assuming a 10% return on capital, they calculate that each $5,000 of annual tax payments over 40 years slashes your net worth by $2.2 million. They evidently view Canada as one of these high-tax jurisdictions, although one that is not quite as bad as the United States, which recently imposed a punitive exit tax on people seeking to move to offshore tax havens.

Some popular Canadian books have suggested the drastic action of giving up Canadian citizenship and liquidating RRSPs at the current 25% withholding rate, rather than ultimately paying 50% or more when the RRSP is taxed as a RRIF.

Leaving the country is, of course, a desperate, last resort, one that no one can undertake lightly, no matter what their tax burden may be. Apart from family and moral considerations, most tax experts say you'd need at least $500,000 to entertain such off-shore fantasies. This is not to say the problem is not serious. A *Maclean's* cover story showed there is a massive "offshore-haven" industry in Canada.

Furthermore, tax havens are now being aggressively marketed to average Canadians, as well as the wealthy, according to Revenue Canada's international audit division. That's why it is beefing up its international auditing staff, and putting special emphasis on tax havens and the reporting of worldwide income.

Canadians have always been obliged to report foreign income. Now they must disclose if they own more than $100,000 in foreign investment property, and must file an information return if they transfer or loan property to a non-resident trust or if they own an interest in a foreign affiliate.

The tax department also intends to use international tax organizations to exert pressure on tax-haven countries to eliminate secrecy laws. Assets moved offshore often return to Canada, either for reinvestment or distribution to heirs. At that point, Revenue Canada will become aware of the money, at which time the penalty provisions of the reporting requirement will kick in.

But a legitimate tax haven for wealthy Canadians may be a country that taxes its own citizens as much as Canada does, but which offers Canadians a relative haven. It is, surprisingly, the United Kingdom. According to Goodman & Carr and the British law firm Rowe & Maw of London, the key is understanding the difference between the terms "domicile" and "residence." If a British native is "domiciled" in Britain, from a tax perspective that means Britain is considered his or her permanent home. A Canadian living and working in Britain, however, may become "resident" for tax purposes but not considered domiciled there, provided they intend to return to their native country eventually. Anyone considering this must seek expert advise. "Emigration is not a step to be taken lightly, and experience shows that many who choose their destination purely for tax reasons will return home without achieving their objectives," says Titmuss Sainer Dechert, a London, U.K., law firm.

## *Educating the next generation*

Readers of this book have shown a willingness to work hard and work smart to ensure their long-term financial health. Often a major long-term result of building wealth is that children or grandchildren will inherit significant assets. Investors pay a lot of attention to building wealth but often pay little attention to ensuring that the next generation will be able to handle that wealth.

Start early with the next generation. If you are saving for your children's education, involve them in the investment-planning process. It is a wonderful opportunity to teach them how the structure of the investments must be related to the objectives, time horizon, and liquidity required. At different ages children will see that the time horizon is different, so the portfolio structure must be different.

We note that with the 1998 federal budget, the Canadian government has made it more attractive for parents to save for their children's post-secondary education. Many financial planners are now revisiting Registered Education Savings Plans (RESPs) because of the new 20% grant per $2,000 contribution per child per year. That amounts to a $400 annual gift per child, plus the savings can grow tax-free until they are needed for education.

Grandparents who intend to leave their estates to their children should discuss the structure of their investments and relate that structure to their objectives—whether you are educating your 35-year-old child or your 12-year-old grandchild.

If you are a victim of the Divorced Dad Syndrome—building a large estate to compensate for the time you weren't with your children—make sure your children know how to manage the estate they will receive.

For families that have decided to use trust and other estate-planning techniques, consider involving your children in that planning process and in the resulting planning and implementation.

If the next generation is to begin their investing with more knowledge than their parents and grandparents, they need to be involved. People learn by doing, especially when they learn from bad decisions. Better a bad decision today that might cost

$1,000 than a bad decision later that may cost $100,000. In 20 years, today's lessons will seem cheap and it will have been money well spent.

## For more information

Web site under construction: **www.wealthyboomer.com.**

The authors are also happy to share insights with readers by e-mail.

Jonathan Chevreau can be reached at *The National Post* at jchevrea@finpost.com or at home at **chevreau@istar.ca**.

Michael Ellis can be reached at **mbmellis@idirect.com** or by phone at (416) 560-1063.

S. Kelly Rodgers can be reached at Rodgers Investment Consulting: **RodgersInv@aol.com**. To order the investment counseling directories, call (416) 483-4198.

# Index